Destination Detroit

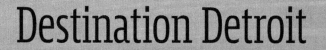

Destination Detroit

Discourses on the Refugee in a Post-Industrial City

RASHMI LUTHRA

University of Michigan Press
Ann Arbor

Published in the United States of America by the
University of Michigan Press
Manufactured in the United States of America
Printed on acid-free paper
First published January 2024

A CIP catalog record for this book is available from the British Library.

Library of Congress Cataloging-in-Publication Data

Names: Luthra, Rashmi, author. | Michigan Publishing (University of Michigan),
    publisher.
Title: Destination Detroit : discourses on the refugee in a post-industrial city /
    Rashmi Luthra.
Other titles: Discourses on the refugee in a post-industrial city
Description: Ann Arbor [Michigan] : University of Michigan Press, 2024. |
    Includes bibliographical references (pages 175-191) and index.
Identifiers: LCCN 2023027184 | ISBN 9780472076451 (hardcover) |
    ISBN 9780472056453 (paperback) | ISBN 9780472904624 (ebook other)
Subjects: LCSH: Political refugees—Cultural assimilation—Michigan—
    Detroit. | Political refugees—Cultural assimilation—United States. |
    Refugees—Cultural assimilation—Michigan—Detroit. | Refugees—Cultural
    assimilation—United States. | Political refugees—Michigan—Detroit—Social
    conditions. | Political refugees—United States—Social conditions. | Refugees—
    Michigan—Detroit—Social conditions. | Refugees—United States—Social
    conditions. | Detroit (Mich.)—Race relations.
Classification: LCC HV640.4.U54 L884   2024 | DDC 362.8709774/34—dc23/
    eng/20230828
LC record available at https://lccn.loc.gov/2023027184

DOI: https://doi.org/10.3998/mpub.11473711

The University of Michigan Press's open access publishing program is made possible
thanks to additional funding from the University of Michigan Office of the Provost and
the generous support of contributing libraries.

Cover and title page illustration: *Forced Displacement*, mixed media and collage, by
Syrian artist Oroubah Dieb (2018), courtesy of the artist.

*I dedicate this book to
my grown children, Shikha and Shamik,
my grandchildren, Ashima and Raina,
and grandchildren still to come*

Contents

Acknowledgments

First, I would like to thank my parents (Sukrita and Kasturi Luthra) for instilling in me a love of lifelong learning and supporting me in every way. I am deeply grateful to my daughter, Shikha Ganguly, and my son, Shamik Ganguly, for being my inspiration to reach high while keeping grounded. I also thank them for always being my cheerleaders. In addition, they provided very useful input for the selection of the book cover. My granddaughters, Ashima and Raina, renewed my motivation as I reached the finish line. To my spouse, Anik Ganguly, goes thanks for his steadfast love through life's challenges, allowing for the peace of mind conducive to my intellectual work. In addition, I thank the many family members and close friends who have been part of my educational journey.

The professors and colleagues who have inspired me and encouraged me, constituting part of the intellectual arc leading to this book, are too numerous to name but I will risk singling out a few. Benjamin ("Benjie") Lozare modeled a passion for using education for social change. Neuma Aguiar modeled feminist thought and action from a third world/postcolonial vantage point. Russell ("Russ") Middleton lit a fire for social justice. Hemant Shah and Roberta Astroff inspired me to do critical cultural analyses of news and other discourses using lenses of gender, race, ethnicity, and nation. My feminist community of friends and colleagues, including Angharad Valdivia, Radhika Parameswaran, Huma Ahmed-Ghosh, Jyotsna Vaid, Leslie Steeves, Suzanne Bergeron, Manju Parikh, and Seema Kapani, sustained me intellectually and emotionally. Carolyn Byerly helped to resuscitate my scholarly life after a hiatus by offering to read my work. My colleagues in Public Communication and Culture Studies at the University of Michigan-Dearborn, Wayne Woodward, Troy Murphy, Margaret Murray, and Nicholas Iannarino, provided great encouragement and an intellectual home. My students provided the horizon that gave my scholarly work, including this book, a larger meaning and they challenged me to be my best intellectual self.

Melody Herr gave me the courage and concrete feedback that made this book possible. Her guidance was indispensable in making this book a reality and I am forever grateful. Scott Ham at the University of Michigan Press understood the heart of my project and helped me to sharpen its focus and elevate its quality. The book would not have seen print without him. I would also like to thank Kevin Rennells for his supportiveness as he expertly and efficiently managed the production process. In addition, my thanks go to freelance editor Kirsti MacPherson for polishing the manuscript to wonderful effect and to Mary Ann Lieser for her thoughtful indexing. I extend my heartfelt gratitude to Syrian artist Oroubah Dieb for generously allowing me to use a version of her magnificent painting for my book cover.

To the Center for Arab American Studies (CAAS) at the University of Michigan-Dearborn, including Sally Howell, goes my gratitude for sharing with me oral history interviews conducted as part of their project, "Unsettled Lives: Displaced Iraqis in Metro Detroit." I'm also very grateful to the Arab American National Museum (AANM) for their enormously useful website, a starting point for many of the artistic "texts" I analyzed for the book. Finally, I would like to thank Marty Hershock for providing course releases to work on the project and funds for the freelance editor.

I also thank the many feminist and social justice groups that work against great odds to make this world more humane, hospitable, and just for the marginalized and vulnerable, including those rendered into the refugee condition.

Introduction

The Refugee Story as Part of the Story of Metro Detroit

We a city of Masjids/Synagogues/Temples
And Baptist Church preachers
We fly hijab/wrapped sisters on Friday/and some of the
finest Church suit brothas
you'll ever see on any given Sunday

    —JESSICA CARE MOORE (2017, 180)

On a warm, sunny afternoon on June 10, 2017, about 200 protestors gathered on Telegraph Road in Southfield, a suburb of Metro Detroit. They held signs proclaiming "No Sharia Law" and "Sharia Law Violates the Civil Rights of Christians, Women, Gays, and Children" alongside signs touting "Trump: Make America Great Again."

The rally was part of simultaneous protests against sharia law organized by the anti-Muslim group ACT for America in twenty states, the first such effort in the United States (Rubin 2017; Dalby 2017). As newspaper publisher Osama Siblani pointed out, Islamophobic groups had been making significant gains, given the international climate of heightened concern about terrorism and the political climate ushered in by the election of Donald Trump (Jackson 2017). Siblani publishes the *Arab American News*, a bilingual weekly newspaper in Dearborn, Michigan.

Early in the century, Dearborn and neighboring cities in Metro Detroit with large Arab American populations had already become "a must-visit location on twenty-first-century America's newly established anti-Muslim protest circuit" (Denvir 2012). The area was therefore an obligatory stop this time around as well.

Just a few days before the rally, the nonprofit organization Global Detroit and the immigration research and advocacy group New American Economy had released a joint report highlighting the contributions immigrants make to the Detroit economy. Underlining the message of the report, New American Economy president John Feinblatt said in a press release, "Immigrants are helping power Detroit's economic recovery" (Walsh 2017).

In September 2017, the Trump administration announced it planned to drastically reduce the number of refugees allowed to resettle in the United States. In response, Global Detroit released another report specifically addressing the contributions of refugees to the southeast Michigan economy. The report concluded that "In total, refugee workers boosted the economy in Southeast Michigan by between $164.3 million and $211.3 million [in 2015]" (Haddad 2017).

Seeing the Pattern

These two episodes are instances of the pitched, symbolic battle in recent times over the figure of the refugee or immigrant "other." The pattern has gone like this: the alt-right or extreme right has released conspiracy theories on social media about hordes of refugees from the Arab and Muslim world implanting sharia law into US cities and towns. Whereas sharia law in actuality provides moral guidance to Muslims for daily living and is not intended to contravene secular law, it has been mischaracterized by the far right as a static, monolithic Islamic law threatening the US constitution (Lean 2018; Quraishi-Landes 2016; Ali and Duss 2011). Milder versions of these concerns have found their way into mainstream media. Refugee advocates have responded to the concerns raised in mainstream media by vividly describing the positive contributions of refugees and immigrants, and refuting myths surrounding refugee flows.

Post-industrial cities in the United States have been at a particular crossroads when it comes to the contest over the meaning of refugees. Do refugees represent opportunity or danger? These cities desperately need to stem population and resource loss, but they also deal with local communities that feel internally displaced by economic and technological flux. Few US locations provide a more vivid case study of this fight than Metro Detroit, where competing interest groups have been waging war over the meaning of the figure of the refugee.

In this book I dive deeply into the discourse on refugees that various institutions in Metro Detroit are producing. How local institutions talk about refugees gives us vital clues about how they are negotiating competing pressures and how the city overall is negotiating competing imperatives. Indeed, the way various groups talk about refugees in Metro Detroit gives us a crucial glimpse into how US cities are defining and redefining themselves today. The figure of the refugee becomes a slate on which groups with varied interests write their stories, aspirations, and fears. Consequently, local refugee discourses can tell us what it means to be a Metro Detroiter now—and by extension, what it means to be a post-industrial US city at this time.

Metro Detroit as an Immigrant or Refugee Hub

Among post-industrial cities in the United States, what makes Metro Detroit compelling as a case study for examining refugee discourses? It has a long-standing position as an immigrant and refugee hub. More specifically, it has the largest Arab American population in the United States. In this section of the introduction, I give a brief history of Arab immigration to the Metro Detroit area, to provide context for the refugee discourses examined in this book. This is not meant to be an exhaustive history, but rather a historical sketch to set the stage for the actual focus of the book: refugee discourses that intersect and diverge in telling ways as various institutions use the figure of the refugee to elaborate their own interests.

I first arrived in Metro Detroit over three decades ago to work at the University of Michigan-Dearborn. Little did I know of the outsized complexity awaiting me. The region has come to embody in extreme form processes of deindustrialization and selective revitalization, segregation of communities, and tensions between suburbs and city core. Most pertinent to this project, Metro Detroit has been a long-standing hub for immigrants and refugees from the Arab world (Doucet 2017a; Schopmeyer 2000; Schopmeyer 2011).

The Metro Detroit area consists of Wayne, Oakland, and Macomb Counties. The cities of Detroit and Dearborn are both in Wayne County, with Dearborn just eight miles west of Detroit. From World War II until today, the center of gravity in terms of population and economic activity has shifted drastically away from Detroit to its various suburbs. Detroit's population went from less than 300,000 in 1900 to 1.85 million at its peak in 1950, and then down to less than 700,000 currently. The Metro Detroit region, by contrast, has grown to more than 4 million inhabitants. White flight has been a significant factor in the depopulation of the city. A telltale sign of the part race has played is that while in 1950 Detroit was 84 percent white and 16 percent black, by 2010 it was 11 percent white and 83 percent black (Doucet 2017a).

Just a few miles from Detroit, Dearborn has developed its own distinct character over the years, becoming home to the largest Arab American population in the United States. The presence of the Arab American community is evident in the many institutions it has built over more than a century. These include the Arab American National Museum, the only one of its kind in the country. There is also the *Arab American News*, the country's oldest and largest Arab American newspaper. In addition, there is a human services agency called the Arab American Community Center for Economic and Social Services (ACCESS). The presence of the community is palpable in the Arab American business district on Warren Avenue in East Dearborn but also in the Dix-Vernor corridor in the South End of Dearborn, with signs in Arabic and English. It is also noticeable in the schools, city councils, and elsewhere.

As a portion of the Arab population, the Muslim Arab community has also made its mark in terms of institution building. The largest mosque in North America, the Islamic Center of America, sits within walking distance from the University of Michigan's Dearborn campus. And halal food (food made in accordance with Islamic law) is commonplace, including on campus.

Arab Americans, both Christian and Muslim, are part and parcel of the story of Detroit's glory days as an industrial city, its decline since the 1950s, and its ongoing selective revitalization. Even as African American culture and leadership are necessarily at the heart of a just and sustainable revitalization of Detroit—making "a way out of no way," as longtime Detroit activist Grace Lee Boggs so eloquently put it—the story of Arab Americans and Muslim Americans in Detroit is also an important one tucked within the larger narrative.

As Schopmeyer notes, "As early as the 1910s, Detroit was established as one of the major destinations for Arab immigration" (2011, 30). The early Arab immigrants came mainly from Greater Syria (now Lebanon and Syria). They were mainly Christian men, farmers and merchants, attracted by economic opportunities presented by Detroit's industrial growth from automobile production. Their families later joined them. They generally left impoverished rural areas to look for economic opportunities in Detroit. Many initially worked as peddlers. As they gained economic stability they established small businesses and places of worship, such as Orthodox and Maronite churches (Jouppi 2017; Arab America 2022; Cwiek 2014).

As Detroit's economic position continued to strengthen in the early twentieth century, it became even more of a magnet for Arab immigrants. When Henry Ford instituted the five-dollar workday in 1914, it spurred a huge influx of Arab immigrants to the city, including Yemeni, Palestinian, and Chaldean immigrants. The presence of family connections and an Arab community further encouraged immigration, making the transition easier and creating upward progress. Places of faith that provided support and a community that shared the language were sources of comfort and aided in the transition to new lives.

At first the immigrants settled in Highland Park, near Ford's plant. When Ford opened the River Rouge plant in Dearborn in the late 1920s, Arab American immigrants followed and established a community at the South End of the city (Jouppi 2017). They created a vibrant business district that still thrives today, with Arab bakeries, hookah lounges, bookstores, and grocery stores.

The United States banned Arab and Asian immigration from the 1920s to the mid-1960s. This changed in 1965 with the passage of the Immigration and Nationality Act, which spurred another influx of Arab immigration to Dearborn and to Metro Detroit more generally.

From the 1970s onward, the religious composition as well the circumstances of arrival began to change. While poverty still constituted a push factor from the Arab world, a greater share of the movement was now the result of other push factors, including displacement of populations by war, regime change, and other aspects of international geopolitics. A greater share of the arrivals were now refugees. A *refugee* is someone who has been forced to flee their home because of the fear of war, violence, or persecution. In contrast, an *immigrant* generally makes a conscious decision to leave their country to settle in another (International Rescue Committee 2018). The wars between North and South Yemen in the 1970s before their unification into the Republic of Yemen in 1990, but also the civil war in 1994 after unification, created the conditions for Yemenis to immigrate to Dearborn and the Metro area from the 1960s to the present. This combined with the attraction of an already-established Yemeni community to draw these immigrants to the Metro area.

The Lebanese war from 1974 to 1990 displaced Christians, Muslims, and Druze (people from a political and religious sect of Islamic origin). An already-established Lebanese-Syrian community, especially in Dearborn, acted as a magnet for these refugees. The majority of Lebanese refugees at this juncture were Shi'i Muslims "and therefore tipped the religious composition of the region toward Islam" (Schopmeyer 2011, 31).

The US-led Gulf War in Iraq in 1990 and 1991 and then the post-September 11 invasion of Iraq by the United States "and the substantial political and economic turmoil in between" (Schopmeyer 2011, 31) were the next major instigators of displacement. This time those affected were Iraqi Christians and Muslims, contributing to the growth of the Arab refugee population in Detroit. A reasonable estimate of the Arab population in the Detroit area puts it at over 220,000, with the largest estimate for Michigan exceeding 490,000 by some counts (Schopmeyer 2011).

This second major wave of Arab immigration occurred after Detroit's industrial peak, and entailed a complex combination of push and pull factors—including already established communities with welcoming religious, social, and cultural institutions. By dint of the timing of their arrival, these cohorts of Arab immigrants became part of the effort to stem population loss and urban decline.

The Syrian conflict in the 2010s created the conditions for the most recent exodus from the Arab world. The conflict between rebels and the Assad regime had descended into civil war by 2012, escalating over the next several years (BBC News 2016). By 2015 the war had displaced more than 4.2 million people. A possible destination for these refugees, Detroit had declared bankruptcy in 2013. This was the culmination of years of declining tax revenue, population loss, and abandonment of homes (Bomey and Gallagher 2013). This confluence of events therefore presented both an opportunity and a challenge for the Detroit area. The city was looking for a comeback, and it has a unique history of Arab immigration and concentration.

Some, including those on the far right, paint a picture of cultural shifts taking place in Dearborn and other Metro Detroit cities with Arab communities. However, the Arab population is a complex mélange of different nationalities, ethnicities, and religions. Arab Christians predominated until the second wave. Even in 2004, 58 percent of the Arab population in the Metro Detroit area identified as Christian (University of Michigan 2004). In addition, while Dearborn is the main hub for the Arab population in Metro Detroit, there are Arab communities spread through the Metro Detroit area. For example, Iraqis displaced by the wars since 1991 created businesses and religious institutions mainly in the Warrendale neighborhood of Detroit (Center for Arab American Studies 2014). In contrast, Palestinians are mainly in the suburban city of Livonia, just twenty miles west of Detroit. And Chaldeans, a Christian community from northern Iraq, are now mainly in the more affluent northern suburbs of Detroit, such as Sterling Heights, West Bloomfield, and Bloomfield Hills (Carlisle 2015; Arab America 2022). The Lebanese community has a huge presence in Dearborn, but it is sprinkled throughout the Metro area as well.

Adding to the ethnic and religious complexity of the Metro area are towns such as Hamtramck, two square miles surrounded by Detroit. While it has not gained the notoriety in far-right circles that Dearborn has, it has come into the radar of outfits such as Rescue Michigan that have tried to sow fear of the institution of sharia law in the region. Once dominated by the Polish community, the tiny city now has a Muslim majority. However, this Muslim majority is made up of Yemenis, who are Arab, and also Bangladeshis and Bosnians, who are not Arab. This brings home the point, which my students often make, that not all Arabs in the Detroit area are Muslim and not all Muslims are Arab (Bailey 2015).

At the Crossroads of Belonging and Unbelonging, Inclusion and Exclusion

The local discourses examined here were produced at the juncture of many competing pressures and histories. For decades, Arab communities in Metro Detroit have experienced processes of inclusion and exclusion, incorporation and marginalization. As an example, in the 1950s the Dearborn City Planning Commission began a decades-long attempt to tear down the South End of Dearborn and rezone it for industrial use. This area was home to mostly Muslim Lebanese, Yemeni, and Palestinian immigrants, and it still is. Then mayor of Dearborn, Orville Hubbard, was known to have said in that context that "The Syrians are even worse than the n-----s" (Denvir 2012). The local Arab community organized and fought back, obtaining a federal injunction to block the project by 1973, but only after 250 homes had been demolished (Denvir 2012).

The contradictory process of inclusion and exclusion was further intensified with the US military presence in Iraq, US support of Israel in the Palestinian conflict, and especially September 11 (Shryock and Abraham 2000; Shryock, Abraham, and Howell 2011; Howell and Shryock 2011; Howell and Jamal 2009, 2011). In one example, the Detroit Arab American Study (DAAS) from the University of Michigan in 2003 found that 15 percent of Arabs and Chaldeans in the Detroit area said they had had a "bad experience" after the September 11 attacks, including "verbal insults, workplace discrimination, targeting by law enforcement and airport security, [and] vandalism." However, one-third said they had received expressions of support from non-Arabs (University of Michigan 2004). This recalled moments in my classroom after September 11 with some of my students telling me stories about being spat on for wearing a hijab and being told to "go back home."

Arab immigrants and refugees in the Metro Detroit area have established robust commercial and civic institutions. They are involved in every aspect of the city's life. However, the limits of Arab cultural citizenship have also been visible. While the community has about a quarter of a million people and a history of more than a century, it appears that at every key political juncture the dominant white community has once again marginalized the Arab community. The dominant white community holds up to scrutiny the Arab community's cultural citizenship. In this way, the white community holds the Arab community hostage in a sense, accepting it and legitimizing it—but only until further notice.

The more immediate backdrop to the project includes the growing unease that immigrants and people of color (in the Detroit area and nationally) felt during Trump's election campaign in 2015 and after his election in 2016. It also includes the steady mainstreaming of racist, anti-refugee, and anti-immigrant rhetoric since then. The long-standing histories of refugee relocation and community building in the Detroit area form the basis of the institutional discourses examined here, but the Trumpian moment certainly added a layer to the mix. For example, the Rescue Michigan website examined for the project was created in part to bolster Trump's chances in Michigan, and the creators were emboldened by the anti-immigrant rhetoric that constituted a central plank of his campaign.

An event on campus in 2015 crystallized for me the need to understand the position of the Detroit area regarding Syrian refugees. The College of Arts, Sciences, and Letters organized a panel on campus to support the idea of relocating Syrian refugees to the Metro Detroit area. I was struck by the statement of a leader from the Arab American Institute that our stance in terms of Syrian refugees was a matter of "our soul" as Metro Detroiters, and by the testimony of recent Syrian refugees about their arrival in Detroit and their effort to make a life here. They spoke of the difficult circumstances of their departure from Syria and the extensive vetting they experienced to qualify for relocation. They expressed their desire to get jobs and send their children to school, to get on with their lives. Even with an Arab community so well embedded locally, it was possible to see that gestures of reassurance were required, and that the call to conscience was still necessary for the white-dominant community in Dearborn to be comfortable with the relocation of Syrian refugees to the area. How Metro Detroit treated Syrian refugees would have implications for the future of

Syrian refugees, certainly, but it also had implications for the meaning of Metro Detroit. Would it continue its hospitality toward the Arab and the Muslim worlds? Or would it turn in a different direction?

As the Syrian refugee crisis intensified, the question of the US role became part of the public agenda. With its history of resettlement from the Arab world, Metro Detroit became part of the larger debate, and local institutions, such as the press, refugee agencies, cultural institutions, politicians, and local far-right groups, had to respond. They spoke out for or against the relocation of the refugees, or sought to act as cultural mediators between the refugee experience and the cultural mainstream. In this book, I closely examine each of these institutional discourses to understand the complex forces at play and the potential implications of the stories the institutions write on the figure of the refugee.

Another facet of the Syrian refugee crisis also influenced the discourses. The majority of the Arab population in Metro Detroit has historically been Christian. But by the first decade of the century, the Christian and Muslim Arab communities were almost at parity (Schopmeyer 2011). The larger national Islamophobic currents in the United States have found their way into the local discursive environment to some extent, manifesting as local concerns about institutions making accommodations for Muslim practices.[1]

Strong local Arab and Muslim civic institutions and many allies counter these strains of Islamophobia. But to fully understand the local discourses, we must consider how the Muslim aspect has been repeatedly associated with the Arab aspect—especially by those trying to create fear of the Syrian refugee.

While some groups express suspicion of populations from the Arab world, others speak of the clearly demonstrated economic potential of this

1. The issue of accommodations is a vexed one, not only for Muslim refugees in Detroit but for refugees and immigrants from many regions living in different cities in the United States. For example, in an extended ethnographic treatment of the struggle of Asian American populations to make a place for themselves in suburban Fremont, California, Lung-Amam (2017) details the pushback by the white residents who historically dominated the area. The areas of contention ranged from changes in the size of homes to the shape of malls to academic standards in schools. So while the issue of accommodations can become a site of struggle in the different contexts of immigrant settlement in the United States, with Muslim refugees there is a further layering of Islamophobia on top of the resentment felt in accommodating any "stranger."

group. Chords of suspicion are also strongly countered by cultural institutions who work strenuously through their art and exhibits to allay fears and to fully present the humanity of Syrian and Iraqi refugees. In sum, then, the discourse on the refugee became part of the larger story of the belonging and unbelonging of the Arab other, the Muslim other, and the refugee other in Metro Detroit. It also became part of the larger story of whether the refugee other can help turn Detroit around. At the crossroads of economic, political, and cultural imperatives and possibilities, people and groups write stories onto the figure of the refugee. The refugee becomes a palimpsest on which to write the fears, desires, and hopes of the city.

Writing the City's Aspirations and Fears onto the Figure of the Refugee

I was born a citizen and a human being. At four years of age I became something less than human, at least in the eyes of those who do not think of refugees as being human.

—VIET THAN NGUYEN, FROM THE ESSAY "THE DISPLACED"

I am a Muslim refugee from a war-torn country—the sum of many fears.

—JOSEPH AZAM

Among the phenomena bursting into public consciousness in the early twenty-first century has been the massive displacement of people. Just in 2012, 7.6 million people across the world were displaced by conflict or persecution, roughly 23,000 people a day (Fiddian-Qasmiyeh et al. 2014, 3). The United Nations High Commissioner for Refugees (UNHCR) has reported that "the number of displaced people is at its highest ever—surpassing even post-World War II numbers," translating to 1 out of every 113 people globally (McKirdy 2016). Jones (2017) points to the innumerable reports and images in 2014 and 2015 that made palpable the presence of the phenomenon, widely termed a refugee or migration "crisis." These included the heartbreaking images of hundreds dying in shipwrecks in the Mediterranean and the body of three-year-old Alan Kurdi washing up on the Turkish shore. Jones illustrates that there is nothing "natural" or fixed about how events surrounding refugees or any individual refugee are understood. Rather, representations of refugees and the "crisis," as well as the meanings assigned to them, have ideological underpinnings. If authorities and the general public see borders as essential to protect the people of a nation from "others" from foreign lands, the situation is represented as a crisis, and refugees become problems or burdens. On the other hand, if like Jones (2017) we see the "hardening of the border through new security practices" as "the source of the violence, not a response to it," then the complicity of powerful nations in the creation and representation of a refugee or migration "crisis" becomes visible.

The quotations at the start of this section from writers who had themselves been rendered "refugees" by political events are a reminder that there is nothing natural or fixed about the definition of a "refugee." Rather, that definition or signification is an ongoing process, subject to complex and historically contingent economic, political, and cultural forces.

What processes have played a crucial role historically in the struggle over the definition of "others"? Colonialism, neocolonialism, and empire— processes that continue today in varied forms. These processes of "epistemic violence," to borrow from Spivak (1988), reproduce troubling relations between an empire and its subjects, between the center and the periphery, helping to prop up the relations of domination and subordination. The "worlding" of which Spivak speaks—the "assumption that when the colonizers come to a world, they encounter it as uninscribed earth upon which they write their inscriptions" (Spivak 1990, 129; Morton 2003)[2]—is still quite relevant. And refugees today are among the eminently visible "others" on whom powerful institutions can write their inscriptions.

As Mohanty asserts, discourses of the "other" are implicated in the "practice of ruling" (Mohanty 1991a, 21). She also says, following from Edward Said's groundbreaking *Orientalism*, that in defining the East as other or peripheral, the West can define itself as the center, and that this

---

2. While I am greatly influenced by Spivak's writings and ideas in my understanding of postcolonial thought as well as postcolonial feminist thought, I include Morton's book here because it helped to focus my thinking on relevant ideas from Spivak as I elaborated my own theoretical framework for this project.

is a crucial aspect of the logic of domination (Mohanty 1991b).[3] In *Orientalism* Said captures the centrality of discourse in establishing and maintaining relations of ruling between dominant and subordinate regions of the world and their peoples.

> Orientalism can be discussed and analyzed as the corporate institution for dealing with the Orient—dealing with it by making statements about it, authorizing views of it, describing it, by teaching it, settling it, ruling over it: in short, Orientalism as a western style for dominating, restructuring, and having authority over the Orient. (3)

In *Orientalism* the main focus was on discourses elaborated in the post-Enlightenment period. In a later work, *Covering Islam*, Said demonstrated the malleability and persistence of the Orientalist discourse. He showed convincingly that military action in the Middle East in the late twentieth century "has often been preceded by a period of 'Islam's' rational presentation through the cool medium of television and through 'objective' Orientalist study" (28). Hamdi (2013) gives an example of how this kind of "'objective' Orientalist study" becomes the basis for political projects. Bernard Lewis, in 1990 in "The Roots of Muslim Rage," made the case that Muslim anger is based on a fear of modernity. In a telling echo of this argument, as George W. Bush made the case for the invasion of Afghanistan in 2001, he asked, "Why do they hate us?" and then answered it himself: "They hate our freedoms—our freedom of religion, our freedom of speech, our freedom to vote" (Bush 2001).

Said's insights applied foremost to the discursive construction of the Orient, especially as it pertained to the Arab world and/or Islam. However, they have been usefully extended to incisive critiques of the construction and deployment of discourse about the Oriental "other" in a broader sense. Additionally, Spivak (1988) and Mani (1998) show that those who have

---

3. When discussing media coverage of Islam, Said (1981) notes that it is important to "identify the situation out of which statements arise, and why it seems important to note the various groups in society that have an interest in 'Islam'" (xviii). In a similar vein I have tried to trace here the interests that a few local institutions have in the "refugee" and how these interests and projects result in certain discourses about the refugee.

been rendered vulnerable, such as women from marginal communities in the Indian context, are readily spoken for and inscribed on. This process of symbolic appropriation is illuminated by Mani's influential work on how the British used the figure of the Indian woman in the debate over sati (widow immolation) in the nineteenth century to rearticulate traditions. Fair's work (1996) showed how television journalists used images of women to package the African famine for U.S. news consumers and to provide a particular framework of interpretation for the crisis.

In my own work, inspired by Mani's, I have shown how postcolonial women became the ground for the "pro-life" lobby and the population-control lobby to advance their own institutional projects, even as they battled with each other over the fate of Reagan's "abortion clause," which was intended to restrict abortion funding globally (Luthra 1995). Like subaltern women, refugees are rendered vulnerable or marginal, making it possible for them to be spoken for or inscribed on. As Wright (2014) says of refugees, "Rather than being allowed to speak for themselves, they are more commonly spoken about by NGO reps, translators, television reporters, TV studio anchorpersons, and politicians. . . . This is compounded by the fact that the very state of displacement automatically places refugees at a social disadvantage. This increases the likelihood of the media treating them as anonymous passive victims" (462). The "refugee" becomes a floating signifier that various institutions can imbue with meanings suited to their projects. Not only that, but the signifier "refugee" can also be articulated to other webs of signification, such as those attached to another currently visible figure, that of the "Muslim." Following from Stuart Hall's central insights into ideology and the making of meaning, I have tried to be attentive here to the relations between different discourses (Hall 1980, 1984a, 1984b, 1985; Grossberg 1996[4]).

---

4. While I owe a great debt to Stuart Hall for my understanding of ideology, discourse, and the contestation over meaning in society and these ideas are central to the elaboration of this project, I have also listed Grossberg's key article here because it helped me condense and revisit some of Hall's key insights related to ideology and the ongoing struggle over the making of meaning.

Roadmap to the Book

I devote most of the rest of this introduction to a preview of this book's chapters. You can read these in any order based on what most interests you or is most relevant to your needs.

DESTINATION DETROIT: THE REFUGEE AS A MEANS OF ECONOMIC REVITALIZATION. The issue of routing Syrian refugees to Detroit first hit the national news in May 2015 in an editorial in the *New York Times*. It proposed the conjoining of two "humanitarian catastrophes," the Syrian refugee crisis and Detroit's depopulation, to the potential mutual benefit of both. Here, both the city of Detroit and the Syrian refugee are represented as tabulae rasae, blank slates on whom others can write the project of economic revitalization. Detroit, recently in the throes of urban ruin and on the cusp of an economic transformation, had been portrayed as a "beautiful wasteland," a "postindustrial frontier" (Kinney 2016) ready to be populated. The city was discursively conjoined with the figure of the Syrian refugee, who had recently become stateless because of war. The idea is that these refugees are ready to populate the city and to contribute sweat and ingenuity as part of the project of transformation and economic revitalization.

After leaving the spotlight for a few months, the issue hit the headlines again after the Islamic State of Iraq and the Levant (ISIL) attacks in Paris on November 13, 2015. These were the deadliest attacks in France since World War II, with gunmen and suicide bombers hitting several locations almost simultaneously and leaving more than 120 people dead and hundreds wounded, while creating economic, political, and social ripple effects in France and beyond. The attacks brought the Syrian refugee issue to prominence at both the national and local news levels. The national news primarily organized the issue around a security frame, and secondarily around a humanitarian frame. In contrast, the major Detroit outlets— whether conservative or liberal—primarily organized their reporting in terms of the city's economic revitalization and secondarily around a humanitarian frame. Both conservative and liberal outlets pushed back against any security framing that had seeped from the national to the state level.

Relocating Syrian refugees to the Metro Detroit area was painted as an important aspect of the city's economic revitalization strategy, and as the right thing to do. Local papers also included several human interest stories showing the successful process of resettlement of Syrian refugees in the metro area. These stories worked to normalize the figure of the refugee in an attempt to dilute any sense of threat seeping from the national to the local levels. They also helped allay any unease lurking beneath the surface at the local level.

The absences in the news discourse were also telling. At no point were the refugees represented as having either political or interpretational agency. In echoes of the refugee agency discourse taken up in the "Refugees Welcome" chapter, the abjectness of refugees as having lost everything was accentuated by refugee agency spokespersons to dilute any possible association with terrorism, and the process of assimilation was accentuated to diminish a perception of the refugee as burden. As in refugee agency discourse, the refugee was rendered as devoid of agency, reinforcing the idea of the refugee as a liminal figure having come close to "bare life," only acquiring a "right to have rights" through our hospitality as a pathway to becoming a citizen once again (Agamben 1998; Enns 2004; Arendt 2007a, 2007b; Stonebridge 2018).

Also absent is a sense that the economic revitalization project in Detroit is a contested one. Rather, when refugee agency advocates defend Syrian refugees as contributing to the economic revitalization of Detroit, the questions surrounding both the causes of Detroit's ruin and the possible pathways for its revitalization remain unpacked. As even a cursory look at the literature on Detroit illustrates, the future of Detroit and the meaning of revitalization are very much sites of political struggle (Doucet 2017b; Kinney 2016; House 2019; Bradley 2015).[5] By leaving out of the equation alternative visions of Detroit's future, such as those stemming from activists at the James and Grace Lee Boggs Center to Nurture Community Leadership or the Detroit Eastside Community Collaborative, the

---

5. One of the most contentious aspects of the economic revitalization of Detroit has been the selective investment in the greater downtown area or Midtown, to the neglect of other neighborhoods and the long-term residents. As Sugrue (2014) and many other scholars have pointed out, the story of Detroit's decline as well as the story of selective revitalization can only be understood fully through a lens of racism.

news stories on the Syrian refugee privilege the understanding of Detroit's future held by the city's dominant elite.

The gesture of hospitality in the local news stories provided an important counterpoint to the national discourse on the refugee as a possible security threat. It also provided an important contrast to the far-right discourse painting the Muslim refugee as a threat to civilization. Still, however, this gesture of hospitality harbored key contradictions in terms of both the figure of the refugee and the meaning of the city of Detroit.

REFUGEES NOT WELCOME: THE REFUGEE AS A THREATENING FIGURE. Far-right websites such as Rescue Michigan, although exceptional in their extreme discourse of othering and hate, are important sites to examine. On these sites one can view a distilled form of the articulations being made between different facets of othering, such as those between the othering of the refugee and the othering of the Muslim; such a symbolic intersection can have potentially serious implications for Muslim refugees. It is also important to examine these sites because in some sense they are the exception that proves the rule. When comparing the "Refugees Not Welcome" chapter with the "Refugee as Vote Getter" chapter, it becomes possible to see the seepage of far-right discourse into the domain of formal politics at the local level. The political arena can be a bridge between far-right discourse and governance, which has implications for policy, including refugee policy. The linkage between the far-right and mainstream channels of government has become more apparent than ever in the current historical moment (Hartzell 2018; Stanovsky 2017) in the United States.

The main thrust of the far-right discourse has been to suture fear of the Islamic or Muslim other to fear of the refugee. The idea is that the Muslim refugee is the conduit for "civilization jihad" being waged by Muslims against the West and its key institutions. Not only do the creators of the website Rescue Michigan repeatedly associate the refugee other with the Muslim other, but they associate the Muslim other already living in US cities and neighborhoods with the Muslim other threatening to come in from foreign Muslim lands. The website creators point to increasing accommodations being made for Muslim practices across the Metro Detroit area. The Rescue Michigan creators then use this evidence to sow fear of the Muslim refugee as a vehicle for the entrenchment of sharia in the Metro Detroit area, edging out civilizational advancements such as the Constitution and women's rights.

Admittedly, this is a caricature of Islam and the Muslim refugee. But recall Hall's insights (1988) on taking seriously the discourse of the right in order to understand the appeal of such discourse to sections of the larger population. This extreme discourse helps us understand rising political currents that have implications for refugee policy, which in turn has implications for the future in cities such as Detroit.

Issues around accommodations do arise in the Metro Detroit area, such as the controversy surrounding the call to prayer in Hamtramck. These are generally resolved by local residents through deliberation and do not rise to the level of acrimony the far right would like to incite (Leland 2004). Such processes of everyday, messy cosmopolitanism (Georgiou 2013) at the ground level help to provide an important counterpoint to Islamophobic discourses being circulated at local, national, and international levels (Lean 2017; Esposito and Kalin 2011).

THE REFUGEE AS A VOTE GETTER: THE POLITICAL FIGHT OVER THE FIGURE OF THE REFUGEE. The confluence of two events made the issue of refugees and immigrants a visible and contested discursive focus in the United States in 2015 and into 2016: the terrorist attacks in Paris and the US presidential election. Once these issues became news, politicians at every level felt pressure to position themselves rhetorically on the question of the immigrant and refugee other. Political expediency as manifested on refugees was clear in the rhetorical balancing act that Michigan's then-governor Rick Snyder performed. Snyder was a potential vice-presidential candidate. He was also governor of a state with a long history of resettlement of the refugees from the Arab world and an empowered Arab American community. He attempted to walk a fine rhetorical line by being one of the first governors in the country to call for a halt to the routing of Syrian refugees to the United States while also repeating his earlier stance that Michigan is a welcoming state for refugees and immigrants.

The political discourse of local politicians such as Michigan state senator Patrick Colbeck and county executive of Oakland County L. Brooks Patterson carried echoes of far-right discourse. Conservative politicians used the Islamophobic discursive constructs of the far right as a shorthand to advance their own political agendas. They used milder versions of anti-Muslim and antirefugee rhetoric so as not to seem beyond the pale. The discursive work of the far right thus seeped into the mainstream through the bridge of politics and in this way has been able to gain a degree of influence.

Perhaps the most important counterpoint to the politicization of the refugee and the Muslim other that emerged from the analysis was the conscious refusal to politicize at the hyper-local level, in diverse cities such as Hamtramck. In Hamtramck, residents took the fact of a majority Muslim city council in their stride. The non-Muslim mayor and the Muslim city councilor both refused to politicize the issue. City councilor Saad Almasmari's words are eloquent in their ordinariness: "It was a regular election, just like any other election. . . . People choose whomever they want" (Felton 2015).

The rhetoric of politicians such as Colbeck and Patterson painted the Muslim and the refugee as strangers. And politicians such as Snyder attempted to balance security concerns with a long-standing posture of hospitality. Nonetheless, politicians in towns such as Hamtramck neutralized the rhetoric of suspicion by rendering the Muslim and the former refugee as utterly ordinary.

REFUGEES WELCOME: THE REFUGEE AS A TEST OF OUR COLLECTIVE CHARACTER. Both national and local news sources conveyed an aspect of humanitarianism in coverage of the Syrian refugee. But the humanitarian aspect was most clearly present in refugee agency discourse. These agencies depicted all refugees, including Syrians, as deserving people's beneficence and hospitality. The agencies portrayed the host society as poised to transform the refugee from a person shorn of possessions and history to a functioning human being in a functioning society. The refugee was portrayed as a figure of vulnerability and hope, the refugee being vulnerable and the hope coming from the host society. In the refugee-agency context the refugee comes across as an entity to be administered. As with the news discourses, representing the refugee as primarily a recipient of the state's and city's hospitality and beneficence, accentuating the refugee's need and victimhood, resulted in a depiction of the refugee as devoid of agency. More than in any other discourses examined here, the refugee-agency discourse also accentuated the gratitude of the refugee toward the host society.[6] Collectively, these elements constructed a sense of the refugee as a moral obligation, as reflecting the host society's sense of humanity. While such a construction served as an important counterpoint to the discourse of the refugee as threat, it also moved the discourse away from the refugee as a being vested with rights or as having interpretational and political agency.

Further, as in the news discourses, what is absent here is any sense of the political conditions that have led to the large-scale displacement of people, including US responsibility for the creation of Iraqi and Syrian refugees. The refugee is therefore depicted as a moral obligation in abstract terms, an obligation reflecting the moral contours of the host society, rather than an obligation resulting from taking responsibility for the political actions of the host society—in this case, the United States.

Another irony in the humanitarian discourse of the refugee agencies became apparent when contrasted with the far-right discourse on the Muslim refugee taken up in the chapter "Refugees Not Welcome." The refugee agency discourse faced in the direction opposite to that of the far-right discourse, representing the refugee as a figure of vulnerability and hope rather than a figure of threat. But both discourses robbed the refugee of agency. Refugee agency discourse depicted the refugee as a vessel to be filled with our beneficence; the far-right discourse depicted the refugee as the distillation of the Muslim other, as a caricature of the not-West. In what seem to be diametrically opposite discourses, one glimpses different faces of contemporary Orientalism, each allowing the West to position itself as the moral center in contrast to the refugee standing in for the East.

DETROIT AS DEPORTATION CENTRAL FOR CHALDEAN REFUGEES: REPRESENTATION OF A REFUGEE GROUP IN NARROW CHRISTIAN TERMS. In

---

6. Nayeri (2018), an Iranian refugee, has written a poignant story about the burdens and implications of the requirement that the refugee be grateful. She recounts her mother having to repeatedly tell her refugee story to local civic groups, concluding, "The problem, of course, was that they wanted our salvation story as a talisman, no more," so that the host society could take credit for their being still alive but not wanting to know anything about their past.

2017 the Chaldean population in the Metro Detroit area found itself under threat from Trump's anti-immigration policies. As a result of a deal struck with Iraq exempting it from a travel ban imposed on several Muslim-majority countries, in exchange for Iraq agreeing to accept deportees, US government officials threatened members of the Chaldean community with deportation to Iraq. The Chaldeans effectively pushed back against the deportation order, working with the local press and the ACLU to obtain stay orders. The local press framing of the issue was quite sympathetic to the plight of the Chaldean residents, who were former refugees.

Local media portrayed the Chaldean community as a Christian community of ancient lineage. Closely following the dominant themes of the community's own self-representation through community leaders and community websites, the press coverage conveyed the sense of betrayal that a majority of the community felt. Many of them had voted for Trump based on his campaign promise to protect minority Christian communities in the Muslim world. The press coverage also conveyed the sense in the community that the deportation of Chaldeans to Iraq would amount to a "death threat," because the dominant Muslim population would persecute them. While this narrow self-positioning was an effective short-term strategy to gain immediate ends, it was short-sighted in limiting the potential for creating alliances with other groups of refugees and immigrants working to push back against restrictive and damaging immigration policies, including policies pertaining to refugees.

UNSETTLING REFUGEE DISCOURSE THROUGH ART AND CULTURE: ATTEMPTING TO MOVE BEYOND THE STOCK FIGURE OF THE REFUGEE. In chapter 6, I examine diverse artistic and cultural creations to explore the potential for public culture to unsettle the discursive constructs of the refugee created by other local institutions in the Metro Detroit area. Public culture creates a necessary and important space for attempting to go beyond administrative discourses on the refugee; it's an important counterpoint to discourses of suspicion and hate being circulated at different levels. Whether through a documentary, photo essay, graphic novel, or museum exhibit, this discourse attempted to break through the discursive construct of the refugee as an entity to be administered or as primarily a threat or opportunity for communities in the United States. There was an attempt to see refugees as entities unto themselves, as having history, as having experienced deep loss but also has harboring dreams and hopes, and as essentially human. These were all bridge-building projects in which people worked strenuously to create empathy for the refugees. Viewers were asked to try to walk in their shoes, even if only for a moment—to ask, for example, what they as refugees would carry if they had to leave suddenly.

However, the refugee was still curated in these creations, and as a curated figure, the refugee entered into the discourse in very particular ways. While opening a window to the refugee experience as essentially human, as with the other institutional discourses examined here, there was only a limited sense of the refugee as having interpretational agency, and an even more limited sense of the refugee as having political agency. As in the other discourses, there was also a very limited acknowledgment of the political conditions that turned the humans into refugees.

This exercise in bridge-building was also shaped to some extent by an already existing effort by Arab cultural institutions in Detroit, especially in the wake of September 11. These institutions included the Arab American National Museum. They showcased a very particular, Americanized "reception area" or "parlor" version of Arab Detroit, attempting to neutralize any "suspect, incomplete, and contested aspects of Arab/Muslim identity" (Shryock, Abraham, and Howell 2011; Yezbick 2011).

When we do glimpse refugee voices in the artistic creations, we glimpse a self-definition through the negation of the former refugee self, a self-definition through the prism of transcendence.[7] On the rare occasion that someone refers to themselves as a refugee in the created works, it is in the sense of looking back at a transcended former self, or with a self-consciousness about having been turned into a refugee by larger forces. Or it is done as a conscious political act—taking a name created by others and using it to turn a critical eye on dominant institutions and processes. Leila Abdelrazaq is a clear instance of the use of the refugee construct as a

---

7. Arendt begins her famous essay "We Refugees" with "In the first place we don't like to be called 'refugees.'" She points to the layers of complexity contained in the label "refugee" by leading with self-consciousness about the label. Gatrell (2013) points to the varied ways in which refugees understand, position themselves in relation to, and sometimes strategically use the refugee label, depending on their particular circumstances of displacement and aspects of their overall situation once they are resettled.

political act. She writes the story of her father as a refugee "as a testament to the fact that we have not forgotten" the rendering of Palestinians into statelessness; the story constitutes a gesture of resistance. The words of another writer, a former refugee from South Vietnam, are poignant in this regard. "I was once a refugee, although no one would mistake me for being a refugee now. Because of this, I insist on being called a refugee, since the temptation to pretend that I am not a refugee is strong" (Nguyen 2018).

CHAPTER 1

Destination Detroit

The Refugee as a Means of Economic Revitalization

In this chapter I chiefly explore the discourse that sought to smooth the way for routing Syrian refugees to Detroit. My goal is to provide a broader understanding of what has been termed the greatest refugee crisis since World War II (Packer 2015). The debate on whether the United States should help to address the crisis, and to what extent, including the number of refugees it would take in, occurred within a larger global context. The US contribution would at best pale in comparison to the role played by countries in the Middle East, such as Lebanon, Jordan, and Turkey, as well as by some European countries. Closer to home, neighboring Canada took in about four times as many Syrian refugees as the United States in 2016 (Zong and Batalova 2017). The debate occurred within the larger historical context of US military invasions of Iraq, which created a domino effect leading to the Syrian refugee crisis (Cassidy 2015).[1]

---

1. The specific debate over Syrian refugees was taking place at a time when the issues of refugee resettlements and immigration had become central to the shaping of liberal democracies, and at a time when several leaders with autocratic tendencies had been elected on a platform of restricting the intake of refugees and immigrants to their respective countries. Trump was elected president on a platform that vilified refugees and immigrants, in a stark reminder of the material consequences of discourses on refugees.

Methodology

I used a combination strategy to collect and examine newspaper articles addressing the subject of Syrian refugees. While my main focus is local news coverage of Syrian refugees, I also examine national news coverage of Syrian refugees for comparison. As a starting point, to find the largest number of relevant stories in national and regional newspapers, I searched LexisNexis Academic for the terms "Syrian refugees in U.S." and "Syrians in Detroit." I delimited search results for the term "Syrian refugees in U.S." to the date range May 1, 2015, to December 31, 2015, the period when these stories were concentrated. The search term "Syrian refugees in Detroit," with or without a time range, yielded too few stories, so I broadened the search to "Syrians in Detroit" without a time range.

The LexisNexis search yielded 166 national news stories on Syrian refugees, all bunching within the few months after the attacks in Paris, the deadliest to occur in France since World War II. Gunmen and suicide bombers had hit several locations almost simultaneously, leaving more than 120 people dead, hundreds wounded, and creating economic, political, and social ripple effects in France and beyond. The search also yielded 41 news stories on Syrian refugees in Detroit, 4 of which were in *Crain's Detroit Business*. These constitute a universe of articles as located through the database using those particular search terms.

While the searches did yield different kinds of stories, including editorials, columns, and even letters to the editor, the majority were straight news stories. In the discussion below, I indicate the type of story only when it is not a straight news story—for example, when the news item referenced is an editorial.

In addition to the broader LexisNexis search, I reviewed select individual newspapers for relevant stories. For the local press, I chose the best-known and most widely circulating local papers, the *Detroit Free Press* and the *Detroit News*. The *Detroit Free Press* tends to be at the liberal end of the political spectrum, and the *Detroit News* at the conservative end. Reviewing both allowed me to gauge whether the approach to the refugee issue diverged or converged based on a newspaper's political orientation.

I used the search term "Syrian refugees" when searching the two local papers. I used the same search term to examine news stories on the website of Michigan Radio, an Ann Arbor-based affiliate of National Public Radio. In addition, I did a Google search using the term "Syrian refugees in Detroit."

When reading the articles from the local press and local radio station, I learned of a specific controversy surrounding the construction of a housing complex for refugees in Pontiac, Michigan. To get a hyperlocal perspective on this issue, I conducted a Google search using the term "Pontiac and Syrian refugees" as well as the search term "Pontiac Syrians" on the *Detroit Free Press*, the *Detroit News*, and Michigan Radio websites.

My review of the sources discussed above revealed recurring themes in each set of articles and for each area of inquiry. These themes crossed over between national and local news coverage. When examining the coverage of the resettlement of Syrian refugees in Detroit, I separately located recurring themes in the articles yielded by LexisNexis, those from the *Detroit Free Press* website, those from the *Detroit News* website, and so on. In the sections below, I explore these themes in greater detail.

The Paris Attacks: An Inflection Point

During my review of news stories, I realized that the ISIL attacks in Paris on November 13, 2015, were a natural inflection point in both national and local coverage. Before the Paris attacks, President Barack Obama had announced a policy to admit 10,000 Syrian refugees into the United States in 2016. After the attacks, various entities—including governors, Congress, elected representatives at the local level, faith-based and other groups working to settle refugees, and (although rarely) the refugees themselves—either defended or resisted President Obama's stated policy. Twenty-six state governors—including Michigan Governor Rick Snyder—questioned Obama's position, citing security as their primary concern. Congress also passed a bill calling for a halt to refugee resettlement until certain security guarantees were met. On the political stage, both nationally and locally, stances toward refugee resettlement split mainly along party lines. Republicans voiced security concerns about Obama's policy, and Democrats defended the position based on humanitarian concerns.

The tussle between federal and state government entities garnered news attention at every level, while the Congressional response was covered mainly at the national level. Stories not only increased in number after the Paris attacks, but their framing changed. A *New York Times* article encapsulates well the general contours of news discourse at the national level before the attacks. In "Let Syrians Settle Detroit" (2015), the main concern is to persuade national policymakers and administrators that settling Syrian refugees in Detroit would benefit both the refugees and Detroit. The authors ask political and administrative entities to "[s]uppose these two social and humanitarian disasters were conjoined to produce something positive." The rest of the article is devoted to defending the track record of Syrian and other refugees in the United States; to demonstrating the feasibility and suitability of the relocation plan; and to addressing concerns voiced by skeptics, namely "the difficulties of assimilation" for refugees, the possibility of failure should "the most ambitious Syrians . . . leave the city once they achieved economic security," and the political challenges confronting the plan "given skepticism toward immigration, particularly in the Republican Party."

Although the article leads with the benefit to refugees, the rest of it is mainly premised on the idea that the proposal will rise or fall based on the costs and benefits for Detroit and US agencies. Although the economic benefit from refugees is the focus, toward the end of the article the authors speak of the plan's consistency with "America's ethical and moral commitments."

The *Times* piece was one of a handful of news stories supporting the relocation of Syrian refugees to Detroit in the months before the ISIL attacks in Paris on November 13, 2015 (Detroit has space, need for Syrians 2015; Walsh 2015; Opinion 2015). The *Detroit Free Press* and *Detroit News* also carried articles echoing an optimistic outlook for resettling Syrian refugees in Detroit. In one such article, the *Detroit Free Press* quotes Michigan's Republican governor Snyder at length, as he explains "in addition to helping people in need, Michigan can improve its economy by taking in refugees," and says of past refugees in Michigan that "they were great small business people, they were professionals, they were people that hire people, that tend to create jobs" (Eagan 2015).

In the same vein, another story in the *Detroit Free Press* personalized the issue by leading with the story of a Syrian refugee family who had just settled in Michigan, with family members expressing how the "accessibility to everything" familiar because of the local Arab population had made the adjustment easier for them. The authors asserted that "unlike some places where people have been wary about Syrian refugees, Michigan sees them as one solution to the state's population loss" (Karoub 2015).

The *Detroit News*, at the more conservative end of the political spectrum, observed in a story featuring a refugee advocate that "Michigan once ranked first among states for taking in Syrian refugees," but now ranked second. Like the *Detroit Free Press*, the *Detroit News* carried articles before the attacks on the successful relocation of Syrian refugees, and on Governor Snyder's and Mayor Duggan's efforts to increase the number of Syrian refugees coming into Michigan and Detroit. Before the Paris attacks, the economic aspect, absent in stories about the overall Syrian refugee issue, was central to the stories about Detroit and Syrian refugees.

After the Paris attacks, stories on Syrian refugees surged in both national and local news. However, they typically focused on the political controversy in the United States, not on the question of resettling refugees in the country. Taken collectively, the coverage foregrounded two main competing perspectives: humanitarian and security. The Paris attack was the main news hook, but the refugee crisis became a "political football" (LaFranchi 2015), with actors at all levels using the situation to position themselves favorably with their constituencies. This was particularly apparent with candidates in the Republican presidential primary race, who discursively used security concerns about the refugee program to display patriotism, strength, or overall suitability for the position of commander-in-chief. Candidates felt obliged to address Obama's refugee policy in some way because of heightened public concern after the Paris attacks (Fitzgerald and Hanna 2015). This shift in framing also happened at the local level, with coverage of Syrian refugee relocation in Detroit converging around two story lines: Governor Snyder's turnaround on welcoming Syrian refugees to Detroit, and the efforts by Oakland County Executive L. Brooks Patterson to stop the construction of a housing complex for Syrian refugees in the city of Pontiac, Michigan (discussed in more detail below). Although there was some national coverage of Snyder's reversal, local stories predominated.

In a handful of news stories, refugees themselves argued against perceived security concerns by questioning the conflation of "refugee" and "terrorist" in the political rhetoric. In these articles, refugees showed through their own stories that they'd had no choice but to flee violent situations and were merely looking for safety and a chance at normal lives for themselves and their children. The few stories where refugees offered their opinions came to the attention of the media thanks to either organizations in the business of settling refugees or faith-based groups aiding in this area. Representatives from these organizations often described refugees as worthy of entry into the United States and deserving assistance. Refugee organization spokespeople also represented the refugees as regular human beings who wanted the same things as the articles' readers.

Similar to what has been found in research at the national news level in other contexts, almost no mention or critique was made of the nation's (in this case, the United States') responsibility for creating a political context that led to the increased movement of refugees. A similar absence has been found in work on the UK, Germany, and Australia (Pickering 2001; Holmes and Castañeda 2016; Philo, Briant, and Donald 2013). As we will see later in this chapter, this aspect was true of news coverage at the local Detroit level as well.

Local Coverage Maintains More Sympathetic Framing

The stories addressing the general issue of Syrian refugees all had an adversarial frame, balancing the perspectives of those for and against Obama's policy. In contrast, the stories addressing the routing of Syrian refugees to Detroit were almost invariably sympathetic to the idea. This was true of stories both before and after the Paris attacks.

The handful of stories before the Paris attacks echoed the general tenor of the *New York Times* article with which I started this discussion: Detroit is a very suitable place to locate Syrian refugees, and that by welcoming Syrian refugees, Detroiters would be helping not only the refugees, but themselves. These themes occurred in both the local and national coverage.

News stories supported the first point with cultural, administrative, and economic arguments. They noted Detroit's existing Arab population, its social service nexus supporting this population, and the availability of property due to the city's depopulation. Together, these themes created a frame of interpretation that encouraged readers to see refugee relocation as a mutually beneficial policy, with the refugees finding a suitable refuge and a suitable bridge to assimilate to the United States, and Detroit receiving the human capital necessary to revitalize its economy and its neighborhoods.

The lead to an article in the *Wisconsin State Journal* captured well the tone of the arguments.

> We shouldn't do it [help Syrian refugees] just because it makes us feel good. We should do it to help our economy. And one American city, my hometown of Detroit, has the space and infrastructure to welcome tens of thousands of Syrian refugees while benefiting the most from their presence. (Detroit has space, need for Syrians 2015)

Local organs such as *Crain's Detroit Business* echoed this sentiment, positing that "to many, the refugees represent an opportunity to repopulate a Detroit neighborhood [in this case North Town] and boost the local economy." The article goes further: "And there's no question that immigration is an important strategy for Detroit" (Walsh 2015).

It is notable, however, that the overall interpretive frame of the local news continued to be sympathetic to the relocation of refugees in Detroit, even after the Paris attacks, regardless of the various politicians' stances, and even when the stories were organized around a frame of conflicting views. For example, a story published in the *Detroit Free Press* on the day Snyder made his announcement was headlined "Snyder suspends Syrian refugee effort in Michigan," with the subhead "Many in state are outraged, but governor says safety is a key concern after attacks in Paris" (Eagan and Warikoo 2015). The subhead cued readers to realize that Snyder's decision had prompted pushback. Early in the article the authors observed that "Snyder's announcement Sunday is a step backward from recent efforts and comments from his administration offering to aid refugees," extending the critical frame from this being an unpopular move to it being a regressive step and contrary to Snyder's own earlier stance. To drive home the contradiction, the story cited the governor's statements before the attacks, including one referring to himself as "the most pro-immigration governor in the country." The story also gave far more space to the critics of Snyder's move than to supporters of it, allowing local Arab American leaders and refugee advocates to point out how misguided the reversal was and how it sent the wrong message. While two Republican representatives' quotes in support of Snyder's statement were included, these had a marginal position in the story. As another example, Brian Dickerson of the *Detroit Free Press* pointed out in his column that as a governor Snyder had no authority over refugee relocations and that his statement was a matter of "partisan demagoguery" (Dickerson 2015).

A couple of other stories focused on families that had arrived soon after the governor's statement. These stories reinforced the idea that the governor lacked the authority to pause the resettlements. The articles used the story of particular families as a hook to discuss the national mood against Syrian refugees after the Paris attacks. They allowed refugee advocates and Syrian American advocates to voice their concern about the negative rhetoric at the national level. In one of these articles, a refugee advocate said, "This is the worst we've seen." A Syrian American advocate said, "I'm not just concerned about the Syrian refugees, I'm concerned about the future of Muslims in this country." As for Snyder himself, the article pointed to a contradiction, indicating that his statement "was the first in a wave of governors and other politicians moving to halt or block Syrian refugees," but that when it came to actual refugees coming to Michigan, he had changed his tune, saying through a spokesman, "We are happy that people want to come to Michigan to rebuild their lives, and we have a very supportive community here that can help them do that" (Warikoo 2015). Clearly, even a Republican governor in Michigan must tread carefully because of the importance of refugees to the state's economy and the degree of support for the refugees in the state, especially in an empowered Arab American community.

Another story using a personalizing frame focused not on the family next door, but on a scientist—the kind of person who embodies qualities that would be generally considered highly desirable in a refugee or immigrant (Stafford 2015). The story about Rafaai Hamo arriving in Michigan drove home the point that Syrian refugees contribute to the state. The pathos of the story of Hamo losing seven family members to bombing, including his wife and daughter, and then discovering he had stomach cancer had already touched many people around the world through the *Humans of New York* blog on Facebook. In fact, fundraisers collected $450,000 for his family. By the time the local press covered him, the sympathy he had garnered could be seen as support for resettlement of Syrian refugees in Michigan.

Hamo insisted that he wanted to start a new life and contribute a meaningful legacy, that he wanted to be treated as a citizen rather than a refugee, and that Syrians "will give back to the community, they will be good citizens to the countries they are living in." In doing so, he served as an elite ambassador for Syrian refugees. And by carrying his story, the local news was able to piggyback on his positioning as an ambassador, further bolstering the sympathetic covering of the issue.[2]

This general impression grew stronger when newspapers gave prominence to sympathetic letters from readers. One led with a bold headline: "We shouldn't be afraid of Syrian refugees" (*Free Press* readers 2015). A newspaper also carried a piece by guest writer and refugee advocate Sean de Four, who made the case that it's "the American way" to keep our borders and hearts open to refugees, and that "the integrity of humanity" depends on helping them (de Four 2015). Other stories told of Detroit mayor Mike Duggan standing firm on welcoming refugees soon after Snyder made his statement (Warikoo 2015), of Reverend Jesse Jackson saying Snyder was "wrong to pull back the welcome mat for Syrian refugees" (Erb 2015), and of Michigan documentary filmmaker Michael Moore calling Snyder's statement "disgraceful" (Hinds 2015). Thus, even after the Paris attacks, the overall frame that emerged was sympathetic to the relocation of Syrian refugees in Michigan.

---

2. Although Hamo's self-representation included both his Syrian identity and his identity as a member of the Kurdish minority in Syria, refugee advocates mainly represented Hamo as a Syrian, with a view to making the case for the continued relocation of Syrian refugees to the Detroit area. They were able to parlay the sense of Hamo as a model Syrian refugee into the local news coverage.

Convergence of News Frames in the
Local Liberal and Conservative Press

As discussed, news coverage of plans to relocate refugees to Detroit typi-cally took a sympathetic view both before and after the Paris attacks. This pattern is especially evident when comparing coverage by the *Detroit Free Press* and the *Detroit News*.

Although the two papers share a joint operating agreement, the *Detroit News* is to the right of the *Detroit Free Press* on the political spec-trum. Despite this political divergence, the newspapers used similar news frames when covering refugee relocation. This points to the impor-tance of the issue in Detroit, including the importance of reframing the debate from the national level to accommodate local economic and social realities.

The *Detroit News* conveyed a distinct overall impression that the relo-cation was the correct move for the Detroit area and the state as a whole. They did so through a combination of articles about pushback against the governor's decision, opinion pieces arguing that the decision was wrong-headed, an article about Mayor Duggan maintaining his welcoming stance, and articles showing that the refugee relocation to the Detroit area was continuing unimpeded and that the refugees had been assimilating suc-cessfully. Like the *Detroit Free Press*, the *News* allowed refugee and Syrian American advocates ample space to voice their concerns about the nega-tive rhetoric at the national and state levels and to express their strong support for refugee relocation. When reporters or columnists quoted pro-ponents of pausing or stopping the flow, they always gave advocates for the refugees a chance to refute their position and arguments.

In one example, an opinion piece had the headline "Syrian refugees an asset to U.S." (la Corte 2015). Addressing the actions of both state and federal officials who have "rushed to close off the doors on refugees," the author argued that excluding refugees played right into the hands of ISIS propaganda. In contrast, the author asserted, helping the refugees would "[provide] us with allies, intelligence, and counterprogramming to ISIS propaganda, reducing opportunities for radicalization." Although the main thrust of the piece was the wrongheadedness of the overall political reaction after the Paris attacks, the piece culminated with a clear statement of Michigan's suitability for relocation.

One story showcased local activists "demanding" that the governor accept Syrian refugees (Heinlein 2015). Another covered a panel convened jointly by the Reverend Jesse Jackson's Rainbow PUSH coalition and the Arab American Civil Rights League. The coalition and the league were pushing back against Governor Snyder's decision and urging people to welcome Syrian refugees in Michigan (Dickson 2015). Another story, which came out immediately after the governor's announcement, showed the decision to be politically driven, using fear as a political tactic. A Syrian American advocate, an Arab American advocate, and an immigration advocate each got space to make their case for accepting Syrian refugees in Michigan (Berman 2015).

In a story headlined "Snyder among governors not taking Syrian refugees," the *News* presented Snyder's stance as a reasonable one in the context of competing opinions of Republican politicians, the Obama administration, and refugee advocates. However, once again the newspaper always countered Republican opinions with the opinions of those advocating refugee relocation (Burke 2015). Like the *Free Press*, the *News* ran a handful of stories showing that the successful relocation of Syrian refugees was continuing without interruption after the attacks and that Syrian families were assimilating successfully (Rubin 2016; Hughbanks 2016; Ramirez 2016).

Local News Coverage of a Planned Housing Complex for Syrian Refugees

I turn now to local news coverage of an even more locally based issue. Although far fewer stories were written on this local issue than on the larger issue of Syrian refugees coming to Michigan, the way that an overall sympathetic frame was established is instructive, echoing and even amplifying the frames used for the larger Syrian refugee issue related to Detroit. Before proceeding to the news coverage, some background information on the issue will be useful.

Three days after Michigan's governor Snyder called for a suspension of the refugee program in Michigan until security procedures had been clarified, Oakland County Executive L. Brooks Patterson sent a letter to the mayor of Pontiac, Deirdre Waterman. (Pontiac is a city in Oakland County.) In the letter, Patterson expressed his concern about the plan to build a community center and housing for Syrian refugees and others. Mayor Waterman took a middle-of-the-road approach to the issue, sharing Patterson's concerns about security, but she didn't necessarily want to halt the project.

The stories about the development had an adversarial frame, with news outlets pitting L. Brooks Patterson against Oakland County Treasurer Andy Meisner and developer Ismael Basha. This frame included language implying that Patterson was the unreasonable party and those favoring the development were reasonable. How did newspapers use language to discredit Patterson? One *Detroit Free Press* article described the letter he sent to Mayor Waterman as "stern." The article stated he was "demanding" that Pontiac stop its plans. The *Free Press* gave the developer Basha space to refute Patterson's stance at length, including his questioning of the phrase "Syrian Refugee Village" from Patterson's letter. The story also mentioned twice that Patterson's letter came on the heels of the larger pushback against Syrian refugees after the Paris attacks, including Governor Snyder's statement delivered a few days previously. This detail lent credence to County Treasurer Meisner's claim in the same article that Patterson's "comments politicize a project that will bring much-needed economic development to Pontiac and provide housing for people desperately in need who have undergone exhaustive background checks." Basha and Meisner echoed each other's stance that Patterson's actions "could scuttle a plan to help repopulate and develop a city facing economic challenges and declining population" (Warikoo 2015).

Stories in a number of other local organs and on radio stations took a very similar approach. They led with quotes from Patterson's letter, and then allowed extensive comments from the developer, the treasurer, and refugee advocates to challenge Patterson's claims and stance. In a vein similar to the one in the *New York Times* article mentioned earlier, insiders from the Detroit metropolitan area put forward the idea of conjoining two humanitarian disasters, Pontiac's economic decline and the refugees' need for help, as eminently reasonable and commonsensical. The insiders characterized those who resisted this idea as obstructionist.

A *Detroit News* article (Williams and Hicks 2015) exemplifies the general approach. The article devoted four paragraphs to stating Patterson's position, including quotes from his letter. By contrast, it devoted seventeen paragraphs to an eloquent and detailed refutation of Patterson's position by Meisner, the Oakland County treasurer; Basha, the property developer; Dr. Muzzamil Ahmed, the board chairman of the Michigan Muslim Community Council; and Iman Abdulrazzak, the director of the Michigan Muslim Community Council Syrian refugee task force.

The local Fox News television outlet gave more space to Patterson and Waterman than the *Detroit Free Press* and *Detroit News* stories did. Still, the language used undermined Patterson's stance. For example, one Fox 2 news story described Patterson as being "upset" about the development and as saying he planned to "raise hell," even while acknowledging that he has no legal right to stop the development (Asher 2015). A later Fox 2 story had the headline "Patterson fumes as Syrian refugee plan in Pontiac proceeds" (Kelley 2015). Again, the language painted a picture of Patterson as petulant and unreasonable. The television station allowed the treasurer, the developer, or both to make statements refuting Patterson's stance and showing that he was politicizing the issue. Reporters took these statements at face value. All in all, then, local news outlets shared news framing favorable to the development of the housing complex, even though those outlets existed on different parts of the political spectrum.

Economic Revitalization as the Predominant News Frame

When it came to Syrian refugee relocation in Detroit and the building of a housing complex to welcome Syrian refugees, it was clear from the stories that economic considerations were at the forefront, which created a favorable frame of interpretation. Local politicians, particularly Republican politicians, felt the pull of the security discourse after the Paris attacks, but the news media centered coverage on the economic perspective, and secondarily on the humanitarian aspect. Local news media did not always include security considerations when exploring the issue, and when security concerns did make it into the local news, reporters and anchors always showed them to be exaggerated or misguided.

Detroit's population loss and need for revitalization were the issues that created the larger context from which the local news frames emanated. The news strongly tended to play a developmental role, championing and supporting immigration as an instrument of economic revitalization. In addition, it became clear that Detroit's long-standing strength as a hub for Arab immigration (Rignall 2000; Schopmeyer 2000; Schopmeyer 2011) contributed to the favorable frame of interpretation.

It was also clear from the analysis that one factor allowing for this favorable framing was the eloquent advocacy for refugee relocation. There was a range of refugee advocates, including faith-based organizations such as Lutheran Family Social Services of Michigan/Samaritas. Importantly, these advocates included representatives of Arab American and/or Muslim organizations. Some of these were refugee-specific, such as the Syrian American Rescue Network. Others were not specific to refugees, such as the Michigan Muslim Community Council.

The fact that the stories frequently used prominent members of the Arab American community as spokespersons is in accord with Howell and Jamal's argument that "Arabs in Michigan have achieved genuine political incorporation" (97) and that this "compelled officials to recognize that the fate of Michigan, and of Dearborn in particular, [is] intertwined now with the fate of their Arab citizens." Howell and Jamal (2011) were making this argument in the specific context of post-September 11 Arab Detroit and why the public backlash in Detroit was less severe than it was nationally. But the aspect of Arab and Muslim institutional strength was clear in this news analysis, contributing to a sympathetic framing of the refugee relocation issue. Refugee advocates were able to make an eloquent case for refugee relocation. And in economic terms, the fate of Michigan was seen as tied to the prospect of revitalization by immigrant communities, including Syrian refugees.

Local politicians, such as Governor Snyder and L. Brooks Patterson, got caught up in the national pushback against Syrian refugees after the Paris attacks, but they participated in this pushback as part of their own political calculations. In contrast, refugee advocates, Syrian American advocates, and Arab American advocates at the local level were able to effectively reframe their arguments to make a strong case for the uninterrupted relocation of Syrian refugees to the Detroit area.

Although the overall interpretive frame within the news was sympathetic to Syrian refugee relocation to Detroit, there were some important absences or near-absences in the news coverage. The news media allowed some refugees to express their points of view, but these voices were mainly promoted by refugee resettlement agencies to show that the refugees were adjusting well. The agencies featured the refugees mainly to show that they had escaped desperate situations, that they had been stripped of their former networks and possessions, and that they were eager to start new lives for themselves and their families. All of this added up to a sense that the refugees did not represent a threat and deserved support.

But to the people at the news outlets and in the resettlement groups, the refugees had very limited if any self-direction. They seemed like empty vessels, ready to receive Americans' beneficence. They remained largely within what Malkki has astutely described as an essentialized category of "refugee," as having certain cultural traits. These included being associated with loss and needing the help and direction of international, national, and local agencies (1995). A scholar examining national news coverage of refugees in the Australian context described this as the construction of the "ideal refugee," akin to the idea of the "deserving" refugee. The ideal refugee is either very young or very old, and is being persecuted by "an internationally proclaimed oppressive state." Also, the ideal refugee has an invitation from the host government and is "visibly grateful" (Pickering 2001, 177).

Another notable absence was coverage of the political causes of the Syrian refugee crisis and any sense of US responsibility, direct or indirect, for the crisis. What Malkki says about refugee studies literature applies to some extent to the news discourse analyzed here. This discourse locates "the problem not in the political conditions or processes that produce massive territorial displacements of people, but rather within the bodies and minds (and even souls) of people categorized as refugees" (1992, 33). As with refugee studies literature, the political conditions creating the refugee flow were rarely covered in the news. This allows the news coverage to represent refugee relocation as an act of charity rather than an act of responsibility or reparation.[3]

When examining national news coverage of refugees in Germany, Holmes and Castañeda made a similar observation that the representations "shift blame from historical, political-economic structures to the displaced people themselves" (2016, 1). At both the national and local levels, the scrutiny, whether implicit or explicit, shifted from the larger structural causes to the potential danger and/or opportunity that the refugees presented. However, there was also an important countercurrent in the news to the representation of refugees as pathological figures. Refugee advocates worked strenuously to show that refugees are normal people trying to establish normal everyday lives. In rare instances, such as through the voice of a prominent refugee like Rafaai Hamo, we could see the refugees themselves straining against the dominant representation, insisting on being seen as humans or as citizens. On the other hand, the fact that so much effort was devoted to insisting on normalcy points to the larger current against which these voices are working, the larger discourse quite ready to pathologize or even demonize the refugee.

In the end, then, the representation of the "refugee" remains contradictory at the local level. Local news outlets and experts depict refugees as deserving of our sympathy and representing the potential for economic revitalization, but it is also necessary to defend their normality and harmlessness. And although local advocates for refugees effectively reframed the security discourse in the news coverage, this reframing included pointing out that stringent security procedures are already in place. These advocates emphasized that refugees coming to the United States are among the most vetted of immigrants, and compared with procedures in other receiving countries, they are among the most vetted refugees in the world.

---

3. With the exception of one or two phrases from local activists such as Suheila Amen that slipped into the news as quotes, none of the stories broached the larger context of the surge of refugees from Syria or the Arab world. Almost none mentioned the responsibility of the United States in contributing to the conditions leading to the large-scale displacement of Syrians, Iraqis, and others from the Arab world.

Although news coverage of the refugees was largely sympathetic at the local level, the defensive posture sometimes taken in the news stories revealed the larger discourses on the refugee crisis being circulated at this historical moment, even if to some extent they worked against the grain of these larger discourses. By briefly analyzing national news coverage and then focusing more deeply on local coverage of the Syrian refugee situation, I was able to see the finer grain in the discourse. Brought into view were some of the contradictions and layering of the discourse, a result of competing imperatives that become even more visible at the local than the national level.

At the national level, the humanitarian perspective competed with the security perspective. At the local level, the additional considerations of economic revitalization and the suitability of the receiving locale for the refugees entered into the news framing of the issue. Studies of news discourse in other national contexts also point in this direction, as when Pickering observes from the Australian context that "Local political contexts are also important in understanding the engagement of alternative views" (2001, 180). Holmes and Castañeda (2016) observe in the German context, paraphrasing Derrida, that "state interests and local ethics of hospitality are always in tension. On the one hand, states limit the right to residence; on the other hand, local communities may respond with hospitality to newcomers and offer refuge" (13).

At the local level, the contradictory logics and the discursive "war of position" becomes more visible. Local news discourse brings to mind some of the larger news frameworks that have become widespread, such as the security framework. But local news also introduces other frameworks that are relevant to its own survival and historical trajectory, such as the need for the economic revitalization of cities such as Detroit.

From casual perusal of the news coverage of other cities and towns in a similar position, it appears that similarly contradictory logics are at play. For example, a story of manufacturers in Erie, Pennsylvania, told of welcoming Syrian refugees to fill a shortage of willing and able workers worsened by the opioid epidemic (Gillespie 2017). Another story told of immigrants eventually being embraced by a meatpacking town in Iowa (Cohen 2017). An extended study of news coverage of refugee resettlement in different revitalizing cities would help to corroborate the generally supportive and developmental role the local press plays.

Contrasting Relocation of Syrian Refugees with Relocation of Burmese and Congolese Refugees in Michigan

Examining news coverage of refugee resettlement in other revitalizing cities was not within the scope of this project. However, I did examine news stories on the resettlement of Congolese and Burmese refugees in Western Michigan to see whether similar news frames predominated and whether similar tensions and contradictions were present.

Using the search term "Michigan Burmese refugees" in LexisNexis yielded no stories, while the search term "Michigan Congolese refugees" yielded five news stories. I then did a Google search using the search term "Congolese refugees in Michigan," which yielded nine stories. I then used the search term "Burmese Christians in Michigan," yielding seven news stories. Finally I tried the search term "Western Michigan Burmese refugees," yielding another two stories. Using the same combination of search terms at the *Detroit Free Press, Detroit News,* and Michigan Radio sites yielded no additional stories.

Perhaps even more notable than any similarity or difference in news frames in coverage of the different refugee populations in Michigan is the difference in scale of the coverage. The Congolese and Burmese refugees in Western Michigan did not make it into the news to the same degree as the Syrian refugees. Also, only three of the twenty-three stories had a conflictual frame. These news stories pushed back against either Snyder's decision to pause refugee resettlement or President Donald Trump's executive orders leading to a decline in refugee resettlement.

The majority of stories were either human interest stories featuring a refugee family or stories allowing refugee advocates, including Christian churches of different denominations, to highlight the importance and humanity of the work they were doing with refugees. In a news story carried by the newsletter of the Christian Reformed Church, the reader finds out that the Oakland Christian Reformed Church in Hamilton, Michigan, applied to become a cosponsor of a refugee family and then waited two years before actually being able to host a Congolese family. Whereas they had expected to host a family of four, it turned out to be a family of ten, presenting the parishioners with a "God-sized challenge," one they rose to meet (Christian Reformed Church 2018).

A news story in the American Baptist Churches of Michigan newsletter recounted the history of the resettlement of Burmese refugees in Battle Creek, with the First Baptist Church of Battle Creek's having played a crucial role in this history (Bauer and Thawnghmung 2017). And an article in the *Christian Post* features a Christian couple in Sault Ste. Marie that adopted eight Burmese refugee children from the persecuted Karen community in Burma, noting that they are "mostly Christian in the predominantly Buddhist country" (Riley 2009). From a piece in *Michigan News*, a University of Michigan organ, we learn that rising seniors at the university formed a group called [RE]vive and that they hosted a group of sixteen Congolese refugee high school students from Grand Rapids for a day of educational and vocational training (Congolese refugee high schoolers get training at U-M). The focus of the story was on the efforts of the hosting organizations.

The rescue narrative was present here, just as it was when talking about the Syrian refugees. Although the organizations proudly shared the successes of the refugees, the organizations themselves were the heroes of the stories. For example, a story in *LIRS*, the newsletter of the Lutheran Social Services of Michigan, relates at the end that among the Banyamulenge Tutsi refugees they had been resettling in Grand Rapids, one had bought a house within three years and another had joined the US Air Force. However, the main focus of the story was the persecution the Tutsis had been experiencing in the Congo and the work Lutheran Social Services/Grand Rapids had been doing to resettle the refugees (LIRS 2013).

Many of the stories included a Christian dimension, an aspect shared with the Burmese and Congolese refugees they were resettling. Even some of the stories carried in secular news organs such as *MLive Michigan* made the Christian aspect central. One such story applauded the humanity of Hager Reformed Church in Grandville, Michigan, for their "act of faith, hoping to make a life-changing difference for one unknown family," a Burmese refugee family of four (Runyon 2018). Another such story led with a pastor, himself a refugee from the Democratic Republic of Congo, leading a weekly church service in Grand Rapids, addressing fellow Christian refugees from the Congo in French. Later in the story, the reader learned that this unusual sight was made possible by the kindness of the regular pastor at the Lutheran church, who had attended an overcrowded service at the Congolese pastor's house and had decided the Congolese pastor and worshippers needed more space (Airgood 2017).

The news discourse on Congolese and Burmese refugees highlighted the religious aspect of the news stories—an aspect not available in the news discourse on Syrian refugees. To include the religious aspect in that discourse would have risked backlash against Syrian refugee relocation, invoking associations with the threat of terrorism as well as the threat of Muslim cultural shifts. As noted earlier, the local press played a developmental role supportive of the idea of refugee resettlement as a tool of economic revitalization. It therefore made sense for the press discourse on Syrian refugees to emphasize the economic aspect while also making room for the humanitarian aspect and staying clear of the specifically religious aspect.

While the Christian and humanitarian aspects were at the forefront when news sources reported on the Congolese and Burmese refugees, the economic aspect did enter into the picture. An immediate economic aspect the stories recognized was the important gap the Congolese and Burmese refugees were filling in terms of Michigan's position as a key destination for refugees. Readers learned early in the story that although there were generally "waning numbers of refugees to the U.S.," the Congolese refugees were an "exception"; "[o]f the 490 refugees who resettled in Michigan from October through March [2018-19] 319 are Congolese" (Rahal 2019).

As with the Syrian refugees, some stories refer to the actual and potential economic contributions of the refugees to towns and cities in Michigan. One story showcased the success of Burmese refugees in Battle Creek, noting that "most of the early arrivals have since become citizens of the United States and have purchased homes in Battle Creek. There are currently six Burmese Christian churches and four Asian markets operated by former Burmese refugees" (Bauer and Thawnghmung

2017). Another story features a former Burmese refugee, now a community leader, who founded the Burmese American Initiative in Grand Rapids to foster a sense of community in Burmese families in Grand Rapids (Parikh 2012). This same community leader and former refugee, Martha Thawnghmung, shared her perspective on Burmese refugee resettlement in a column in the *Battle Creek Enquirer*. Wielding statistics, she detailed the economic contributions the Burmese were making to Grand Rapids: buying homes, being an indispensable part of the workforce, creating new markets, forming families that became an integral part of the school system, and constituting ten new growing church congregations. She added poignantly that Burmese refugees succeeded on their own, and that it was time they got the "earned recognition as a valuable addition to the community." She reflected that Battle Creek could have done better as a receiving community, and ended the column with a call to the larger community in Battle Creek to invest in the Burmese community (Thawnghmung 2017).

As with the news stories on Syrian refugees, refugee advocates' voices were given the most play. News sources allowed advocates to speak on behalf of the refugees to show that they deserved help. However, unlike the news stories on the Syrian refugees, very few stories about Burmese and Congolese refugees had a conflictual frame. There was no identifiable antagonist against which the advocates were working to normalize the Burmese and Congolese refugees. Further, there was no reference to terrorism or any aspect of threat associated with the Burmese and Congolese refugees.

Perhaps that is also why the stories on the Burmese and Congolese refugees were freer to include details of the difficulties experienced by the refugees, such as trauma, mental health problems, and lack of literacy. For example, the Michigan State University public radio station WKAR carried a story on the mental health challenges Burmese refugees in Michigan faced. These included higher-than-average suicide rates, and "good kids" ending up in jail because of depression and/or alcoholism (Thiele 2018). Another news story spoke of the high level of trauma the Congolese refugees experienced in their homeland, and the resulting medical and mental challenges they faced on arrival in Michigan (LIRS 2013).

In the story about the Congolese pastor in Grand Rapids, he explained his motivation, saying he preached to his fellow refugees "[b]ecause we think that God can repair what has been lost in their life." However, readers also learned from the story, based on the interview with the pastor, that

> Many refugees from Africa suffer from post-traumatic stress disorder. . . . A refugee's whole family could have been killed in Africa. The refugee then has to live with the trauma for the rest of their lives. (Airgood 2017)

Another story pointed out that many of the Congolese refugees had spent roughly twenty years in refugee camps, affecting their ability to adjust and function on their arrival in Michigan.

> Many adults thirty-five and older are not literate in their first language. . . . Those are big barriers. Kids don't get much education, I've met eighteen-year-olds who only went through fourth or fifth grade or never learned how to work for the first time. (Rahal 2019)

The same story also mentions that 68 percent of the Congolese refugees are survivors of torture.

These differences in emphasis suggest that the resettlement of Burmese and Congolese refugees in Michigan was not construed as a potential problem or issue in the way that the resettlement of Syrian refugees was. Whereas both kinds of stories spoke of the desire of the refugees to adjust and to contribute to their new societies economically, there was more room in the stories about the challenges and difficulties Burmese and Congolese refugees faced on arrival. In sharp contrast, when speaking about the Syrian refugees more emphasis was placed on normalizing them and diluting any possible perceptions of threat. The humanitarian aspect was at the forefront when news sources reported on the Burmese and Congolese refugees, including the specifically Christian humanitarian aspect. But the economic revitalization aspect was at the forefront when news sources reported on the Syrian refugees. When religion could not be used to tie US citizens' humanity to refugees' humanity, the local press sutured the story of the Syrian refugees to the story of the economic revitalization of the Detroit metro area as a way to humanize and normalize a refugee population that the far right and right-leaning politicians had vilified. While a Christian agenda was predominant in the stories of the Burmese and Congolese refugees, an economic revitalization agenda was predominant in the stories of the Syrian refugees.[4]

---

4. The economic revitalization of Detroit is highly contested, with the local press supporting a particular vision of economic revitalization that encompasses gentrification. As I was reminded in a talk I attended at the Arab American National Museum by Gloria House (2019), acclaimed poet, educator, and longtime Detroit-based activist, there are two Detroits. There is the Detroit of the rich and white and the Detroit of the poor and people of color, one "flourishing affluent and attractive, the other physically neglected and stripped of essential resources." She also reminded us in the talk of the "curtailment of freedom of speech in the city" and "the literal white-out concerning anything other than the literal promotion of gentrification." I include this here to point to the contradictions of a local press that supported the resettlement of Syrian refugees as a tool for economic revitalization, but only as part of a white, elite-led vision of the economic revitalization of Detroit.

CHAPTER 2

Refugees Not Welcome

The Refugee as a Threatening Figure

The website Secure Michigan was a Manichean world where the lines were clearly drawn between us and them, friends and enemies, the familiar and the strange, and ultimately between good and evil as defined through a narrow anti-Muslim and racist prism. It was also a world that suspended the usual rules used to gauge veracity or validity. Entering the Secure Michigan website was an unsettling and eye-opening experience, like entering an alternate universe, particularly for someone like me. I am anchored to the academic mission of a public university, which is itself tethered to a liberal, pluralist ideal of fostering greater understanding and connections among people of different cultures, faiths, sexualities, genders, levels of ability, nations, and classes.

In this chapter I dive deeply into the far-right, ultraconservative discourse on the increasing presence of Muslims and Islam in Michigan and the Detroit Metropolitan area. I identify central tropes and rhetorical strategies that proponents of this discourse use to create alarm about and distrust of the inflow of Syrian and Muslim refugees into Michigan. Not only did Secure Michigan participants evoke suspicion about the refugees themselves, they created fear about all of the institutions working to facilitate the movement of the refugees into Michigan and to help with their adjustment once they arrive. The refugees' Islamic culture also came into their crosshairs. Further, the website was geared toward inciting not just fear, but citizen action to push back against the routing of Muslim refugees into Michigan.[1]

The institutional backing of the Islamophobia industry and the discourse it produced have been well documented, particularly by Nathan Lean (2017). Here I explore the local manifestations of this industry. While Lean exhaustively documents the intermeshing networks of people, institutions, and money that underpin the systematic vilification of Islam in the United States, I explore how the national networks and the discourse they spawn provide legitimacy and discursive grounding for the local groups that similarly make a monster out of Islam. Also, I investigate how the local groups and people devoted to creating fear about Islam extend the work of the national industry, allowing it to take root in particular communities.

Suturing Fear of the Refugee to Fear of the Islamic Other

The sleight of hand began as soon a user entered the gateway at www.securemichigan.org, a site that has since been taken down. The main graphic at the top of the gateway was of a phalanx of people figurines superimposed on the image of a globe, with the mass of identical figurines marching westward into North America. On top of the image, the main underlined heading said "Secure Michigan," with the subheading "Refugee Resettlement Monitor of Michigan." A mission statement just under the main graphic read "We are dedicated to providing news and informa-

---

1. When attempting to return to the Secure Michigan website to complete the citations for this chapter, I bumped into the interesting phenomenon of the elusiveness of the alt-right's online presence. Clicking on the site's link took me to the message, "Oops! This site has expired." Others have noted the elusiveness of the alt-right (Ellis 2018) as well as the disappearance of several alt-right websites since the clampdown on hate speech by social media platforms such as Twitter (Neiwert 2018). While I am not able to confirm the reasons for the disappearance of the site, it does lend support to the idea that the alt-right gained its strength through a "media bubble" and could lose strength as the bubble bursts. I should also note that while the Rescue Michigan website had disappeared by the time I finished this chapter, the "parent" site Refugee Resettlement Watch was active for several months after, but then it disappeared as well. However, many of the elements posted on the site are still available as stand-alone items on YouTube and elsewhere.

tion regarding the costs and security concerns of the Refugee Resettlement Program and its negative impact on the people of Michigan." The two main menu options at the top right of the page were "Sharia Crime Stoppers" and "Candidate Vetting."

A quick scan of the main page showed stories about the dangers of sharia law and its presence in Michigan, the dangers presented by Abdul El-Sayed's bid to be governor of Michigan, the "Islamist infiltration" of the FBI in Michigan, and the complacency of Christians in the West about the persecution of Christians in Muslim-majority countries. None of these prominent elements had any direct connection to the purported focus of the site, which was refugee resettlement in Michigan.

Only when a user moved to the sidebar was it possible to find videos and pointers to books that directly connected refugee resettlement and the takeover of Western civilization by Islamic supremacists. The idea was (and is) that the "importation" of refugees from Muslim-majority nations is a "stealth invasion" and a principal vehicle for the defeat of Western civilization and the rise of global Islamic supremacy.

The founder of the national Refugee Resettlement Watch website with which Secure Michigan is affiliated, Ann Corcoran, was the principal proponent of this argument, through both her videos and a pointer to her book, *Refugee Resettlement and the Hijra to America*.[2] But there were other key supports for this discursive construct. These included a video with James Simpson expounding on key points from his book, *The Red-Green Axis: Refugees, Immigration, and the Agenda to Erase America*. There were prominent pointers to his book as well as Leo Hohmann's book, *Stealth Invasion: Muslim Conquest through Immigration and the Resettlement Jihad*. These works purported to share original research on refugee resettlement as a vehicle for Islamic conquest. Videos of local presentations made by Secure Michigan participants repeated the same key points and connections. The works making a direct connection between refugee resettlement and "civilization jihad" were interspersed with more general videos about the dangers of the spread of sharia law and Islamic supremacy, the latter

---

2. In Islamic history the hijra refers to Muhammad's migration from Mecca to Medina with his followers. Ann Corcoran subverts its use for her own purposes, evoking fear of Muslim refugee resettlement by speaking of their "hijra" or migration as a primary vehicle of "civilization jihad."

echoing the stories in the main part of the page. Overall, then, an interpretative frame was created that fostered suspicion and fear of all things Islamic. This in turn prepared the ground for a positive reception of the argument that relocation of Muslim refugees to Michigan will speed up the Islamic invasion.

From the site we glimpse the adeptness of the radical right in evoking fear of the "other," in this case the Islamic other. Moreover, because this was a site mainly addressing a Michigan audience, we can glimpse how a discursive articulation is created between fear of the general Islamic other and the more concrete and actionable fear of the specific Islamic other in people's own backyards.

An example of the evocation of fear about Islam in general was the link on the website to a slickly produced, animated video titled "Killing for a Cause: Sharia Law and Civilization Jihad." The video was produced by an organization calling itself Counter Jihad, which described itself as "a response to the ongoing incursion by Islamist groups and their ideology into American life" (Barrett 2016). A caption below the video explained that "This video is a primer on Sharia law, violent jihad and what the Muslim Brotherhood calls 'Civilization Jihad.'" The video started by explaining that sharia, or Islamic law, demands jihad. After explaining that there are two kinds of jihad—violent jihad and civilization jihad—the video elaborated on the latter, saying, "Civilization Jihad has the same goal as the Violent Jihad—to conquer land for their Caliphate—but instead of waging war or staging terror attacks like their brothers in the violent jihad, these Civilization Jihadists wear suits and ties, and their work is much more subtle."

At this point in the video, an image of marauding Muslim invaders on horses appears. Then there's an image of a Muslim terrorist wearing a suicide vest, drawn in the most caricatured way, that morphs into the image of a Muslim man wearing a dark suit, clenching his hands in fists at his sides as in the previous image of the suicide bomber. Through image and voice-over, the video creates the impression that the United States is being taken over from within, without Americans even realizing it. The creators next show us how the two aspects of jihad are really two sides of the same coin, except that civilization jihad is more subtle, more effective in the long term, and happens at the everyday level in ways that we might not recognize. The video then breaks down the concrete mechanisms through which civilization jihad is conducted:

> They file lawsuits for Muslim truck drivers who don't want to drive beer. They convince schools to hold Muslim Day, where the girls wear head-scarves and the kids say Muslim prayers. They complain when our government watches to see if their violent buddies are hanging out with them. They call anyone critical of Islamic Law an "Islamophobe," a term they invented to make people scared to speak out. . . .

The video creators then point out the enemies who are engaged in civilization jihad. In a direct parallel to the beginning of the video where they pointed out the "bad guys" of violent jihad, such as Boko Haram, ISIS, and al-Qaeda, they now point out the "bad guys" of civilization jihad: the Council on American Islamic Relations, the Muslim Student Association, and the Islamic Society of North America.

The entire video is full of unsubstantiated claims. Right after naming the enemies in suits, the video uses a clearly unsubstantiated claim to create guilt by association. The video says, "The Justice Department found that these groups were, in fact, started by the Muslim Brotherhood." The video clinches the matter by saying that not all Muslims believe in sharia, but that an "awful lot do," and "they have to go." They break down sharia for us thus:

> They believe that anyone who insults Islam can be killed; they believe that women are property; that gays should be killed; and that little girls should be mutilated and forced to marry old men they've never men [sic].

They point out that these things go against the Constitution. Finally, the video exhorts everyday citizens to help and to visit counterjihad.com.

Another illustrative video featured on the website is a talk by Raheel Raza titled "By the Numbers: The Untold Story of Muslim Opinions and Demographics." The Clarion Project, a right-wing Israeli settlement group, funded the talk (Lean 2017). Raza, a Muslim woman, functions as a "native informant," which lends credibility to her anti-Islamic rhetoric, giving her the potential to extend the reach of anti-Muslim discourse into the mainstream, or even into liberal or progressive circles. Lean has convincingly documented the use of such native informants by the national Islamophobia industry, and here the strategy is deployed by a website targeting Michigan residents.

Raza positions herself carefully and at some length at the beginning of the video, as being rational and reasonable, a facilitator of "an open, honest, fact-based conversation" about Islam that she claims has become increasingly difficult to conduct in the United States. In opening this conversation, she also positions herself as standing for freedom of speech. At one point in the video, she addresses a clip from an episode of *Real Time with Bill Maher*, shown on Fox News, in which actor Ben Affleck defends Islam against writer and podcast host Sam Harris.

Raza positions herself as an authentic representative of Islam by saying that she doesn't need Ben Affleck to defend her and her religion. She then goes on to paraphrase Sam Harris's argument that people need to be concerned not only about hardcore jihadists or Islamists but also about the very large number of conservative Muslims who hold radical views. She effectively positions herself as the voice of reason, but she insists that the majority of Muslims are radicals who believe in honor killings to punish women who have premarital or extramarital sex and believe it is justified to kill someone who leaves the Muslim religion. These are stated as self-evident facts, but they are actually statistics taken out of context from a Pew Research poll and selectively used to construct a particular portrait of Muslims as carrying radical ideas dictated by sharia. The way she presents herself to the audience throughout is telling, as one seemingly reasonable person talking to another.

In the video, Raza frequently picks out a practice that she says a majority of Muslims believe in, such as the justified execution of those who leave their faith. Then she faces the audience and asks, "Do *you* think that's a radical belief?" Every time she equates a horrific belief with Muslims, she asks again, "Do *you* think that's radical?" In this way she underlines the alterity between the rational self and the radical Muslim other, which in her scheme includes most Muslims.

Networking Fear of the Refugee/Islamic Other

Both the video and the website included a key element that allows inter-mediaries on the radical right to create a bridge between the national anti-Muslim discourse and a locally inflected discourse that speaks directly to the concerns and motivations of residents in towns and cities in Michigan. These intermediaries include Ann Corcoran of Refugee Resettlement Watch and Dick Manasseri of Refugee Resettlement Monitor of Michigan/Secure Michigan. This discursive bridge is the construct of sharia as a stealth invasion and as something to fear, a construct that has already been effectively disseminated by the national Islamophobia industry (Lean 2017) and on which emissaries of the far right can build. A secondary but effective connection is the role of refugee relocation in the stealth invasion of sharia into our midst. The three-step maneuver allows for the articulation between fear of all things Islamic, fear of sharia, and the fear of the implantation of sharia in our towns by Muslim refugees and immigrants.

The networked aspect of the anti-Muslim, anti-refugee discursive operation, as well as the articulation between the national and local aspects, is clearest in videos of presentations by Dick Manasseri to local groups in Michigan. Manasseri has been described as a "spokesman for Secure Michigan" by Leo Hohmann (2017) and as "Secure Michigan Communications Director" by *Morning Sun News* of central Michigan (Bradley 2017). People like Dick Manasseri are indispensable intermediaries linking national rhetoric that creates fear of an Islamic invasion through refugee resettlement to locally inflected rhetoric along the same lines, customizing the main talking points to hit home with communities in Michigan.

The Rescue Michigan website appears to be an affiliate of Ann Corcoran's national-level Refugee Resettlement Watch website, directly using many of her works and videos but also ventriloquizing her ideas through local emissaries such as Manasseri. This networking aspect is a powerful strategy in that it allows national activists such as Corcoran to reach deeply into particular communities such as those in Michigan, but it also allows local activists such as Manasseri to use material and templates from the national activists and websites, and to piggyback on the ample influence that national activists have gained (Goyette 2016; Beauchamp 2017).

This strategy is recursive in that Manasseri amplifies his influence through the better-known Ann Corcoran, while Ann Corcoran in turn piggybacks on the influence of better-known and better-funded outfits than her own, such as Frank Gaffney's Center for Security Policy, which published her book and videos. Gaffney's video is featured on the Secure Michigan site because of Corcoran's connection "upward" with Gaffney and "downward" with Manasseri (Goyette 2016; Lean 2017). Within this "counter-jihad" network various outfits with varying resources and degrees of influence constantly reference and publish each other. In this way, they bolster each other and help each other to go mainstream (Beauchamp 2017; Lean 2017).

Diving into the videos of the local presentations by Manasseri gives us a close look at this mutual implication among different tiers in the network. It also lets us zoom in to the language and methods used to customize the national rhetoric for Michigan communities.

An example is Manasseri's presentation to the Tea Party in Eaton County, Michigan, on May 18, 2017. He starts by bolstering Secure Michigan's legitimacy, showing his work as connected to that of James Simpson, Philip Heaney, and Ann Corcoran, all of whom were better-known "counter-jihad" activists. Very early in the presentation, he shows a video by Ann Corcoran; he makes a point of saying it was made specifically for Michigan. This video, also found on YouTube as "Ann Corcoran: Michigan on the Brink," pays special attention to Michigan as a leading edge of civilization jihad. She points to Southeast Michigan as the "region most likely to become a collection of shariavilles, where large numbers of sharia-compliant residents will live according to Islamic sharia law instead of the U.S. Constitution," and where people of other faiths adhering to the Constitution "will live in fear until they are forced to leave." She then points out that Michigan receives a greater percentage of Syrian refugees than any other state, and that 99 percent of these "unvetted" refugees are "sharia-compliant Sunni Muslims."

Corcoran goes on to apply these themes to sites across the country, while pointing out that the major sinister trends are more present and more pertinent in Michigan than elsewhere. For example, she talks of "Welcoming Michigan," an advocacy group working to make Michigan more welcoming to immigrants, as "infiltrating" entire counties and cities in Michigan. She also describes the "outrageous secrecy" of the "refugee resettlement industry," most evident in the case of Oakland County, Michigan, where she contends that 11,000 refugees have been placed in the last eight years without consultation with the county government.

As in her national website, Corcoran "uncovers" the stealth operation of the federal government, in cahoots with refugee resettlement agencies or "volags" (voluntary agencies), in relocating Syrian and other Muslim refugees to particular locations without the consent of local governments and local citizens. In this presentation, however, she brings in facts and figures specific to Michigan and names enemies specific to Michigan. These include Governor Snyder, State Senator Arlan Meekhof, county executives, city council members, and others. She also mentions the building of more than 100 mosques in Michigan, claiming that the "Muslim Brotherhood, operating as the CAIR [Council on American Islamic Relations]" has teamed up with the Department of Justice to create an environment where municipalities do not dare to challenge the building of mosques for fear of lawsuits. She then points to Pittsfield Township in Michigan as one such case.

Going further, she claims she has personally witnessed the transformation in Michigan (although she lives in Maryland), where the "once vibrant" cities of Dearborn, Hamtramck, Sterling Heights, and Warren are "succumbing to the shariavilles within them." She then points to the practice of women in the "shariavilles of Michigan" covering themselves and says that this is a sign of their accepting that "they are the property of men under Sharia." She says this is a problem for all women living in or around the shariavilles. Finally, she points to the accommodations that Michigan schools and governments are making to sharia practices, such as allowing Muslim prayers at some schools. She says that Michigan is undergoing this "fundamental transformation" faster than any other state.

Two other local presentations posted on the site were in a very similar vein, except that we more directly see Manasseri's interpretive work in translating the ideological template provided by Corcoran, Simpson, and Hohmann for a local Michigan audience. Manasseri interprets and elaborates on the stock themes with local facts and figures, local events, and local personalities.

One is a presentation to the Macomb County Republican Women's

Forum held on March 18, 2017, at Ryan Palace, Sterling Heights, Michigan. The other is a presentation to the Bloomfield Republican Women's Club on November 9, 2015. In the latter presentation, Manasseri only briefly uses a video from Corcoran. He paraphrases the main themes of Simpson's book early on, and then he uses most of the time to explain the situation in his own voice while borrowing heavily from the national ideologues. He is thus able to make extensive local connections and pitch the dangers as closely relevant to Michigan audiences. Very early in the Bloomfield presentation, he frames Secure Michigan and himself as truth tellers providing information that the mainstream media in Michigan are failing to impart. He deflects scrutiny from his own truth claims by casting himself as the purveyor of truth and the media as the purveyor of lies, even if by omission.

Manasseri asks poignantly, "You're going to hear things you've never heard before. So the real question is, why would the information that we're going to talk about today not be in the *Detroit News*?" He never answers the question, purposely leaving the audience to fill in the blanks of a particular part of his conspiracy theory. Later in the presentation he comes back to the role of local media in facilitating the propaganda of the "refugee resettlement industry." He asks, "How many articles have you seen in the *Detroit Free Press* talking about humanitarian stories about refugees?" He says there are a lot of stories in this vein because agencies such as Samaritas are using the local papers to disseminate their propaganda, casting themselves as humanitarians while hiding the fact that they benefit financially from the inflow of refugees.

Manasseri further positions himself as a revealer of the truth by saying that the figures on how many refugees from which countries have been relocated to Michigan and to Southeast Michigan came from Freedom of Information requests filed by Secure Michigan and are being shown for the first time in the presentation. In both presentations, detailed breakdowns of the actual and planned placement of refugees appear, giving a sense of sharia-compliant refugees coming to a town near you.

In the same vein as on the Secure Michigan website overall, Manasseri cherry-picks local facts and throws them together to create an impression of the growing threat of sharia. Because there is no evidence to link actual refugees to any actions that would cause alarm, the proponents of the anti-Muslim discourse must work to create an association between the growing presence of sharia practices in Michigan on the one hand and the stealthy placement of sharia-adherent refugees in Michigan on the other.

Bending the Truth in Service of Hate

The local presentations include several instances of the creative use of association to engender alternative truths and foster a misleading impression of the impending threat that Muslim refugees and Muslims in general present to Michiganders. I home in on a few of these to give a flavor of the strategies the radical right has used to root fear in particular communities.

One such association in the videos and presentations is that between Europe's "no-go zones," areas in Europe with concentrations of Muslim immigrants that are supposedly reeking of sharia-dictated male suprem- acy, and the sharia-dictated male supremacy in the shariavilles of Mich- igan. Lean (2017) has convincingly shown how far-right, anti-Muslim activists picked up and propagated the myth of "no-go zones" in Paris, spreading it even into the mainstream media, and repeating it in radical- right media even after "nearly every major news outlet had decided that, indeed, there was no such thing as 'no-go zones'" (96). On the Secure Michigan website, this myth continued to be propagated, and local ambas- sadors of the Islamophobia industry repeated it. This alternative fact was placed next to the idea of shariavilles in Michigan to create a false impres- sion that women's freedoms are under threat due to shariavilles estab- lished by Muslim refugees past and present. The point was that if the cit- izens of Michigan didn't act vigilantly to push back against the spread of sharia, Michigan would go the way of Europe, where women are allegedly terrified to go into the "no-go zones."

As Lean points out, the representatives of the far right are not build- ing their careers based on an objective evaluation of the actual situation. Rather, their "expertise" is based on an extension of already existing anti- Muslim narratives (2017, 96). As Stanovsky (2017) points out, fascist discourse thrives on remix and repetition, and its audiences derive pleasure from these practices. While he was referring primarily to visual images, his insights can apply to both visual and textual elements on the Secure Michigan website.

How do these insights illuminate the discursive methods that anti-refugee, anti-Muslim activists use in Michigan? Another example of stretching the truth to sow fear is illustrative. It is true that a number of women wear hijab in cities in Michigan such as Dearborn and Hamtramck. However, it is a giant leap to say that this constitutes gender slavery or presents a threat to non-Muslim women, yet these are precisely the kinds of associations Manasseri has made in his presentations. For example, when addressing the Bloomfield Women's Republican Club, he prepared the ground for a particular "revelation" by saying that an audience of women should be particularly concerned about what he is about to say. He then continues,

> I think you already know by definition that sharia is a male supremacy way of living. Every woman who lives under sharia is a second-class citizen. They're one of four wives. They might be ten years old and be married. They are treated absolutely terribly. It's basically a second-class, almost slavery condition that women live in. So when we talk about sharia-adherent people moving in. . . .

He says that this should get every woman's attention and that they should be concerned about what this means for their children. In a similar vein, when talking to the Macomb County Republican Women's Forum, he says

> Women are property in shariavilles in England and in Michigan. If a woman is living under sharia, and it's happening right here, they don't have any rights. How could America, how could Michigan, ever allow . . . Would we bring a slave ship to Michigan and put slaves who happened to have darker skin to be slaves? [sic] Of course we would never do that. Yet we allow the refugee resettlement program to open up a door on an airplane and bring a family of people into Detroit and to Sterling Heights who are living as property! It's unbelievable!

Gendering Fear of the Refugee/Muslim Other

This is an apt example of the weaving of small bits of truth—the fact that a number of Muslim women cover their heads in particular cities in Michigan—with a large number of alternative facts. It is a standard modus operandi of the alt-right. To give another illustration, it is true that at one point three out of five people on the Hamtramck city council were practicing Sunni Muslims. But it is quite a leap from there to Manasseri's claim that Hamtramck is "well on the way to being a shariaville." And yet the truth of these kinds of utterances is very difficult to evaluate. Their strength is in their fit with a particular ideology and their resonance with like-minded and persuadable audiences. Also, the repeated focus on the oppression of women as evidence of the spread of sharia is reminiscent of the widespread use by colonial and neocolonial actors of the trope of the oppression of Third World women to legitimate the subjugation of particular populations by a dominant power. Spivak (1988) most famously described this as a narrative of "saving the brown women from brown men." Other scholars have pointed out this mindset in contexts as diverse as British India (Mani 1998) and the US invasion of Afghanistan (Abu-Lughod 2013). Mani has shown how the figure of the victimized Indian woman was used symbolically by British colonists to argue that the practice of sati (widow immolation) should be abolished. Abu-Lughod has shown that the figure of the oppressed Muslim woman, the Muslim woman victim of the Taliban, was used to help justify the US invasion of Afghanistan after September 11.

Inspired by Mani's approach, I showed in earlier work how postcolonial women became the symbolic grist in the struggle between the New Right economists, the pro-life lobby, and the population-control establishment. The issue in that paper involved an "abortion clause" policy that President Ronald Reagan introduced in 1984 requiring nongovernmental organizations to certify that they would not perform or promote abortion using funds from any source, as a condition of receiving U.S. government global family planning funding. The trope of brown women as victims has also been used by anti-refugee, anti-Muslim activists in Michigan, which is a testament to its persistence.

Another aspect of the oppression of women trope deserves more elaboration here. Uma Narayan (1997) has pointed out that when US news covers violence against women in the US, it often carries the label "domestic violence." But the US news represents the same violence against women in the Indian context not as episodic and specific, but rather as being associated with an entire culture.

On the Secure Michigan website, it was clear that the far right had done ideological work to dissociate violence against Muslim women from violence against non-Muslim women in Michigan. Anti-Muslim activists have worked assiduously to provide an interpretive frame of honor crimes for the former and of domestic violence for the latter. A story on World Net Daily for which the link was prominently highlighted on the Secure Michigan website illustrated this ideological work. The link lured readers with the headline "Sharia Honor Killing in Michigan Mirrors Threats of Violence Against Womn [sic] Worldwide." Clicking it led readers to the World Net story headlined "Death Threat Allows Muslim Woman to Evade Deportation." The main picture in the story showed a Muslim woman, face veiled except for her eyes. The caption stated, "A Jordanian woman living in Michigan is seeking court protection from being deported back to her homeland out of fear that she will be killed as soon as she returns in accordance with Islamic sharia law." The lead of the story takes a very sarcastic tone: "Her crime?" The next paragraph started with, "The woman who came to the United States on a student visa but has overstayed, got pregnant out of wedlock. Her cousin has vowed to kill her to preserve the family's honor."

The rest of the story takes pains to show that the US mainstream media has suppressed the aspect of this being a sharia-based, specifically Muslim crime by using phrases such as "traditional taboos" or "local tribal customs," as in an Associated Press story. Later in the story the author quotes Robert Spencer, host of the website "Jihad Watch," and Dick Manasseri. In the quotes, Spencer distinguishes honor killings both from local tribal custom and from other kinds of domestic violence, to make a strong equation between the particular honor killings and Islam at large. Spencer is quoted as saying that honor killing is no "tribal custom" and that "it's deeply Islamic."

In a similar vein, when readers clicked the menu option "Sharia Crime

Stoppers" on the top right of the Secure Michigan website, they saw stock videos on sharia and male supremacy taken from the counter-jihad nonprofit United West. These short videos had titles such as "Women and Sharia—Male Supremacy," "Women and Sharia—No-Fault Rape," "Women and Sharia—Honor Killing/Violence," "Women and Sharia— Child Brides/Forced Marriage," and "Women and Sharia—FGM," referring to female genital mutilation.

These videos hammered on the association between Islam, sharia, and the oppression of women. For example, the video on honor killings repeatedly asserted how important it is for police and prosecutors to understand the difference between regular domestic violence and honor violence. According to the video, the mainstream white community shunned domestic violence and considered it illegal; its occurrence was an aberration. On the other hand, the Muslim community allegedly allowed honor killings, as dictated by sharia law. Supposedly, domestic violence was the act of a repentant man cognizant of the wrongness of his actions, whereas honor killings were perpetrated by the entire family in cahoots with the imam and the community, and the perpetrator was valorized. The video draws the contrast in the most simplistic terms.

Narayan has described how the West frames the murder or suicides of women in India related to disputes over their dowry as "death by culture." Similarly, a Western source described violence against women within the Muslim community in Michigan and elsewhere in the United States as an aspect of "death by culture," where the culture is Muslim culture through sharia. We see here how an anti-Muslim source uses the trope of oppression of women to vilify Islam at a time when multiple discourses have converged to demonize Islam and those who follow it.[3]

---

3. To point out the deployment of the trope of Muslim women's oppression is not to detract from Muslim women's experiences. While there might be occurrences in Michigan where Muslim women fear that someone will hurt or kill them if they return to their home country, and while in some of these instances there might be an element of "honor" involved, it is pertinent to examine the selective use of and the prominence given to the honor crime aspect in a publication devoted to sowing suspicion about Muslim refugees and Muslims more broadly. The argument could be made that a Muslim woman might fear for her life on return to her home country because of the violence of war or domestic or sexual violence similar to what non-Muslim women experience. The intense focus on honor crimes here and the visible effort to associate them with Islam and to dissociate them from domestic violence, when placed into the overall context of

A deliberate mistake becomes evident when the exact turns of phrase are examined more closely. The headline in Rescue Michigan, "Sharia Honor Killing in Michigan Mirrors Threats of Violence against Women Worldwide," turned out to be patently false in light of the actual story. The whole point of the story was that a Muslim woman sought court protection from deportation because she feared being killed in accordance with sharia law; she had not already been killed, as the headline implies. The World News Daily headline, "Death Threat Allows Muslim Woman to Evade Deportation," also contains a contradiction. The headline portrays the Muslim woman as a victim of a sharia-based death threat, but also as possibly a trickster. According to the headline, she could have been using honor killing as a pretext to "evade" deportation. Such contradictions provide further evidence that the intent here is not to "save Muslim women." It is to deploy the figure of the oppressed Muslim woman to create fear of the Muslim other.

Inverting Progressive Discourse in the Service of Hate

Another discursive method that was common on the Secure Michigan website was a kind of perverse mimicry of progressive discourse. The site used this mimicry to cast suspicion on every utterance from groups dedicated to defending the civil rights of Muslims in the United States. The site's creators were apparently dedicated to tainting every word from progressive activists even before they opened their mouths.

As Bhabha (1994) theorized, mimicry is a strategy of "partial representation," a process of imitation with a twist. But the irony is that Bhabha was concerned with the practice of mimicry by the colonized, a subjugated entity, whereas here we see it being practiced by groups participating in the vilification and targeting of a minority population in the United States. This strategy was apparent in the description above of the video "Killing for a Cause," where the Council on American Islamic Relations was

---

the website and its purpose, speaks to the use of the trope of the oppression of Muslim women to create fear and suspicion of Muslims and Muslim refugees.

equated with the Muslim Brotherhood. But it is worth examining this strategy a bit more here.

The discursive construct of "Islamophobia" within the civil rights struggle of Muslims in the United States has made available another lens for understanding and creating conversation around anti-Muslim perceptions and actions. Within the far-right discourse on the Secure Michigan website, the idea of Islamophobia was painted as a ruse for establishing Islamic supremacy in the West. To the site's creators, Islamic supremacists used the idea of Islamophobia as a mechanism to silence or co-opt various institutions, from the mainstream press to the FBI to the Department of Homeland Security.

According to the far-right logic in evidence here, people such as former Department of Homeland Security employee Philip Haney were forced to shred documents by their superiors about possible terrorists. Police personnel and FBI personnel were supposedly given sensitivity training that blinded them to sharia crimes. The mainstream press allegedly covered sharia crimes as instances of domestic violence or tribal custom. And people were supposedly silenced and forbidden from discussing Islam frankly. All this allegedly happened because of the Muslim Brotherhood's strategy of indoctrinating various US institutions and our entire society with the Islamophobia discursive construct. In this logic, the far right's discursive constructs are just plain facts, and the groups who support Muslim civil rights are instilling false consciousness in people through the Islamophobia construct, among others.

Another inversion that takes place is that Muslims, a minority population in the United States who are vulnerable to discrimination, labeling, and hate crimes, are portrayed as the perpetrators and far-right activists become the victims of propaganda and labeling. The haters become the hated; the perpetrators become the victims. This is clear when far-right sources paint not only Muslim-oriented organizations such as the Council on American Islamic Relations as instilling false consciousness, but also mainstream organizations such as the Southern Poverty Law Center (SPLC).

In his presentations to the Tea Party and to the Macomb County Republican Women's Forum, Manasseri cast the SPLC as a group that intimidates people by labeling them as haters. He proudly mentioned that Secure Michigan and he himself had been labeled as haters on the SPLC website, holding up this description as a badge of honor. He painted himself and his organization as victims of a left-wing campaign. Rather than Muslims being the targets of a well-organized industry dedicated to vilifying them, or Muslim refugees being victims of war and neoliberal policies, in the discursive world of the far right, Islamic supremacists and the left become co-conspirators. These groups are supposedly using Muslim refugees to achieve domination. Muslim refugees become civilization jihadists, and refugee agencies become the facilitators of this process for their own economic gain.

It is also worth considering another kind of mimicry or mirroring that might be occurring, although I have not had a chance to delve into it deeply here. Abbas (2017) has pointed out that in the British context, far-right extremists and Islamist radicals are two sides of the same coin. Both are marginalized communities growing in a context of "lack of social mobility, persistent unemployment, growing anomie, and political disenfranchisement" (57), and both are "pro-totalitarian." Further,

> These groups wish to instill a sense of purist identity politics and both have a utopian vision. Furthermore, both have a narrowly defined vision of the self, which is exclusive of the other, where identities are *domaine de l'imaginaire* [the realm of imagination]. . . . Both groups are the structural and cultural outsiders of society *and* directly opposed to each other. (57-58)

Abbas also observes that the two extremisms feed off of each other's rhetoric. This brings home the importance of not only locating the contours of the national and local radical right's anti-Islamic and anti-refugee discourse, but of understanding the relationship between the far-right discourse and other prevalent discourses circulating in a particular context at the same time. It would be useful to explore how far right discourse feeds into the discursive environment within which others make their claims, such as the mainstream press, refugee advocates, and proponents of Muslim civil rights. Each actor in the discursive contest generates possibilities, but also creates constraints for the others.

Material Effects of Fearmongering

Finally, it is important to keep in mind that the far-right, anti-Islamic discourse matters. It not only feeds into the discursive environment, it influences citizen action and institutional policies and actions. Racist rhetoric, including anti-Muslim rhetoric, has gone increasingly mainstream, particularly in the Trump era (including during the period leading up to the election). This points to growing links between far-right discourse and political processes and outcomes (Stanovsky 2017; Hartzell 2018). I will discuss a few obvious examples of how the anti-Muslim and anti-Muslim-refugee discourse "becomes material" or has actual or potential consequences for people's daily lives in Michigan, including in the Detroit metropolitan area.

The Secure Michigan website included numerous calls for Michigan citizens to push back against the supposed growing influence of sharia. The site included calls to resist the supposedly secretive efforts of the refugee agencies to move Muslim refugees to Michigan as if they were "UPS packages," and in doing so helping to "seed" sharia in Michigan towns and cities. As an example, the website included a "Citizen Toolkit" with an introduction saying that the kit

> provides you with tools that can help [protect] you and your family from the onslaught of Refugee Resettlement (RR) in your neighborhood, city and county! You can prepare yourself to present a brief RR introduction to your city council and/or county council, ending with a request for an RR agenda item at an upcoming meeting and the consideration of a Resolution.

This modus operandi had already been put to action. In October 2016, the Waterford Township Board of Trustees passed a resolution by a vote of 7-0, saying the township would not participate in the federal government's resettlement of Syrian refugees. Although the resolution carried no legal weight, it was meant to send a message to the federal government and to set an example for other townships and counties in Michigan. The Secure

Michigan website repeatedly valorized this resolution as an example of what citizen action can accomplish.[4]

The intermeshing of anti-Muslim discourse and local politics was also visible in the frequent valorization of Oakland County Executive L. Brooks Patterson in Manasseri's local presentations. Manasseri pointed to Patterson's pushing against building a development in Pontiac mainly for Syrian refugees, describing it as "standing up against the shariaville enclave." He offers strong praise for Patterson's "noncooperation" and "non-welcoming techniques" and for not being bullied into the "Islamophobia notion." In one presentation, Manasseri proudly inducts Patterson into what he calls the Michigan "pockets of resistance."

Pushing back against the development, as had been valorized by Secure Michigan, had potential consequences for the lives of Pontiac residents. They stood to lose not only an opportunity to revitalize foreclosed properties, but opportunities for housing for residents, including Syrian refugees. The website also made anti-sharia training available to local law enforcement officers, incited local action against the building of mosques, and provided forms for vetting candidates for local elections. These forms included questions such as "Do you support the U.S. Refugee Resettlement Program?" and "Name examples of sharia compatibility/incompatibility with the U.S. Constitution." At the hyper-local level, the Secure Michigan website reached down to address the composition of committees in particular towns, such as the ethnic committee in Sterling Heights, pointing out that committee members had participated in welcoming refugees.

In all of these ways the site incited concrete local action to keep Muslim refugees out and to stymie Muslim culture as a whole. That a handful of Michigan candidates actually felt obliged to fill out the candidate vet-

---

4. Among the material consequences of the local alt-right discourse on refugees might very well be the actual reduction in the number of refugees coming to Michigan, down by 75 percent in 2018 compared to the previous year (Warikoo 2018). While residents of Michigan might not swallow the most extreme and outlandish aspects of the alt-right discourse vilifying refugees, there is some indication that the lighter and relatively polite aspects of this discourse could have enough influence to affect policy. While Trump's policies were probably the most proximate cause of the drop in numbers, local constituencies' doubts about refugees and immigrants may have given Trump permission to enact anti-refugee and anti-immigrant policies.

ting form shows that the discourse and tactics of the far right were not always dismissed out of hand.

The tendencies already established by the extreme right at the national and local levels received further encouragement leading up to and after the election of Donald Trump. Even at a discursive level, the linkages are apparent. The clearest example of this discursive articulation on the Rescue Michigan website was Dick Manasseri's identification of his organization as providing "ammunition" to "Trump's army." This army supposedly included the women of Macomb County who he was addressing, because, as he pointed out, Macomb County supported Trump.

Seepage of Far-Right Discourse into the Mainstream

The sheer excess and phantasmagorical aspect of the local far-right discourse might encourage people who are committed to social justice to dismiss it. But this discourse has become part of mainstream forums such as county and city meetings, Republican Party women's clubs, and local political campaigns. Therefore, it is vital to take notice and deconstruct this discourse and to trace its seepage into other discursive domains.

Mainstream news organs such as the *Detroit Free Press* and *Detroit News* and mainstream organizations such as the refugee relocation agencies refuse to dignify this discourse by directly acknowledging it. Still, there are indications that the outer tentacles of this discourse are part of the discursive environment within which these organizations enunciate their claims and defend their actions. For example, local refugee agencies spend a lot of time and effort normalizing and rendering safe the figure of the refugee. This expenditure of effort points to the potency of the counter-discourse painting the refugee as a figure of danger and threat.

In the chapter on "Refugee as Vote Getter" in this book, it became clear that one of the avenues through which far-right discourse seeps into the mainstream is through politics. Far-right discourse became increasingly normalized by President Trump at the national level. Local Republican politicians have also used echoes of the far-right discourse, thereby contributing to its mainstreaming and normalization. To give an example at the state level, Patrick Colbeck, an unsuccessful Republican candidate for Michigan governor in 2018, used the far-right language of "civilization jihad" to sow suspicion and fear of the Muslim other. He did this as a means of denouncing a rival candidate, Abdul El-Sayed.

In the documentary *Stateless*, the viewer sees how Tim Kelly, then a Republican member of the Michigan House of Representatives, used language typical of the far right. Kelly called the resettlement of Syrian refugees a "dangerous movement of people" and said that Christians aren't "lopping people's heads off." Combined with his blog posts saying that people should assume that all Muslims are interested in blowing things up, the implication is clear that Muslims present a threat.

L. Brooks Patterson's language was more measured when raising alarm about building what he called a "Syrian refugee village" in Pontiac. But in backing his effort to stop the housing development that would include Syrian refugees, he brought in James Simpson as a keynote speaker at the Oakland County Business Roundtable in 2016. Simpson was "known for his virulent anti-refugee stance" and was prominently featured on the Rescue Michigan website (Laitner 2016). There were also echoes of far-right discourse in the language *New York Times* readers used to debunk the proposal by Laitin and Jahr to "Let Syrians Settle Detroit." Readers referred to Muslims as "jihadis," a "nest of vipers," and more, indicating that such discourse occasionally finds a home in forums not usually considered conservative.

Another possible avenue for mainstreaming far-right discourse was the local Tea Party. For instance, a Tea Party group invited Dick Manasseri to present at their forum in Eaton, Michigan. Gary Kubiak, president of a Southeast Michigan Tea Party chapter, backed Patrick Colbeck's resolution supporting Governor Snyder's stance on halting the resettlement of Syrian refugees in Michigan after the Paris attacks.

At "Grassroots in Michigan," a website for Tea Party chapters across Michigan,[5] using the search term "Muslim" yielded three relevant stories. The first defended Representative Tim Kelly, saying he had been unfairly kept from running for a post in the Trump administration at the US Department of Education. While Kelly had actually been taken out of

---

5. Their website was no longer available as work on this book was finishing.

the running because of offensively blogging that people should assume that all Muslims are interested in blowing things up, the story on the Tea Party site characterized the development as "obstructionism" conducted by "Never Trumpers" and "deep state operatives."

The second story urged readers to support a bill in Michigan to limit the application of any foreign law, including sharia. The Tea Party movement was at the forefront of pushing for anti-sharia laws in the United States (Elsheikh, Sisemore, and Lee 2017).

The third story urged readers to oppose particular candidates for the 2018 midterm elections, including Abdul El-Sayed. The story referred to him as a "devoted Muslim" and said in bold lettering that it was "rumored he is Soros-backed and also has the backing of the powerful Muslim Brotherhood-linked network of Islamic organizations." The American billionaire, investor, and philanthropist Soros, who often contributes to liberal and democratic causes, has been painted as a devil figure by the far right, and associating El-Sayed with Soros was a rhetorical maneuver intended to vilify El-Sayed.

A Haas Institute report from UC-Berkeley points out that groups such as the Tea Party advancing the anti-sharia movement have also been spearheading campaigns in support of anti-refugee legislation. Their efforts are generally concentrated during the periods before presidential and midterm elections, providing a platform to normalize anti-Muslim sentiment. The Michigan Tea Party is among the institutions propagating anti-refugee and anti-Muslim discourse at the local level, tying in with conservative Republican candidates in doing so.

As the far-right discourse seeps into the mainstream, it tones down its rhetoric. When the Rescue Michigan emissary Dick Manasseri speaks to different groups, such as local Tea Party chapters or Republic Women's Clubs, he tailors his message to make it palatable. With the Tea Party group, he mentioned "shariavilles" in Michigan because that term was acceptable in that group. With the Republican women's groups, he didn't use the term "shariaville" per se, but discussed how the women should be concerned about "sharia-adherent" Muslim refugees moving into their towns, being placed there stealthily by refugee agencies without citizens' consent. With both the Tea Party and the Republican women's groups, Manasseri emphasized the meaning of sharia for women. This phrasing travels well as it meshes with existing notions of the oppression of Muslim women across a broad political spectrum.

When it is local politicians and not the far right itself that is raising suspicions about Muslims and Muslim refugees, the language further softens and is used very selectively. Patrick Colbeck evoked suspicion of Muslim refugees by merely speaking of "fundamentally transforming America." When attempting to pass a resolution supporting Snyder's decision to temporarily halt Syrian refugee resettlement in Michigan, he did not need to spell out that this fundamental transformation had to do with sharia or undermining the Constitution. He could use a shorthand to evoke fears of sharia, honor crimes, accommodations, and more because of the work the far right had already done in spreading its discourse. In other words, local politicians could piggyback on a discursive rubric being disseminated by the far right in a way that allowed them to look more respectable and less overtly racist.

As mentioned earlier, during the gubernatorial election in 2018, Colbeck borrowed from far-right discourse. He used the term "civilization jihad" and mentioned the Muslim Brotherhood, with the goal of creating distrust of a rival (and also unsuccessful) gubernatorial candidate, Abdul El-Sayed. Similarly, it suffices for Tim Kelly to talk about a "dangerous movement of people" and of Christians not "lopping people's heads off" to elicit a whole slew of images and phrases in people's minds to evoke fear and suspicion of Muslims and Muslim refugees. The Michigan Tea Party, too, could simply associate Abdul El-Sayed with the Muslim Brotherhood to evoke suspicion of the candidate because the far right had already used their rhetoric to place the Muslim Brotherhood within the "civilization jihad" complex.

Thus, the tone and the specifics of the discourse vary in different parts of the political spectrum. However, the selective use of elements from the far-right network by more mainstream politicians and groups still works to create fear and suspicion of the Muslim other. Many institutions in Michigan work to counterbalance the far-right discourse, including refugee resettlement agencies, the local press, Democratic candidates, and an empowered Arab American community. But the fact that far-right discourse seeps into the rhetoric of more mainstream institutions makes it worthy of examination. Taking our cue from Gramsci and Hall, then, we should step beyond our incredulity at the burgeoning parochialism and xenophobia of our current historical moment. People need to ask why these attitudes take hold, why they are so appealing? And what part do local and national far-right discourses play in their increased success?[6]

Footbaths and Controversy

I will end with a vignette from my institutional home, the University of Michigan-Dearborn. The incident I describe and the discourse surrounding it are not about Syrian or Muslim refugees per se. But it does point to the long-standing existence of some level of anxiety in Michigan about making accommodations for Muslims.

In July 2007, the university administration announced that it would be installing a few $25,000 foot-washing stations on campus, including in the library bathroom. As reported in the *New York Times:*

> When pools of water began accumulating on the floor in some restrooms at the University of Michigan-Dearborn, and the sinks began pulling away from the walls, the problem was easy to pinpoint. On this campus, more than 10 percent of the students are Muslims, and as a part of ritual ablutions required before their five-times-a-day prayers, some were washing their feet in the sinks.
>
> The solution seemed straightforward. After discussions with the Muslim Student Association, the university announced that it would install $25,000 foot-washing stations in several restrooms. (Lewin 2007)

In the same story, a sophomore at the school, Zahraa Aljebori, is quoted as saying, "I think this was the school's way to draw more Muslims, by showing that they were more welcoming." This was a plausible explana-

---

6. Gramsci's concept of hegemony opened up the study of the process of ruling by the dominant classes or blocs. Rather than assuming the dominance of the ruling classes, Gramsci pointed to the need to understand how power was maintained, with the need to maintain the consent of the working or subordinate classes being a cornerstone of maintaining a dominant position. Using a Gramscian approach, Hall conducted a careful study of how Thatcherism was able to take hold in England. By taking the popularity of Thatcherism seriously, Hall urged the left to move beyond their incredulity to understand the societal shifts that Thatcher had exploited to carve out a powerful authoritarian, populist ideology.

tion, given the aggressive push the university was making at the time to increase enrollments.

Whereas a combination of enrollment and practical concerns drove the decision to install footbaths, the decision gave right-wingers such as blogger Debbie Schlussel a chance to sow further anxiety about the purportedly growing Muslim influence in Dearborn. The fact that our campus, otherwise invisible at the national level, made a *New York Times* headline is itself a testament to the influence of the xenophobic rhetoric spawned by figures such as Schlussel. She was among the first from outside the university to latch onto the footbath decision, which meant she could drive the news agenda pertaining to it and construct it as an issue. On May 30, 2007, the blog entry on the footbaths carried on her website led with

> Forget about the Constitutionally mandated separation of church and state . . . at least when it comes to *mosque* and state.
>
> When students return in the fall, the University of Michigan-Dearbornistan is set to have Muslim footbaths in at least two locations. (Schlussel 2007)

Taking out of context campus spokesperson Terry Gallagher's comment that the footbaths were a result of "years of ongoing negotiations with the Muslim Student Association," Schlussel cast suspicion at the motives of the student group purportedly behind the decision. She added, "The *Chicago Tribune* exposed the radical Muslim Student Association (MSA) as an American branch of the Egyptian terrorist group, Muslim Brotherhood."

Associating the MSA with the Muslim Brotherhood is an oft-used tactic on the political right. The Rescue Michigan website's "Killing for a Cause" video, discussed earlier in this chapter, used this same tactic. Schlussel also took aim at the MSA's role in instituting a "reflection room" on campus that she insists was established for Muslim students. She remarked, "I wonder what would happen if Christian or Jewish students went there to pray or hang out." When juxtaposed with the fact that the reflection room had actually been used by Christian groups without incident as noted in the *New York Times* article (Lewin 2007), the rhetorical tactic becomes visible: to instill suspicion of the Muslim "other," anti-Muslim sources create issues out of the smallest accommodations.

As we saw earlier in this chapter, the far-right discourse speaks of accommodations to Muslims as a sign of "civilization jihad." The more Muslims arrive in a particular location such as Michigan, the argument goes, the more they demand accommodations. And the more accommodations people make, the more "their" culture takes over "ours."

Debbie Schlussel's amplification and politicization of an otherwise minor and little-contested accommodation is an example of the fodder right-wing bloggers provide. Far-right outfits later use such fodder to create fear of Muslims and Muslim refugees as threatening "others." As Youmans (2011) points out, Schlussel's website was "read by thousands of supporters and critics" (278), and her "characterization of Dearborn as a town run by 'Hezbos' [affiliates of the Islamist political party and militant group Hezbollah] has spread throughout much of the right-wing punditry." Further, "She sees the city as a place marked by a high level of Arab and Muslim influence and believes that taking over the United States is the aim of immigrants from the Middle East and their offspring" (281).

Schlussel's comment on the reflection room brings to mind a small incident that occurred when I was serving as the chair of a department on campus in 2008. A longtime lecturer in the department came to my office. He was perturbed that a student was using a student lounge on the same floor to roll out a small rug and conduct prayers. He was concerned that the room was being used for an illegitimate purpose and wanted me to be aware as the chair.

This was a minute occurrence among the daily complaints and concerns shared with me as chair. But it is an indication of the suspicion that can bloom even in the minds of otherwise enlightened faculty when those such as Debbie Schlussel create a climate of suspicion. This climate also becomes fertile ground for the associations made by outfits such as Rescue Michigan, joining the particular issue of accommodations to the larger discursive rubric of "civilization jihad," and then associating the construct of "civilization jihad" with the issue of Muslim refugee relocation. Through these tactics, groups such as Secure Michigan create unease or even fear about what the movement of Muslims into our neighborhoods might mean for us.

CHAPTER 3

The Refugee as a Vote Getter

The Political Fight over the Figure of the Refugee

We glimpsed the intersection of politics with the Syrian refugee issue in the "Destination Detroit" chapter. This chapter takes a more in-depth look at how the Syrian refugee issue was politicized leading up to the 2016 presidential election. It became a "political football" with consequences for refugee flows nationally, but more pertinently for refugee flows to Michigan.

Politicians in Michigan found themselves navigating multiple currents flowing from local, national, and even international levels. They crafted their politics and rhetoric in response to these multiple currents. In the process, they wrote a shifting story of expediency regarding the Syrian refugee. The refugee served alternately to bolster the story of economic revitalization, to showcase the security chops of politicians with political ambitions, and to allow politicians to address the conservative sections of the electorate.

The routing of Syrian refugees to the Detroit Metro area transcended local discourse. It caught the attention of the national news and of politicians at the national level. The position of Michigan as a key destination for Syrian refugees (Ramirez 2016), combined with the fact of Michigan having been a "battleground" state in the 2016 presidential election (Mahtesian 2016), catapulted the issue of routing Syrian refugees to Detroit into the national spotlight.

The heightened visibility of the issue at the national level in turn created the larger discursive environment in relation to which state and local politicians positioned themselves. They used the figure of the refugee to enhance or maintain their electability. Examining key moments in the political discourse at various levels allows us to see what purposes the figure of the refugee served in this discourse. We grow to understand the contours of the figure of the refugee that emerged, and we learn some of the consequences of painting the figure of the refugee as political expediency dictated.

Using insights gained from a careful reading of articles located for the "Destination Detroit" chapter, I decided to start by examining Governor Snyder's balancing act. He was a Republican governor in a state with a generally welcoming attitude toward refugees from the Arab world, particularly as a tool for repopulation and revitalization. But he came from a party that was increasingly engaging in fear-based politics, including with regard to the issue of refugees and immigrants, particularly at the national level.

I also decided to bring in the *New York Times* opinion piece "Let Syrians Settle Detroit" early in the analysis. This piece urges the governor to bring 50,000 Syrian refugees into Detroit. From there I used the hyperlink function of the web to lead me to related stories. In doing so, I located "political moments" relevant to the issue of Syrian refugee resettlement in Detroit.

I went back to the articles on Snyder in the *Detroit Free Press* and the *Detroit News*, and I located a key article in *Politico* through the recursive method of following relevant hyperlinks. It became clear that the presidential election was the discursive terrain on which Governor Snyder crafted his own rhetorical balancing act. The terrorist attacks in Paris added a layer along the way—they were an aspect that had to be taken into account by the politicians in relation to the larger environment of the campaign season.

The campaign season continued to be the overarching framework within which a number of political actors—and surrogate political actors such as Fox News and Breitbart—fashioned their discourse about Syrian refugees. But the hyperlink method led me to other political moments within the election season. These included Chobani founder Hamdi Ulukaya's interview with Bill Clinton, in which Clinton advocated bringing Syrian refugees to Detroit. Breitbart and Fox News both picked up the interview and tried to use it to discredit Hillary Clinton. I accordingly considered this to be a significant political moment in the campaign season and examined it in depth.

The refugee issue was a minor note in the 2018 midterm elections in Michigan. However, the closely related issue of fear of the Muslim other was politicized in the fight for Michigan's governorship. I will therefore include this aspect as a secondary emphasis in this chapter. The fear of the Muslim other also manifested in another hyperlocal election, that of the Hamtramck city council. I will fold this aspect into the discussion of the politicization of the Muslim other as associated with the fear of the Muslim refugee.

The Politicization of Syrian Refugee Resettlement in Detroit and Governor Snyder's Balancing Act

In January 2014, Rick Snyder, the Republican governor of Michigan, asked the Obama administration to use its executive powers to designate 50,000 extra visas to bring high-skilled immigrants to the Detroit Metro area. This was well before the presidential campaign season. Economic considerations were at the forefront, and immigrants were part of the program to revitalize Detroit. Snyder also created the Michigan Office for New Americans at this time. At this early stage, the focus was on immigrants more broadly and not on refugees per se.

In May 2015 a professor of political science from Stanford University and a former president of the New York City Housing Development Corporation teamed up to write an opinion piece in the *New York Times*. In "Let Syrians Settle Detroit," the authors urged Governor Snyder to focus his immigration efforts on Syrian refugees and bring 50,000 of them to Detroit. The authors described the scenario as a win-win situation. It conjoined "two social and humanitarian disasters," Detroit's decline and Syria's refugee crisis, for mutual benefit. The opinion piece emphasized the potential benefit that entrepreneurial Syrian refugees would offer in the economic revitalization of the Detroit Metro area. However, the focus was not on immigrants in general but on Syrian refugees specifically. This focus, combined with the fact that the presidential campaign had already kicked off by the time the article was written, put the issue in a political context.

Governor Snyder had shown great enthusiasm and leadership on the issue of bringing immigrants to Metro Detroit before the campaign started. But he began to do a much more careful rhetorical balancing act once the issue focused on Syrian refugees and the campaign season began (McGraw 2015).

Before broaching his balancing act and how it intensified after the terrorist attacks in Paris, however, I would like to dwell for a moment on reader reception of the idea proposed in the *New York Times* article. The article received more than 466 reader comments, and an examination of the comments showed that by this time the issue had become highly controversial. Of the 466 comments, 51 were about topics that had nothing to do with the focus of the article. This left 415 comments, which I read carefully and coded as either positive, negative, or neutral. I coded as positive the comments that agreed with the overall proposal to relocate Syrian refugees to the Detroit area. I coded as negative the comments that disagreed with the proposal, thought it was a bad idea, or were highly sarcastic in their characterization of the proposal or the authors. I coded as neutral the comments that mulled the pros and cons of the proposal or thought through specific obstacles or logistics without passing judgement on the proposal. This coding scheme yielded 111 positive comments, 201 negative comments, and 102 neutral comments. The idea had clearly become controversial early in the campaign season, pointing toward its politicization.

The negative comments fell into several categories. A number of readers contended that this proposed solution to Detroit's situation was inappropriate in some way. This category included 59 comments, 14 percent of the total. Others expressed some version of not wanting a concentration of Muslim refugees to be resettled in the Detroit area (there were 123 of these, 29 percent of the comments). Xenophobic comments expressing fear of Muslim refugees as the cultural other were very much present at this early stage of the presidential campaign. Negative comments emphasized the Muslim aspect of the refugees. The commenters referred to these refugees as "terrorists," "jihadis," a "nest of vipers," "religious fundamentalists," "suicide bombers," "ISIS lovers," and "primitive third world Muslims." The commenters considered these immigrants to be unassimilable. Some commenters described them as "having a hatred of Western ideology" and being "unwilling to live with the American culture," with their culture being "misogynistic, homophobic and anti-democratic."[1]

Once the issue had become politicized, Republican politicians such as Snyder had to balance economic considerations with the suspicion of Syrian refugees expressed by conservative sections of the population and members of the Republican party. By September 2015 Snyder had toned down his call for 50,000 immigrants and was careful in his rhetoric about Syrian refugees. He continued to say that he would "love to see" the Middle Eastern population in Michigan grow, and that immigrants would be an economic plus. But he was also careful to say that there was no specific number or timeline (Gov. Snyder wants more Syrian refugees 2015). Economic revitalization was a high priority for his constituents, and the Arab American community was keen to take advantage of President Barack Obama's plan, announced earlier the same month, to resettle 10,000 Syrian refugees in the United States in the fiscal year beginning October 2015 (Harris, Sanger, and Herszenhorn 2015; McCarthy 2015). However, immigration was becoming a hot-button issue in the presidential campaign, with the conservative stance of Republicans at the national level creating its own pressures. Snyder attempted to thread the rhetorical needle by saying he still wanted Michigan to be a welcoming state, without getting into policy specifics (McGraw 2015).

On June 15, 2015, candidate Donald Trump said that Mexican immigrants were criminals and rapists. On September 30, 2015, Trump said that if he were elected, all Syrian refugees would be "going back." These assertions fed into the focus on immigration and refugee issues and encouraged xenophobic sentiments about immigrants and refugees (Vitali 2015; Gamboa 2015).

The focus on refugees, as well as the conservative rhetoric sowing suspicion of refugees, received further grist with the terrorist attacks in Paris on November 13, 2015. There were rumors of a possible connection between the attacks and Syrian refugees (Kingsley 2015). Trump was the most vocal candidate after the attacks. He redoubled his rhetoric sowing

---

1. Although the rhetoric here was not as consistently extreme as that on the far-right site Rescue Michigan and its parent site Refugee Resettlement Watch, themes and language in these comments echoed the themes and language of the far-right sites.

suspicion of refugees and Muslims, calling for surveillance of "certain mosques" and creation of a database on Syrian refugees. He repeated the line that if he were elected, "they're going back, we can't have them."

It was in this political and discursive environment that several Republican governors across the United States expressed grave security concerns about Syrian refugee resettlement. Governor Snyder was the first governor to publicly express such concerns, calling for a temporary halt to the program to relocate Syrian refugees to the United States until security procedures were clarified. In an interview with NPR, he was clearly attempting to balance the generally favorable political climate for refugee resettlement in Michigan and the sentiments of an empowered Arab and Middle Eastern community that generally favored Syrian refugee resettlement with the growing security concerns being expressed both nationally and locally, particularly by Republican politicians, but also by everyday citizens.

In the NPR interview, Snyder said, "I just want to make sure we're doing the appropriate balancing between what we stand for as Americans . . . and also at the same time assuring national security by keeping the few bad people out of our country." He and his representatives still maintained that he was the most "pro-immigration" governor in the country, even though he was the first to call for a halt, "triggering a national debate about refugee resettlement" (Inskeep and Taylor 2015; Lawler 2015).[2]

The Michigan Senate's Politicization of Syrian Refugee Resettlement

In January 2016, State Senator Patrick Colbeck attempted to pass a Senate resolution urging Governor Snyder to continue his position of pausing

---

2. Snyder conducted a careful balancing act regarding the issue of relocating Syrian refugees to Michigan after the Paris attacks. In contrast, Detroit Mayor Mike Duggan remained constant in support of refugee resettlement in Detroit. He was more free to do so than the governor because of the generally favorable stance of the Democratic Party toward refugees at the national level (Warikoo 2015b), and he had support from his constituency as well. This stance put into relief the efforts of politicians such as Trump and former presidential candidate Ben Carson to paint Detroiters as potential victims of refugee location, exposing the political expediency of that positioning and that representation of Detroit and Detroiters.

resettlement of Syrian refugees into Michigan (Gray 2016). The Senate tabled the resolution. Colbeck represented the most conservative sections of the Republican party, along with other local politicians such as Oakland County Executive L. Brooks Patterson and State Representative Tim Kelly (Pluta 2016; Klein 2017).[3]

Colbeck explained the main purpose of the resolution. He said, "As the frequency and severity of ISIS attacks increase, measures are needed to protect the citizens of Michigan and the United States." He argued that even though "America will always be a nation of immigrants," in the past these immigrants "have loved America and were not seeking to fundamentally transform America."

Gary Kubiak, then president of the Southeast Michigan 912 Tea Party, backed Colbeck's resolution. Kubiak underlined the distinction between past immigrants and Syrian refugees, saying that the latter were not only "unvettable" but that "they're changing Michigan dramatically."

It becomes clear at this point that beneath the recent security concerns lay more deep-seated fears of the Muslim other. This was a fear that we saw expressed fully on the Rescue Michigan site and that had leaked into local Michigan politics. Concerns about Syrian refugees were sutured to longer-standing concerns in sections of the local population about the changing cultural character of the Detroit Metro area with the growing Muslim populations. Even if these sentiments were marginal in the Detroit area, highly conservative local politicians readily exploited their existence (Egan 2018).[4]

---

3. The "Detroit Destination" chapter of this book covers L. Brooks Patterson's opposition to resettling Syrian refugees in Pontiac. Tim Kelly, a Republican state representative in Michigan, encouraged suspicion of Muslims by blogging about the issue, among other actions. Kelly wrote, "Instead of assuming that all people are interested in, let alone capable of, blowing up Western, Christian, or Jewish things, let's assume all Muslims are" (Klein 2017).

4. Colbeck got his inspiration to join politics from a local Tea Party event (Egan 2018).

Politicization of Syrian Refugee Resettlement in Detroit in the 2016 Presidential Election

The issue of routing Syrian refugees to Detroit resurfaced in February 2016, when Bill Clinton sat down with Hamdi Ulukaya, founder and CEO of the yogurt company Chobani, at a Clinton Global Initiative meeting. Ulukaya discussed his journey as an entrepreneur and as a humanitarian using private-sector resources and talent to address the refugee crisis. Bill Clinton suggested during the conversation that routing Syrian refugees to Detroit would be very beneficial, saying:

> Detroit has ten thousand empty structurally sound houses, ten thousand! And a lot of jobs to be had repairing those houses. But Detroit just came out of bankruptcy and the mayor is trying to do an innovative sort of urban homesteading program there. But it just gives you an example of what could be done. And I think any of us who've had any personal experience with either Syrian Americans or Syrian refugees think it's a pretty good deal.

Clinton acknowledged the fears that the Paris attacks had evoked. But he went on to make a strong case for refugees, especially Syrian refugees. The conversation occurred as the primaries were heating up, Bernie Sanders and Hillary Clinton were vying for the Democratic Party's nomination, and Trump was fending off his rivals for the Republican Party nomination. The sit-down with Ulukaya was timed in such a way as to distance the Clintons and the Democratic Party from the anti-refugee rhetoric that Republican party candidates—especially Donald Trump—were using.

The conversation then lay fallow for several months. Breitbart picked it up in August 2016, by which time Hillary Clinton and Trump had won the nominations of their respective parties and were ready to face off. The first presidential debate was scheduled for late September. Breitbart had already positioned itself as a champion of Trump, and the timing was perfect for the politicization of the conversation (Benkler et al. 2017). In four careful steps, Breitbart did just that.

On August 25, Breitbart published a piece on Ulukaya with the title, "Turkish Chobani owner has deep ties to Clinton Global Initiative and Clinton campaign." The article attacked Ulukaya's credibility, presenting him as a prime example of how "in the era of globalism, big government and big business are intermeshed" and contending that the Tent Foundation he established to help refugees was part of "a loose affiliation of millionaires and billionaires whose supposed altruism always seems to pay off handsomely for them." The piece lent a conspiratorial air to the connections between Ulukaya, the Clintons, "globalists" such as Warren Buffett and Bill Gates, and the Hillary Clinton campaign, including campaign manager John Podesta, with each person or group scratching the others' back for mutual gain (Stranahan 2016b).

Close on the heels of this article, Breitbart published another on August 29. This one took a jab at the video described above, in which Bill Clinton made a pitch for relocating Syrian refugees to Detroit (Hahn 2016). The author wrote, "It is unclear from the video why Clinton seems to think it would be better to fill these Detroit jobs with imported foreign migrants rather than unemployed Americans already living there, who could perhaps benefit from good-paying jobs."[5] The article painted resettlement of Syrian refugees as a zero-sum game, with Americans losing as Syrian refugees gained jobs and new homes.

The article notes that Bill Clinton was discussing the "migrant crisis" with Ulukaya, characterized as a "mass migration enthusiast" of the "Chobani yoghurt empire." In concert with other articles by Breitbart casting suspicion on Chobani and/or Ulukaya (Stranahan 2016a; 2016b), associating Clinton's suggestion with Ulukaya was meant to detract from the idea's legitimacy. The article also makes a direct connection between Bill Clinton's suggestion and Hillary Clinton's campaign, using an excerpt from a speech Donald Trump gave the same day in Dimondale, Michigan:

> The unearthed video seems to underscore Donald Trump's recent declaration that "Hillary Clinton would rather provide a job to a refugee from overseas than to give that job to unemployed African American youth in cities like Detroit who have become refugees in their own country."

---

5. This was also a refrain in the comments on the *New York Times* article "Let Syrians Settle Detroit." It is suggestive of the influence of alt-right sites such as Breitbart, which stretches toward the mainstream but also toward more extreme-right websites such as Refugee Resettlement Watch. The fact that the three shared some themes and language indicates how extreme ideas bled into the mainstream.

Hillary Clinton has called for a 550 percent expansion to the importation of Syrian refugees. Based on the minimum figures she has put forth
thus far, a President Hillary Clinton could potentially import a population of refugees (620,000) that nearly equals the population of Detroit
(677,116). (Hahn 2016)

In a classic alt-right maneuver also seen at the Rescue Michigan website,
the website positioned itself as a sleuth uncovering conspiracies and the
secrets of liberals—specifically, the Hillary Clinton campaign. Breitbart
pitted refugees against displaced Americans, in this case displaced African
Americans in Detroit. In a bid to court a city in the battleground state of
Michigan, Trump not only politicized but also racialized the refugee issue,
and Breitbart accentuated its politicization in its role as Trump's booster.[6]

Breitbart's next move was to invite and broadcast an interview with
noted neurosurgeon, Detroit native, and former presidential candidate Ben
Carson, on September 2, 2016. Although Carson had already dropped out
of the race at this point, his Detroit connection made him an appropriate
spokesperson to debunk Bill Clinton's idea. The interview was billed as a
"preview" for an interview with Trump to be aired the next day. Trump
and Carson worked in tandem to bolster each other's credibility, and their
main points closely echoed each other's. Carson said, "You know, there are
plenty of people in Detroit who you could almost look at as refugees. I
mean, we need to take care of our own people" (Hayward 2016).

The fourth story in the series of stories debunking the Clinton-
Ulukaya plan to bring in Syrian refugees to Detroit was an interview with
Trump that aired on September 3. The reporter pointedly asked him to
react to Clinton's suggestion, just as Carson had been pointedly asked
to do. The interview was billed as an "exclusive" with Trump, describing
him as "blasting" Bill Clinton's suggestion as "crazy" and "unfair" to the
American workers already living in Detroit.

Trump then spoke of the Syrian refugees as a possible "Trojan

6. Omi and Winant, in *Racial Formation in the United States*, define racialization
as "the extension of racial meanings to a previously racially unclassified relationship,
social practice, or group." Here I am using the term to say that the association being
made by Trump and Carson between the issue of resettling Syrian refugees in Detroit
and the economic hardship of African Americans in Detroit put the issue into a racial
mold.

horse." He would repeat this figure of speech on the campaign trail and during the presidential debates. Carson's comments from the story aired the day before were folded in, with Carson being referred to as a "Detroit native" and as echoing Trump's sentiment. The story culminated with a long quote from an immigrant policy address that Trump had given the previous week, during which he challenged the media to ask Hillary Clinton about her "radical" immigration platform (Boyle and Hahn 2016).

Read backward, the related sequence of stories can be seen as a strategy of Breitbart's to vilify Hillary Clinton at a crucial time in the election cycle. In the process, the issue of Syrian refugees, including the resettlement of Syrian refugees in Detroit, became further politicized. The folding in of Carson's invited comments added an air of authenticity to the claim that bringing Syrians to Detroit would harm its current residents.

Further, Breitbart amplified the competition between refugees and African American youth that Trump and Carson described. It did so by highlighting and uncritically reporting this aspect, thereby contributing not only to the politicization of the refugee issue but to its racialization. The refugees therefore became part of the Trump campaign's strategy to court African American voters. Not only was Michigan a battleground state, but the African American vote was considered to be crucial to victory.

On the campaign trail, Trump had already been exploiting growing unease about refugee resettlement, partly spurred by the terrorist attacks in Paris. Soon after the attacks, he competed with other Republican presidential candidates, and particularly with Ted Cruz, as the two tried to outdo each other in criticizing Obama's plan to bring in 10,000 refugees. Both Trump and Cruz called for a halt to the resettlement of Syrian refugees for security reasons, thereby attempting to demonstrate their suitability to serve as commander in chief (ABC 2015).

The Bill Clinton video and quotes allowed Breitbart to associate the refugee issue with the concern about jobs in the African American community, and particularly in Detroit. Both Breitbart and Fox played roles as mouthpieces for Donald Trump during the 2016 election. The issue of relocating Syrian refugees to Detroit was an instance of politicizing a particular issue in support of Trump's campaign (Benkler et al. 2017; Illing 2019; Novak 2017).

Writing the Story of Political Expediency on the Refugee

Trump's policies on immigration, particularly immigration from Muslim-majority countries, led to a sharp decline in refugee resettlement, especially from Muslim countries. In Michigan, the resettlement of refugees declined sharply, particularly of those from Iraq and Syria and in Muslim refugees especially (Rahal 2018a). The intentions expressed as presidential campaign rhetoric materialized into actual consequences for the nation, for Michigan, and for the Detroit Metropolitan area.

People protested Trump's travel ban in Detroit, and the protests received local news coverage. A few news stories detailed the sharp drop in refugees from Syria and Iraq coming into Michigan and the potential harm this would probably cause (Rahal 2018a, 2018b). Other than that, there was relative quiet on the refugee issue after the 2016 presidential campaign.

This quiet lends further grist to the argument that the refugee issue, especially the Syrian refugee issue, had become closely pegged to the larger political shifts taking place at every level, from national to state to local. The issue became associated with concerns about security, shifting culture, and economic decline and revitalization. Politicians positioned themselves in relation to various constituencies and power brokers, depending on the political environment and circumstances at the time. The story of political expediency thus was written onto the refugee issue, including the Syrian refugee issue, and onto the figure of the refugee. The very presence or absence of the issue in local discourse followed political seasons such as those defined by elections, becoming most salient and most available for symbolic manipulation during periods of campaigning.

Politicizing the Muslim Other in the 2018 Midterm Elections in Michigan

The next election season of note in Michigan was the midterm election in 2018. As in the United States as a whole, the midterms were highly anticipated due to the possibility of a "blue wave" of Democratic voter support at the state level. The refugee issue was a minor note in the midterms, but the Muslim other became politicized in the race for governor. Politicizing the Muslim other provided fodder for those trying to create fear of the Muslim refugee other.

Political rhetoric can worsen the fear of Muslims among Americans. Those who create this fear or worsen it in sections of the Michigan citizenry can then create resistance to the Muslim other in the form of the refugee as well. After all, if the Muslim other in American towns and cities can be made to seem sinister, it becomes even easier to sow suspicion of the Muslim other from foreign lands.

As noted earlier, former state Senator Patrick Colbeck, a Republican, had attempted to pass a resolution supporting Snyder's pause on Syrian refugee resettlement in Michigan. As part of his run for governor in 2018, Colbeck attempted to vilify a Democratic candidate running for governor, Abdul El-Sayed. In 2016 Colbeck's comments on Syrian refugees were fairly restrained, and he only parenthetically and indirectly referred to Muslim refugees "seeking to fundamentally transform America." In 2018, when the political stakes were higher, he used far more overt language attempting to sow fear of the Muslim other.

In an event held by United West, characterized by the Southern Poverty Law Center as an "active anti-Muslim group," Colbeck spoke of the rise of political aspirants such as El-Sayed as part of a "civilization jihad" plot by the Muslim Brotherhood. His slide presentation indicated that a key "civilization jihad" technique was to "Place Muslim brothers in positions from which they can exercise influence."

Colbeck then asserted that various kinds of "pressure" were being applied. He gave examples of Muslims in the state legislature, of Hamtramck having the first majority-Muslim city council, leading up to the most important example for his current political purposes, saying "but you also have somebody that I will likely be running against in the general election, Dr. Abdul El-Sayed, whose parents have apparently have ties to Muslim Brotherhood back in Egypt. This is scary stuff." He then made a spurious connection between this alleged association and El-Sayed's support of Michigan becoming a sanctuary state.

Colbeck went on to connect El-Sayed with Bill Clinton, political activist Linda Sarsour, and philanthropist George Soros, all of whom had already been painted in a highly negative way in far-right circles. He pointed out that El-Sayed was already being touted as likely to be Michigan's first

Muslim governor, and he said repeatedly, "It's a big deal." Finally, he cautioned his audience not to be lulled into ignoring the threat El-Sayed represented by thinking that Gretchen Whitmer would win anyway (Ansari 2018). (Whitmer did win.)

By using conspiracy theories spouted by the far right, which are reminiscent of those encountered on the extreme right website Rescue Michigan discussed in another chapter of this book, politicians such as Colbeck normalized and brought into the mainstream language that vilified the Muslim other. This language then became a baseline for vilifying the Muslim other in the form of the refugee. As they wrote their political ambitions and ideologies onto the figure of the Muslim other, these politicians propped up the idea that the Muslim other, and by extension the Muslim refugee, represented a threat.

The news website BuzzFeed first reported on Colbeck's comments on April 24 (Ansari 2018). In the ensuing days, Democrats in the state Senate called out Colbeck for his comments. Also, the Michigan Republican Party tried to distance itself from his conspiracy theories (Nashrulla 2018). Colbeck continued to stand by his stance on El-Sayed and "civilization jihad" (Oosting 2018a). The sparring culminated in a tense exchange between Colbeck and El-Sayed during the debate on May 10 that included all gubernatorial candidates from the two major parties. Colbeck repeated his claims that El-Sayed had affiliations with the Muslim Brotherhood because he had been part of the Muslim Student Association at the University of Michigan. Colbeck also raised fears about sharia law creeping into Michigan.

El-Sayed called for Republican gubernatorial candidates to condemn Colbeck's racist and Islamophobic comments. He chose not to dignify Colbeck's comments by directly addressing them, instead saying that whoever is elected governor will be taking an oath to uphold the US Constitution, noting that the document "guarantees me the right to pray as I choose to pray."

At one point, after Colbeck refused to back off, El-Sayed responded with "You may not hate Muslims, but Muslims hate you." The fact that El-Sayed finished second behind Whitmer in the Democratic primaries is an indication that his progressive message generally played well in Michigan, and that the fearmongering about sharia law and the Muslim other had a limited hearing (For Abdul El-Sayed "the path hasn't changed" despite primary loss 2018).[7] However, the politicization of the issue constituted a moment in Michigan's political history when far-right rhetoric about Muslims entered the mainstream political discourse.

The national press was quick to politicize the issue of the Muslim other at the state level. Still, many other politicians worked to find a balance between calling out Colbeck for his bigotry and redirecting the conversation away from the issue to avoid further politicizing it. Gretchen Whitmer, for example, worked to bring the conversation back to the core issues, saying of the gubernatorial debate, "I think you saw a lot of people foraying into things that don't really matter to Michigan voters." She continued, "That's why I try to always get back to making sure that we've got Michiganders who have skills so they can get into higher-wage jobs, who clean up drinking water for Michigan families, that we protect health care and fix the damn roads."

Abdul El-Sayed also tried to redirect the conversation back to core issues. He said, "Every second we're talking about this is a second we're not talking about fixing roads for people, making sure schools stay public, making sure people have access to the water they deserve as citizens of the Great Lakes state" (Oosting 2018b).

Refusing to Politicize the Muslim Other in Hamtramck

I now turn briefly to a hyperlocal election. We saw earlier the careful balancing act that Governor Snyder attempted to do after the terrorist attacks in Paris. Similarly, in the case of Colbeck's vilification of the Muslim other during the midterm elections, we saw Democratic candidates calling out Colbeck on his comments and trying to redirect the conversation to practical issues.

The city council elections in Hamtramck are a useful vantage point to examine a bit further the stance that politicians take when Islam becomes politicized in an electoral race, and the implications of the stance that is

---

7. Of course, one could argue that El-Sayed might have done even better had suspicions not been evoked about his hiding connections with the Muslim Brotherhood. But there is no way of knowing exactly how the discourse affected his chances. At the end of the day, we know that the vilification did not take him out of the running—but also that he did not end up becoming the first Muslim governor of the state.

taken. A Muslim candidate was elected to the city council on November 3, 2015, making it the first city council in the country to have a Muslim majority. But the council took pains to refuse to politicize the issue. They did so alongside local white politicians, such as the mayor, and local residents of different religions and ethnicities. Newly elected city councilor Saad Almasmari made a point of saying that he served every single citizen of Hamtramck (Warikoo 2015a). As reported in a *Detroit News* story, "Almasmari stresses that faith wasn't a selling point during the election campaign" (Hicks 2015). In the same story local activist Bill Meyer made the point that "Hamtramck, I think, was saved in a large part due to the presence of Muslims."

In a story by the *Guardian*, Almasmari could be seen working against the framing of the election as an exceptional event because of the majority-Muslim aspect, saying "It was a regular election, just like any other election" and adding "People choose whomever they want" (Felton 2015). A *Teen Vogue* story homed in on the contrast between the politicization of the Muslim aspect in national discourse and its lack of politicization at the local level, other than by a few fringe actors. The author, Liana Aghajanian, made the point that the 2015 election led to an "international media feeding frenzy," with everyone from the *Washington Post* to German media getting into the act. According to Aghajanian, these media created an impression that Hamtramck residents were nervous about the changing demographics.

Aghajanian said the far right also latched onto the event, inventing the moniker "Shariaville, USA" for Hamtramck. We saw this nomenclature in the "Refugees Not Welcome" chapter as being part of Ann Corcoran's anti-refugee discourse. Drawing a sharp contrast with perceptions in Hamtramck itself, Aghajanian continued, "For the people who actually live and work in the city, however, the suggestions [that sharia was going to replace the U.S. Constitution in Hamtramck] weren't just inaccurate—they were laughable." The article also mentioned the reaction of Hamtramck mayor Karen Majewski to a CNN reporter who asked her in November 2015 if she was afraid of being in her own city. Majewski, who has Polish roots, said the question "was one of the strangest she'd ever gotten."

Aghajanian pointed out that in contrast to the tone struck by the national and international media when covering the city council election, the elected councilor Saad Almasmari himself did not think of it as an extraordinary event at all. He rejected the foregrounding of the religious aspect in national and international news coverage of the election. Reminiscent of statements made by Abdul El-Sayed in the gubernatorial debate, Almasmari said, "My roof is the Constitution, not religion" (Aghajanian 2017). Hamtramck residents also rejected the politicization of religion by their actions. City council candidate Susan Dunn attempted to politicize the issue of the call to prayer that has from time to time become controversial in the city. Hamtramck residents rejected this politicization when they elected Almasmari.

I began the chapter by examining how the issue of Syrian refugee relocation to Detroit became politicized at the national level, with actual consequences for Michigan and the Detroit area in terms of the substantial drop in numbers of refugees settling here. Now I end the chapter broaching how in a hyperlocal election, residents of a Metro Detroit city refused to politicize the Muslim aspect. Through their own version of "vernacular cosmopolitanism" or an everyday, messy, bottom-up kind of cosmopolitanism, Hamtramck residents worked to reframe the election as an ordinary event in their city (Georgiou 2013).[8]

---

8. In *Media and the city: Cosmopolitanism and difference*, Georgiou shows the opposition between an everyday, lived, street-level, bottom-up, vernacular cosmopolitanism and a neoliberal, top-down kind of cosmopolitanism. Vernacular cosmopolitanism is messy because it is informed by complicated histories of a place, including histories of migration by working-class people. Georgiou points to the robustness of vernacular cosmopolitanism, with people having to create solidarities and conduct transactions across difference daily. In Hamtramck, the election of Muslims to the city council was an example of this kind of bottom-up, street-level cosmopolitanism.

CHAPTER 4

Refugees Welcome

The Refugee as a Test of Our Collective Character

If the far-right discourse in Michigan was mainly geared toward creating fear and suspicion of the refugee other, the discourse of the refugee agencies and their allies has the opposite goal: to allay fear and suspicion of the refugee and to portray the refugee as fundamentally similar to the general public, even though in very different circumstances. In the far-right discourse, the refugee is impossible to assimilate. In the refugee agency discourse, the refugee is eager to assimilate, and the agencies' mission is to help them do so as quickly as possible. While the far right seeks to recruit people who will work to stop refugees from entering towns and cities, the refugee agencies recruit people who can make the passage of the refugees into towns and cities easier.

In many ways the two discourses are opposites. The far-right discourse targets the refugee agencies as one among many entities engaged in a conspiracy to relocate refugees in people's backyards without their knowledge. In contrast, the refugee agencies don't target the far right or even acknowledge its existence. To go a bit deeper, however, the agencies do expend a lot of rhetoric normalizing the figure of the refugee, showing them to be harmless. This could be an implicit gesture acknowledging that the agencies are working within a broader discursive environment that is influenced by the far right, where refugees and refugee relocation remain highly contested.

A handful of organizations work with the US State Department to resettle refugees from many parts of the world in Michigan. These organizations include Samaritas, the US Committee for Refugees and Immigrants (USCRI), Catholic Charities of Southeast Michigan, Jewish Family Services, and Bethany Christian Services. Secondary organizations work with these agencies to resettle refugees from particular countries or regions, such as the Syrian American Rescue Network, or SARN. As is reflected in the sophistication of their websites or lack thereof, the levels of funding available to the different agencies vary greatly.

I carefully examined the websites of all these organizations, as well as the websites of two allied organizations doing advocacy work for refugees and immigrants, Global Detroit and Welcoming Michigan. I focused mainly on the self-representation and discursive approach to refugees on the website of the largest and best-known such agency at the state level, the faith-based Samaritas.[1] Secondarily, I examined the websites of USCRI Michigan and the smaller, community-based agency focused narrowly on the resettlement of Syrian refugees, SARN.

To locate similarities and differences between different types of agencies, I confined myself to one-faith based agency and then examined the main secular agency working in the Detroit area, USCRI, and the main agency working to resettle Syrian refugees in the Detroit area, SARN. By examining all three agencies—Samaritas, USCRI, and SARN—I was able to tease out differences and similarities between the faith-based and non-faith-based groups, and between a small, narrowly focused group versus a large, broadly focused group. Each of these agencies had a substantial web presence, allowing me to do a thorough analysis of their approach.[2]

---

1. Although it is not a focus of this study, organizations such as Global Detroit have played an important advocacy role for refugees and immigrants in the Metro Detroit area. They do so by gathering and disseminating credible, well-respected research on the significant economic contribution of refugees and immigrants to the region. Refugee resettlement agencies and local news organs have used their research as a source, and that research has played a part in explaining the economic rationale for keeping the doors open to refugees.

2. There is asymmetry in this book, with my emphasis sometimes being on Syrian refugees, at other times on refugees more broadly, or on Muslim and/or Arab refugees and immigrants in Michigan. This asymmetry stems from my building up from each

How Samaritas Speaks of the Refugee

When I entered the Samaritas website at www.samaritas.org, it immediately became clear that this was a mainstream, well-resourced organization.[3] The site looked fully and carefully constructed, with the text, visual imagery, and hyperlink structure working together to craft an image of the organization, but also of the figure of the ideal refugee. The website overall had a professional look, as did the "New Americans" page at samaritas. org/New-Americans, the main focus here. The elements on the page were well balanced, with even amounts of print, graphics, and white space. The menu choices were clearly and logically laid out, making the site easy to navigate. There were many links to learn more about particular facets of the organization's refugee resettlement program in Michigan. There were two pictures of brown children smiling directly at the camera, with a prominent caption, "Refugees Welcome." They could be from any Third World country. The main text then led with a definition of the refugee.

> Refugees are people of all ages who are forced from their own countries by war or political unrest and who cannot return for fear of persecution because of their race, ethnicity, religion, or political affiliations. Many spend years in refugee camps before they are given permission to enter the United States. They arrive with little more than the clothes they are wearing.
>
> Refugees come here seeking protection and a chance to build a new life. They are eager to learn, to work, and to become productive contribu-

---

case I study to the conclusions I reach. To do a grounded textual analysis, I followed the scope of the issue or denoted population as defined within the universe of discourse produced by the various institutions.

3. Like alt-right organizations and the organizations involved in spreading Islamophobia, refugee agencies engage in resource and information sharing. They network with each other at the same level and across levels (such as the national, state, and local levels) to increase their reach and effectiveness. This networking aspect was clear from the way USCRI Detroit localized the mission and content of USCRI at the national level. It was also evident from the connections between Refugees to College (R2C), Samaritas, and Washtenaw Refugee Welcome that I experienced when I attempted to volunteer for Refugees to College. For example, R2C, a student group at the University of Michigan, used Samaritas's orientation materials to conduct my orientation and also sent me to Samaritas for my background check. Samaritas is a key node in this network and therefore an appropriate focus for this study.

tors to society. As they become settled, they build businesses, create jobs, revitalize neighborhoods, fuel the economy, and strengthen the tax base, enriching their communities.

We can see here that the refugee agency discourse is consistent with the already existing discourses on the "refugee." Historically, a number of organizations generated and elaborated these discourses, beginning after World War II. Chief among these is the administrative apparatus that has been in place since then to regulate the movement and resettlement of those forced to migrate.

Samaritas can be placed within the genealogy of this apparatus, so it's not surprising that it borrowed from already-existing understandings of the refugee as a problem to be administered, specifically a Third World problem (Malkki 1995). As occurred in existing administrative discourses, the organization here dehistoricized and depoliticized the refugee (Malkki 1995, 1996). "They arrive with little more than the clothes they are wearing," shorn of possessions, history, and the ability to tell their own story in politically meaningful terms.

However, in the second paragraph of the quote, we see an interesting change in the discourse. The refugee was afforded one kind of agency: the agency to contribute economically to the host society. According to Samaritas, refugees were grateful beneficiaries of others' assistance and had the potential to convert this assistance into economic benefit for others in the host society.

As Castles (2003) points out, from the 1970s onward, an upsurge in forced migration occurred at the same time as economic restructuring. This resulted in the politicization of forced migration and asylum. Castles also points out that after September 11, the refugee issue became politicized in another way, with the refugee coming to be seen as a security threat.

At the time of writing, we were once again seeing these processes at play, with the combination of political and economic shifts intensifying the politicization of the refugee issue. It is ironic, but also a logical outcome, that as the refugee issue becomes highly politicized globally, refugee agencies such as Samaritas respond by further apoliticizing and dehistoricizing the refugee. These agencies paint the refugee as a clean slate ready on which others can write their beneficence. But they also depict the refugee as a potential contributor to the host society, rather than an economic burden.

Contrast this portrayal with the far right's exploitation of the fear of the refugee as a security threat, a cultural threat, and an economic burden. Partly in response to the growing mainstream influence of the far right, the refugee agency devotes its discourse to allaying these fears by portraying the refugee as a figure of both vulnerability and hope—as anything but a threat or a burden.

Video testimonials of the refugees figure prominently in the middle of the page, reminiscent of the importance of testimonials in human rights work (Gilmore 2005; Smith 2005; Hesford 2005). The testimonials, through a combination of narration, imagery, and snippets of interviews with a refugee, develop the major themes of the website. The idea is that refugees are normal human beings like other members of the general public, looking for safety and a secure future for their families, grateful for assistance, and trying to fit in, become self-sufficient, and contribute to the host society.

The Samaritas website presented carefully selected slices of refugee narratives to build on this idea. This is in accord with a key insight from Hesford and Kozol (2005) that victim narratives enter the mainstream on particular terms and are used in particular ways, which are not always in the long-term interests of the victims (in this case, refugees) themselves.

The video testimonial featuring Dr. Rafaai Hamo, "The Scientist," was a case in point. Dr. Hamo already had national recognition and was therefore an apt choice to project a positive, upbeat image of the refugee agency and of Syrian refugees. Hamo, his son, and his three daughters had fled from Syria to Turkey after a missile attack killed seven members of his family, including his wife and another daughter. After two years in Turkey and after having contracted stomach cancer that he was not eligible to have treated there, he and his family received refugee status to move to Troy, Michigan. Soon after he was featured in the blog *Humans of New York*, where he caught the eye of President Obama and his family, resulting in an invitation to the State of the Union address in 2016 (Winsor 2016). As a figure of both pathos and dignity, Hamo became not only an attractive signifier for refugee advocates in Michigan, but an attractive news hook for the national and local press.

In the video itself, he was shown arriving at Detroit Metropolitan Airport to a warm welcome, with four people holding up a banner saying "Welcome Home!" in English and Arabic. As the viewer sees the sign, they can hear Hamo's voice-over in Arabic with English subtitles below, saying of Americans: "How loving they are! How generous they are! And how they appreciate science and all humanity!"

Here is a person who was once a renowned scientist in Syria, but as a refugee became a shiny blank slate on which to write the story of American generosity—in the words of the refugee himself, no less. His former status was still relevant to the extent that it provided gloss to both the self-presentation of the refugee agency and the representation of refugees. And Syria, rather than being a place that had fostered such talent, became the dangerous place where Hamo's family was bombed and from which he was admitted to the United States. Also, rather than being one among many scientists as part of a functioning research infrastructure within Syria, Hamo became "The Scientist" from Syria, the exception rather than the rule.

The figure of the refugee is funneled through various representational regimes and becomes available for signification by various entities, including refugee resettlement agencies. And so does the place from which he or she comes. This place becomes the negation of the host society. It is the place where the refugee can no longer reside, the place they have to flee, the place of violence and rejection, the very foil of the United States as the host society, which is portrayed as a place of welcome, acceptance, and safety.

Hamo's words did the work of allaying the concerns of Michigan residents. He announced his love for the American people and professed his strong desire to assimilate and to give back to American society. He said toward the end of the video,

Because I know that American people really do love all people, I hope my future will be like those Syrians who came before me, and like every natural-born American citizen. I need to be a productive person and I hope to enjoy all the rights and responsibilities of being an American citizen. I don't want to feel like a guest or be a burden on the American society. I want to be treated equal and give back to this country.

Throughout the website, in various testimonials, refugees voiced their gratefulness and their love of America. Also throughout the testimonials, refugees either voiced their strong desire to contribute to American society or were actually shown contributing to society or working actively to assimilate to it. Those themes had already been clearly demonstrated in Hamo's words, and the website user could see these themes clearly enunciated again in the second video testimonial on the New Americans page, featuring local entrepreneur Albert Yousif. In that video, Yousif explained in English that he served in the Iraqi army for nine years in Iraq. He said that after serving in three wars, "I said enough is enough. I cannot keep living my life serving in the army and then I always hear that this is America's land of opportunity, so I said, where is my opportunity?"

As he spoke, the video showed various indications of his having established a successful business in Michigan. He signed papers in a well-appointed office. The website viewer could see his employees hard at work. The video showed a prominent poster of his A2Z Facility Maintenance company. He explained how after arriving in Michigan he had struggled, working jobs from morning till night, but that it had all paid off because he was able to start his own business. He explained proudly that he hires employees from different ethnic and national backgrounds, adding

the United States built on melting pots [sic] from all nations. Different brains, different thoughts, different ideas. And this is what make [sic] this country strong; really strong, and great, and unique actually. And then I find out that there is a need for refugees to be hired. And then I thought about it and I said okay, this country gave me something, it is my time now to give back. And I tried to find the best way to give back by hiring people who they come new [sic].

Among the refugees Yousif has hired was an electrical engineer from Iraq. The young woman echoed Yousif's sentiments when she said,

I came as a refugee to the United States from Iraq because people there are killing each other. There is no peace. Even when I was going to my work, I don't know if I will return to my home or not. So I thank God for everything he gave me till now. And I thank all the people who support in bringing me here because there is no danger. It is very beautiful.

She also strongly endorsed the hiring of refugees, saying,

As a human thing, we have to support people when they are in fear, and they don't have a safe life, so we have to help them. Every person is looking for happiness. And to live in peace. What do we need more?

Once again, we see refugees voicing their gratefulness to the United States, their love of the United States, and their desire to give back to the society. She also reiterated the image of the country from which she came as a place of violence and instability, a place of disorder. In addition, she hammered home the idea that refugees are normal people like the video viewer—simple, ordinary people wanting to live in peace, even if their circumstances are different from most other people's.

The same basic storyline was clear in the third video testimonial as well. This one showed a young family with the children enjoying a normal American pastime, horse riding at Pine River Stables in Michigan. The father explained that when the war started in Syria, they fled to Jordan, and after staying there for two and a half years, they had arrived in the United States about five months previously. He added, smiling broadly, "America is amazing." He then explained the circumstances in greater detail.

When the war started, the bombs were very close to where we lived. They were killing everyone; children and adults. There are many groups that are involved, but nobody knows who is against who, or who is with whom.

Once again, the place he came from was painted as a place of chaos, and the United States became by contrast a place of order and possibility. The contrast is made all the more stark with images of bloodshed in Syria and green stables in Michigan. Painting this stark contrast between the two places reinforces a dominant epistemic map, and also underlines the legitimacy of the work the refugee agencies do and the humanitarian underpinnings of that work.

When asked how his life is now, the father said:

Very good, thank God. Here there is peace and future for my family. And my children are just so excited and happy now. I want to thank God first, because he opened the doors for us to come here. I also want to thank the Samaritas agency for their help and support. They make us feel very comfortable and safe here.

When asked about his plans for the future, he said:

I want my children to learn English and continue their education. I also want to learn the language and work and be stable financially. I want to forget about my painful past. Just be safe, healthy, and live in peace.

Once again, all the major themes the refugee agency would like to project are included here—themes that allay any concerns Michigan residents might have about refugee relocation. The video presented a young, respectable-looking family who had fled dire circumstances and wanted only to leave the violence behind and live in safety. They were eager to assimilate and to become financially stable. They were also very grateful for the help they were receiving, and they loved America.

Following the link from the New Americans page to the New American Alumni page led a user to a repetition of the same discursive rubric. This one was part of a coordinated public communication strategy on the part of Samaritas. The page showcased the accomplishments of three "alumni" of Samaritas's relocation efforts, including Albert Yousif (already featured on the New Americans main page); a former interpreter for the US Army in Iraq relocated to Grand Rapids, Michigan; and a young family from the Congo relocated to Grand Rapids via Uganda. Without exception, all of them said they were grateful to the United States and Samaritas, grateful to be able to start a new life in Michigan, and eager to assimilate and give back.

Following the link from the New Americans page to the "Refugee Foster Care" page led the user to another version of the same story. This one was embodied and voiced by youths. Five of them told their stories on video: one from Burma, two from Eritrea, one from Ethiopia, and one from Guatemala. They were all soft-spoken. Shyly and briefly, they told the interviewer about the circumstances that led them to flee their home countries, how they made it to the United States, and what struggles they experienced in adjusting to life in the United States. They described their success in adjusting and their dreams and aspirations.

These youths came to the United States when they were between fourteen and eighteen, and at the time of the interviews were in their late teens or early twenties. Viewers watching the interviews can clearly understand the impact of relocation and see the potential waiting to be unlocked. Early in the video, two or three of the interviewees described their experience in their home country or in a refugee camp as "futureless." This creates a powerful story arc that culminates with them speaking of purposeful futures; one wants to own a farm, another to pursue a degree in dental hygiene, and another to go to college. The refugee agency and the United States are both the protagonists here, making the upward journey possible.

An associated theme on the website was the potential disruption of the story of the United States as a welcoming society and a beacon of human rights by political developments, especially in the Trump era. On the left-hand bar of the New Americans page, a user could see two news stories, one from MLive.com and one from the *Detroit Free Press*. Both stories stemmed from a Samaritas press conference featuring six refugees. The refugees shared their experiences in light of Trump's ban on immigrants from seven Muslim-majority nations. Both stories were dated February 2, 2017, the day of the press conference, a few days after Trump announced the ban.

Samaritas carefully managed the refugee narratives in the press conference, and then selectively used the news stories to make a political statement in accord with their mission. The idea was to push back against political currents that were cultivating fear of refugees and immigrants, particularly Muslim refugees and immigrants. The refugee narratives served Samaritas's advocacy mission, with the inadvertent outcome that the refugees themselves were not allowed to be political beings capable of independently interpreting world events. This difference becomes apparent even in the headline to the MLive story: "Refugees in southeast Michigan ask Trump to reconsider immigrant ban."

The press conference itself featured short speeches and testimonials from the refugees. Their telling of their experience was framed in terms of the refugee agency's struggle to influence policy on refugee resettlement. The "asking," the demand, was very specific to the current predicament and very specifically tailored to Samaritas's objective. The first sentence of the story, introducing the refugee narratives, expressed that mission:

> They want to build a better life for their families in a free country. They want to feel safe from violence in the Middle East. They want to live like anyone else.

Before the refugees even opened their mouths, the creators of the video and website unwittingly bleached them of the political. When the refugees did speak, they asked the United States to live up to its hallowed reputation as a beacon of human rights. They spoke of the current political moment as a possible exception in an otherwise illustrious history. One refugee was quoted as saying, "Trump got the wrong picture about Islam," and "His decision about the seven count[r]ies [is] absolutely incorrect. Muslims want to live a better life." Another refugee said, "We expected these orders from third world countries, not the United States." That refugee continued, "We didn't expect this from the most democratic country in the world." Another refugee quoted later in the story said, "We love Americans, and I hope Americans love us, too." Throughout the Samaritas website, the refugees' voices were safely contained within the same general discursive rubric.

How USCRI Speaks of the Refugee

As a user navigated the US Committee for Refugees and Immigrants (USCRI) website at www.refugees.org, a slight discursive difference from the Samaritas site was noticeable, although the main discursive contours were similar.

The term of choice for those being served here was "the uprooted." This is an umbrella term encompassing refugees, immigrants, unaccompanied migrating children, and survivors of human trafficking. Perhaps because USCRI serves both those uprooted by force and those uprooted by choice, and perhaps because it is a secular rather than a faith-based organization, the language of rights tends to be more central here than the language of charity or humanitarianism, although both are present.

The USCRI site invoked American citizens' responsibility for the uprooted and emphasized the dignity of the uprooted. As the uprooted move along their path to independence, USCRI wants the general public to fight "alongside" them. There was an attempt here to move beyond the giver-receiver binary. Under the heading "Rebuilding Livelihoods," USCRI said that a goal was to "guide resilient people to recover their financial independence." To this organization, the uprooted were not blank slates; rather, they had already had functioning lives. Similarly, the site included a heading, "Restoring freedom, dignity, and independence." While USCRI was still the hero in this story, freedom, dignity, and independence were not being *given*, but rather *restored*. The refugees already had these qualities, but their condition of uprootedness changed that. Under "Empowering Survivors," the site listed this goal: "help people reclaim the basic human needs and rights to rebuild their lives." The refugees already had rights—these rights just had to be reclaimed.

Yet the USCRI in Detroit page at www.refugees.org/field-office/detroit/ led with:

> In the neighborhoods across Detroit, Michigan, we open doors for uprooted people, helping the world's most vulnerable rebuild their lives. We are a part of a nationwide network that breaks through social, cultural, and economic barriers so previously interrupted lives can flourish. The first welcome begins with navigating American culture, laying solid foundations for a fresh start, and making essential community connections to successfully integrate into the community.

As a user went deeper into the site, the resonances with the discursive rubric of other refugee agencies such as Samaritas became clear. The rhetoric gestured toward already functioning places and already functioning lives before a disruption. However, there were no details about these places or these lives prior to the disruption or arrival in the United States. As with Samaritas, the places the refugees came from remained abstract, even interchangeable, and what truly mattered was the "fresh start" in the United States for the "world's most vulnerable."

The gesture toward already existing lives and homes remained a token gesture. Instead, the emphasis was on the role of the agency and of Americans in writing a new life onto refugees, who became in some measure blank slates. The theme of gratefulness also resonated loudly here, particularly when featuring refugee testimonials.

Clicking the link "Learn more about the empowered survivors living in your community" took the user to "[s]tories of strength and resilience" that "can be found every day in our own backyards." A picture board showed the faces of refugees of different ages and backgrounds, relocated in different parts of the United States, each being an entry point to a sketch or vignette. Some of the stories had only a picture accompanying them, while others had a video testimonial. A number of the stories didn't indicate the location of resettlement, lending an element of universality to the stories, including the video testimonials.

A theme running through the videos was the refugees' love for America and their gratefulness. The thankfulness came through prominently. In fact, even though the introduction focused on stories of strength and resilience, once a user clicked each story, it appeared under the banner "Refugees Love America—[name of refugee]." The scripts were very similar, even though the details were different. In that sense, the stories appeared interchangeable, even though they were specific. Leaving out the location of resettlement in many of the stories reinforced this sense of interchangeability. In a sense, it didn't matter where in the United States the refugees were. What was important is that they were in America writ large, an America of mythic proportions.

As an example, under the thumbnail "Refugees Love America— Rukhsara" was this blurb: "'Now I know that I am human and now I know my rights'—Rukhsara, who was welcomed to the United States with her family seven years after fleeing Afghanistan. Watch Rukhsara's story of going from fearing death every second to having the 'opportunity to be a successful woman' in America." In the video itself, Rukhsara briefly told the story of coming to the United States via Pakistan after a seven-year wait. The video ended with her saying, "I love this country." An "America the Beautiful" soundtrack accompanied her narration throughout. As with Samaritas, USCRI was here the enabler, the hero, making possible a new life—a life full of promise and possibility, the exact opposite of what the refugees left behind.

Another example under the thumbnail "Refugees Love America—Abraham" begins with this blurb: "Abraham lived in a refugee camp without hope until America opened its doors. In 2009, Abraham and his family came to the United States after years in a camp. They found hope, identity, and happiness. They are thankful for the ability to call America their home!" In the video, Abraham explained that his family left Bhutan when he was four "due to religious and political persecution" and went to a refugee camp in Nepal. He said, "We lost everything—our home, our land, our wealth, including our future, hope, and identity back in Bhutan." He says that after living for eighteen years in the refugee camp with no hope or identity,

> the great nation on the planet, also known as the land of opportunity, the United States of America, opened its gracious door to the Bhutanese refugees. In 2009 me and my family got the opportunity to come to this great nation and we found ourself hope, identity, and happiness. Me and my family are so grateful to this great nation and the wonderful people here who holds our hand and give a second chance to start a new life and letting us say the great nation is our home. Thank you.

As with the other video, he ended by saying, "I love this country."

The similarity in story and format is striking enough that, as with the Samaritas press conference, it becomes clear that the refugee testimonials were scripted and shaped to serve the refugee agency's purpose of advocating for its mission. As with the refugee narratives on the Samaritas website, the figure of the refugee entered the discourse as an apolitical being, voicing a script that fit within the overall mission and discursive rubric of the refugee agency.

The "empowered survivors" link from the "USCRI in Detroit, MI" page led to thumbnail sketches with no tie to specific places in the United States. But the "Learn more about Detroit services and ways you can get involved" link from the page took the user to a more intimate space. A video under the heading "Meet Your Neighbors" anchored the refugee story in Detroit. In fact the video began with shots of ruins in Detroit, with the voice-over saying:

You are about to witness a very exciting story of a city and its people. It will be an adventure that will open new sights in a familiar surrounding, the story of a city seeking a new horizon in a resolute contest with great challenges. That city is Detroit.

The generalized refugee story on the USCRI website was one where America as the hero gave back life, identity, and a future to the refugee. But in the video for the localized refugee story, the story of Detroit interlaced with the story of the refugee. Each was trying to find footing again after devastating losses and disruption. Both were "seeking a new horizon." As with the general discursive rubric on refugee agency websites, here too there were few details about the place they left behind. And as with the general contours of that discourse, the refugees had suffered great loss in the past and had a chance to start afresh in the United States. The blurb for the video was in accord with the larger refugee agency discourse:

> There's a thriving Arab-American community in Michigan, and the U.S. Committee for Refugees and Immigrants has resettled around 4,500 Arabic-speaking refugees there since 2007, mainly from Iraq. Meet Jasem Al-Khalidi and Oudai Al Aamiri, and their families. The kids are doing well, but their parents must reinvent themselves, starting from the bottom up.

So the viewer got a sense of the refugee as being ready for rescue, and a sense of the United States as a foil for the places left behind. However, the video itself provided a little detail and context about the refugee's adjustment and the specifics of relocation in a specific city. The video featured the nitty-gritty of the process of resettlement, including such details as putting the electrical bill in the landlord's name for the first month of the refugee family's stay in their new apartment, taking the refugee family to their first appointments, and placing toys on the children's beds to welcome them.

The concreteness and level of ordinariness in the video worked against the sense of an America of mythic proportions. While there was still a sense of an upward trajectory for the refugee families on arrival in the

United States, it was presented as a gradual climb with twists and turns. For example, the video depicts Jasem Al-Khalidi from Iraq struggling to speak English as he tries to pay for items at a cash register. We hear him saying at one point,

> For me and my wife we are done, there is nothing left for us. I'm over 50 and she is almost 50 years old as well. The future is the reunification with all my children. So they get a better future, them and their children and become good citizens. So they feel safe and secure and live just like the people of this country. My small daughter is at ease, she has adapted and likes school. She likes the teachers and her classmates and they love her too.

It had not been an easy adjustment for him. In Iraq he used to buy and sell cars; in Detroit he packed materials in a factory, on his feet eight hours a day. The overall story arc was still one of the United States offering a fresh start, a future, even if it was for the next generation. And the overall effort was still to normalize the refugee, to showcase their earnest desire to assimilate, their willingness to work hard and make sacrifices, melting into the longer-standing story of the refugees who came to America and reinvented themselves.

How SARN Speaks of the Refugee

When entering the Syrian American Rescue Network (SARN) website at www.mscrc.nationbuilder.com (no longer active), a user again saw echoes of the larger refugee agency discourse—in some aspects even further intensified. For example, the video featured Nidal and Hyeeda, who relocated from Dara, Syria, to the Detroit Metro area. After Nidal told their story, the narrator expounded that

> the story of Nidal and Hyeeda and their family is the common story of so many Syrian refugees, the safety and security of their families as they ran from the bullets and the bombings. They ran from the death and the

destruction. They ran from everything they knew and loved and headed into uncertainty with the hope and trust that God would guide them on the straight path. As the hearts of all human beings are between the two fingers of God so he can use them as he pleases. Even as the Syrians began pouring out of their homelands, God was moving in the hearts of faithful people thousands of miles away.

As in the discourse on the other agency websites, the place the refugees fled was drawn as a place of death and destruction. As the narrator's voice-over played, the viewer saw a series of photos of Syrian refugees in dire straits. They showed the refugees in rickety boats on the Mediterranean, and being rescued from the boats. The video showed several children standing together by themselves, and in another shot parents and grandparents hugging their children tight. One mother tried to hang on to her child as an officer tried to take the child from her. There was a child being wrapped in yellow foil sheeting, a woman being wrapped in sheeting, the child shivering and the woman shivering violently. Here too the refugees were painted as having lost everything and as being ready for the beneficence Americans have to offer, ready for a new start in life. The main heroes here were Syrian Americans, but Americans nonetheless.

SARN was more narrowly focused on the relocation of Syrian refugees rather than refugees from different locations like the other agencies. Also, the website and video creators were Syrian Americans with a greater understanding of and involvement in Syrian politics as well as a shared history with the refugees they were relocating. For these reasons, Syria and the Syrian refugees were drawn with a bit more complexity than in the other narratives. The Syrians who fled their country were not blank slates. They were seen as having had agency, having been political beings. In the words of Nidal, one such refugee:

> The city I'm from, Dara, was the first place of the revolution so that was one of the first places where things got very heated. I call it a revolution because what happened in Syria began exactly that way, a group of young people peacefully asking the government for their rights of freedom, rights of democracy, rights that would make us similar to other countries like the

U.S. and those in Europe. And the governmental forces at that time faced our peaceful protests with bullets. *They* are the ones who transformed it into a war. I took my family and we fled for our lives.

The Refugee as a Reflection of Our Soul

At the end of the day, however, the overall picture is very similar across the different agencies. The overarching story is of refugees losing everything, fleeing places of violence and disorder, being shorn of possessions and politics when entering the United States, and becoming templates for Americans to write the story of American beneficence on them.

The far right depicted the refugee as a figure of menace and threat. But the refugee agency discourse depicted the refugee as a figure of both vulnerability and hope, and as renewing Americans' own sense of a beneficent, collective self through their transformation. Both the far-right discourse and the refugee agency discourse painted the places from which refugees came as a foil to the United States. These were seen as places of disorder and dysfunction. However, in the far-right discourse, the refugees bring the disorder with them, threatening to infect Western civilization with their Islamic one. In the refugee agency discourse, on the other hand, the disorder was left behind. The refugee became shorn of history—became an apolitical being, a template for Americans to write a new story, a new history.

In the far-right discourse, the refugee was a knowing or unknowing instrument of civilizational jihad. In the refugee agency discourse, the refugee was primarily a victim of violence and political disorder. In both discourses, the refugee became a signifier on which to inscribe various projects, whether of rejection or acceptance. Both discourses strip the refugee of interpretational and political agency. Ironically, although the intentions of far-right outfits and refugee agencies face in opposite directions, certain aspects of their discourse on refugees carry echoes of each other.

CHAPTER 5

Detroit as Deportation Central for Chaldean Refugees

Representation of a Refugee Group in Narrow Christian Terms

In this chapter I broach an aspect of border regulation and control on the opposite side of refugee relocation—the attempted or actual deportation of Iraqi Chaldeans (a Christian ethnic community from northern Iraq) from the Detroit Metropolitan area. The main focus here is the national and local news discourse surrounding this issue. Later in the article I examine the news representation of Mexicans in the Detroit area with regard to *their* possible or actual deportation. I also briefly examine how the self-presentation of the communities might feed into the news representation of their possible deportation. I do this with a view to deepening my understanding of the possibilities and limits of the news representations of the Chaldean deportations.

Before delving into the news coverage itself, I will lay out the chronology of events that provided the impetus for the stories. One of Donald Trump's key promises during his campaign leading up to the 2016 presidential election was a tightening of US borders, as part of the larger strategy of putting "America First." After his election as president, Trump continued his anti-immigrant rhetoric and started to enact policies restricting immigration and stepping up deportation.

In January 2017, Trump announced a temporary travel ban targeting particular Muslim countries, including Iraq. In February 2017, he went further, announcing new rules stepping up the deportation of undocumented aliens, including those who had lost their status due to committing a crime. In March 2017 he struck a deal with Iraq exempting it from the travel ban in return for its repatriation of deported nationals. Before the deal, Iraqi nationals would have been exempt from stepped-up US Immigration and Customs Enforcement (ICE) efforts to round up "criminal aliens." But the deal the Trump administration struck with Iraq, combined with the stepped-up deportation efforts, created the conditions for the attempted or actual deportation of Chaldeans in Detroit.

In April 2017, eight Iraqis were deported on a chartered flight (Hauslohner 2017a). On June 11, 2017, more than 100 Chaldean Catholics were rounded up from Detroit suburbs and taken to detention centers. On June 15 the American Civil Liberties Union (ACLU) of Michigan filed a class action lawsuit on behalf of the detained Chaldeans to halt their deportation (Ferretti 2017). On July 24 a federal judge in Detroit blocked the deportation of not only the Chaldeans detained in Detroit but of 1,400 Iraqi nationals living in the United States (Smith 2017).

In all, I found forty-one stories in the national press (including national blogs that carried news stories) on the issue of deportation of Chaldeans from the Detroit area. I used a combination of LexisNexis and Google searches. In all, I found thirty-two local stories on the issue through searches on Google and on the *Detroit Free Press*, *Detroit News*, and Michigan Radio sites. I used the search term "Chaldean deportations" to search for newspaper stories, blog stories, and national stories in major world publications on LexisNexis. I used the search term "deportations" to search for relevant stories on the *Detroit Free Press* and *Detroit News* sites, and the search term "Chaldeans" on the Michigan Radio site. I also did a direct Google search using the search term "Chaldean deportations."

For the secondary focus, on the DACA-related deportations of Mexicans from the Detroit area, I first did LexisNexis searches using several relevant search terms, with no results. I then used the search term "DACA" to search the *Detroit Free Press*, *Detroit News*, and Michigan Radio sites and the search terms "DACA Detroit" and "deportations of Mexicans in Detroit" on Google. The searches yielded seven national stories and twenty-one local stories in all. The search terms were chosen dynamically; I tried different terms until I hit on the term that yielded the largest number of relevant stories. Trump had made threats during and after his 2016 presidential election campaign to rescind DACA (Deferred Action for Childhood Arrivals), and this had created a negative anticipation of increased deportations of Mexicans, including from the Detroit area.

I examined all the relevant national and local news stories, editorials, and columns that the searches yielded. The examined stories thus constitute a universe and not a sample. When identifying patterns, I first located recurring themes in each set of articles and for each area of inquiry. For example, when examining the coverage of Chaldean deportations, I separately located recurring themes in the articles from LexisNexis, the articles from the *Detroit Free Press* website, the ones from the *Detroit News* website, and so on. Then I combined insights from across the sites. I followed the same process for the articles on DACA-related deportations. Finally, I compared the patterns across the two issues, looking for similarities and differences in themes. I expected the comparison of news representation of two ethnic communities in Detroit facing similar circumstances to yield deeper insight into the dynamics of representation of the Chaldean community, my main emphasis here.

For the Chaldean deportations issue, both national and local stories converged around a few central themes. Because I found that themes overlapped almost completely between national and local coverage, I have interspersed examples below for each main theme from both national and local papers. On occasion, the local stories added an advocate not heard from in the national stories. Some local stories gave a little more detail on the detainments, such as how detainees were moved around from one location to another, or they gave more specific geographic details such as street names. But on the whole, the themes and language of national and local stories were very similar.

The themes and language also completely overlapped between local news organs from different parts of the political spectrum, such as the *Detroit Free Press* and *Detroit News*, for both the Chaldean deportations issue and the DACA-related deportations issue. I have therefore used examples from these interchangeably as well.

The searches yielded different kinds of stories, including straight news stories, editorials, columns, and even letters to the editor. But the majority were straight news stories. In the discussion below I indicate the type of story only when it is *not* a straight news story—for example, when the news item referenced is an editorial.

Deportation as a "Death Sentence" for a Christian Community

The foremost theme was that deporting Chaldeans to Iraq would expose them to potential harm and was therefore the wrong thing to do. A related theme was that Chaldeans would face religious persecution if sent back to Iraq, because of their status as a Christian minority that has historically been persecuted in Iraq. In many stories the potential harm if they were deported to Iraq was characterized as a "death sentence," following from the words of a prominent leader of the community, Martin Manna of the Chaldean Community Foundation.

As an example, a story in the *Christian Science Monitor* led with a personal detail about a Chaldean man detained as part of the sweep:

> Like many thirty-somethings, Allen Hirmiz has tattoos. His—a large one of a cross and one of Jesus on each arm—bear witness to his Christian faith. His sister and family are now afraid they could endanger his life. (Bach 2017)

Later in the same story, the reporter paraphrased advocates and family members as saying that "sending Christians to a region where they're actively hunted by terrorists amounts to a death sentence." A little later in the same story, the executive director of ACLU Michigan asserted, "not only is it immoral to send people to a country where they are likely to be violently persecuted[,] it expressly violates United States and international law and treaties."

As another example, an editorial from the *Washington Post* said, "According to the American Civil Liberties Union of Michigan some of the detainees fled Iraq as refugees and many could face torture and reprisal if sent back. Iraq is notoriously dangerous for its minorities." A little later in the same story, we read that "[a]dvocates have likened the deportations to a 'death sentence'" (Editorial Board 2017). In his column in the *Detroit Free Press*, Mitch Albom explained:

> This is the story of one of one hundred-plus Iraqi immigrants around Detroit, many of them Christians, who came to this country seeking asylum from persecution (much like many of our ancestors did) and who now, twenty, thirty, even forty years later, are being rounded up to be sent back to that same persecution in Iraq, a place few Americans would set foot in. (Albom 2017)

In yet another example, a *Detroit Free Press* article started with the information that advocates fear "[the detainees will] be killed if returned to their home country." Later in the same story, as in many other stories, Martin Manna of the Chaldean Community Foundation was quoted as saying that sending detainees back to Iraq "is like a death sentence" (Allen 2017).

Deportation as Uprooting

Another aspect of potential harm detailed in the stories was the uprooting the deportees would experience. They would be going to a changed Iraq where many people in their community had been killed or displaced, where they did not know the main language, and where they would be strangers. The fact that many of the detainees had been in the United States for decades was also stated repeatedly. As an example of this aspect, a *Christian Science Monitor* story said about a detainee in his thirties that "barring an emergency stay—he will be sent back to an Iraq he hasn't seen since he was a teenager" (Bach 2017). Another example from a *Washington Post* blog asserted that the Trump administration's policy of deporting criminal aliens "could lead to the deportation of thousands of Iraqis back to a war-torn country many haven't seen in decades" (Hauslohner 2017a).

In yet another example, when giving glimpses of the lives of detainees included in the ACLU lawsuit, a *Detroit News* story said, "Also detained is Jihan Asker, forty-one, a Chaldean mother of three who arrived in the United States at age five and has spent much of her life near Warren [Michigan]" (Ferretti 2017).

Deportation as Heartlessness

Another prevalent theme was of the heartlessness of the detentions, including the way they were carried out. The detentions and potential deportations separated family members from each other, causing great anxiety and anguish. Many stories emphasized that the detentions were carried out without warning on a Sunday morning, the Christian day of worship, at homes, outside churches, and outside eating establishments the community was known to frequent.

Another aspect of this theme was that families were not only being disrupted by the detentions and possible deportations, the community as a whole was being disrupted and experiencing anxiety and panic. As an example, a *Voice of America* story described how "immigration officers positioned themselves outside Ishtar" restaurant, "a piece of home" for Iraqi nationals in Sterling Heights, Michigan. A local resident was quoted as saying, "People stopped in their place and were just taken aback by fear. They didn't know what to do" (Barros 2017). In a story in the *Detroit Free Press*, local Chaldean school owner and advocate Nathan Kalasho said that people were targeted outside churches by ICE. He added, "As mostly Christians, many were taken from their families on a day set aside for their faith," and "It was deliberate to me, and vicious." At another point in the story, Kalasho explained that after the raids there was "anger and nervousness" at his school, which had a large proportion of Chaldean students (Allen 2017). A CNN story led with "A family Sunday at the beach turned out to be a nightmare for the Barash family and for Metro Detroit's Chaldean population," with his eighteen-year-old daughter saying that the authorities "seized him" and "whisked him away" from the beach without warning (Lah et al. 2017). In a *Slate* article, Chaldean lawyer Nadine Kalasho said that when they heard about the raids, "We all went into panic mode" (Gelardi 2017).

Deportation as Betrayal of a Christian Community

Yet another recurrent theme was the hypocrisy of the Trump administration and its perceived betrayal of the Chaldean community. A number of stories mentioned that the support of the Chaldeans in Detroit was crucial in Trump's narrow electoral victory in Michigan. According to the stories, Chaldeans gave this support with the expectation that Trump would follow through on his rhetoric during the presidential campaign to protect Christian minorities, particularly those from Muslim-majority nations. Instead, the stories indicated, Trump had decided to use the community as a chip in a deal it struck with the Iraqi government.

Some stories went a step further to convey the sentiment from the Chaldean community that Trump was using them as pawns to show that he was not exclusively targeting Muslims. A *Christian Science Monitor* article expressed the community's sense of betrayal clearly:

> [T]he case of the Iraqi Christians offer[s] a window of a deeply conservative people of faith who now find themselves baffled at their loved ones being caught in raids by the Trump administration. Chaldeans overwhelmingly favored the Republican candidate, ultimately helping deliver a close victory in politically crucial Michigan. They thought, many of those interviewed said, that the president would safeguard their families because of their Christian faith. (Bach 2017)

In another example, a *Foreign Policy* blog entry laid out how members of the Chaldean community were being used as political pawns. After pointing out that in January "President Donald Trump promised to prioritize the resettlement of Christian refugees" and that many members of the community had voted for him because of his many assurances to protect Christians, the blog writers posited that the timing of the sudden turnaround seemed suspicious. This led to the theory that targeting Iraqi Christians with prior removal orders would help the travel ban pass constitutional muster, showing that there was no discriminatory intent against Muslims.

Later in the same story, community advocate Nathan Kalasho was quoted as saying that that Christian Iraqis have now become "collateral damage" (Brayman 2017).

Deportation as Injustice to a Christian Community

Another prominent theme was the defense of the Chaldean community's credentials, and the defense of individual Chaldeans caught in the deportation dragnet. The defense of the community noted their economic contributions and success, their assimilation into the American mainstream, and their ancient Christian lineage. The defense of individual Chaldeans showed that most of those targeted had committed minor crimes, or had committed the crimes long ago, and that they had paid their debt to society by serving their punishment. The defense also showed that these Chaldean individuals had come to the United States legally and had redeemed themselves by being upstanding members of their communities after serving their sentences—establishing businesses, raising families, and being integral members of their community.

As an example, the wife of Sam Hamama, a detainee whose case was well publicized, was quoted in a *Washington Post* blog as saying, "He served his time—a year in prison and thirteen months on a tether program—it was over by '94. We got married and started our lives." Later in the same story, Chaldean American advocate Martin Manna said that the men who were arrested "entered the country legally," that "they're no longer criminals" and that "they did their time" (Hauslohner 2017b).

In another *Washington Post* blog entry, the editorial board asserted, "While the administration is within its rights to remove undocumented immigrants with prior convictions, its willingness to send residents who in some cases have complied with the law for decades to a country where they may face violence shows remarkable callousness" (Editorial Board 2017). Another story encapsulated the language and tone of the defense by showcasing the rehabilitation of a husband and father who had been arrested by ICE pending deportation:

Dorid Marogi, his family explains, came here as a child refugee in the 1980s. He was seven. A few years after high school graduation he was convicted twice for marijuana-related charges. He served nine months in jail and nine months in a work release program. And he lost his green card.

Maybe you say "You commit a crime. You lost the right to be here." Maybe you have an argument. But it's not the only argument. Here's another:

Marogi, forty-two, learned from his youthful mistakes, found work as a cook, found Jenny, a U.S. citizen, at a church bingo night, married her a couple years later, and for the past fourteen years has been raising a family of three kids. (Albom 2017)

And while I mentioned earlier that the Chaldeans being a Christian minority in Iraq who faced persecution was a recurring theme in the coverage, the Christian aspect was also brought up in news coverage as part of the defense of the community, as an aspect of the community that makes it worthy of sympathy or support. Sometimes this took the form of news coverage simply mentioning that most of those rounded up were Chaldean Christians, or by mentioning the church aspect parenthetically, as in the story above that noted that Dorid met Jenny at a church bingo night. Other stories, as previously mentioned, described people being picked up outside their church or as they were getting ready to go to church on a Sunday morning. Other stories explicitly foregrounded that the Chaldeans are "Eastern Catholics who trace their ancestry to Mesopotamia, in present-day Northern Iraq, and traditionally spoke Aramaic," the language of Christ (Bach 2017). In a *Seattle Times* blog, the author indicates early in the story that "Chaldeans are among Iraqi Christian denominations that emerged in the faith's early days and many speak languages similar to those spoken at the time of Christ" (Karoub and Caldwell 2017).

The analysis here focuses mainly on mainstream news and mainstream blogs. Still, it is worth mentioning that a few right-wing news items carried a quote from Chaldean Nation, a group that purports to represent the Chaldean diaspora, to this effect:

> In addition to facing a racist Sterling Heights mayor Mike Taylor that wants to build a mega mosque the persecuted Iraqi Christians are now facing heartless federal authorities that are forcing them to go back to Iraq to destroyed Chaldean towns and villages. (Hohmann 2017)

I include this here to show that it was partly the self-presentation of the community as exclusively Christian that allowed the news to highlight the Christian aspect in their representation. Later in the chapter I note that the self-presentation of the Chaldean community in alterity to the Muslim community, whether explicit or implicit, also encouraged a frame of exclusivity.[1]

Contrasting Chaldean Deportations to DACA Deportations

Before turning to reader reception of the news discourse on Chaldean deportations, I will attempt to deepen my insight into the possibilities and limits of this discourse by briefly contrasting it with the news discourse surrounding the possible or actual deportations of DACA (Deferred Action for Childhood Arrivals) recipients, DACA-eligible persons, and families of DACA recipients in Detroit. Before delving into the comparison, it is useful to give some context on Trump's policies and actions that occasioned the news coverage on the actual and possible deportations of DACA recipients and their families.

---

1. Part of the Chaldean community in Metro Detroit has been taking pains to distance itself from the anti-Muslim rhetoric of other parts of the Chaldean community. In particular, the Arab American and Chaldean Council has worked to create positive relations with the rest of the Arab community, including the Muslim Arab community, and also with other communities of various ethnicities and races in Metro Detroit. In an article on the mosque issue carried by the *Arab American News* (Hijazi 2015), the vice president of community relations at the Council pointed out that it's only a small minority of Chaldeans who are participating in the resistance to the building of a new mosque in Sterling Heights and that the press had amplified this minority voice. He also took pains to distance the community from the organ *Chaldean Nation*, characterizing it as representing a fringe group. However, although the ethnic media organ the *Arab American News* acknowledged an internal differentiation within the Chaldean community, the mainstream media did not. Rather, it amplified a narrow and exclusivist frame when referring to the Chaldean community.

In 2012, President Barack Obama announced Deferred Action for Childhood Arrivals, or DACA. This program would defer deportation for Dreamers, or children of undocumented immigrants, who met certain criteria. The administration put the program into place as a stopgap measure, on a renewable two-year basis. In 2014, Obama announced DAPA, Deferred Action for Parents of Americans or Lawful Permanent Residents, protecting parents of DACA recipients from immediate deportation (Savage 2019).

Trump started saying during his campaign, from June 2015 onward, that he intended to end DACA. After his election in 2016 he said he wanted "to deal with DACA with heart," but then he sent out the message in September 2017 that he was rescinding DACA (Valverde 2018). During the campaign and after his election, Trump also stated his intention to step up deportations of "bad hombres" from Mexico (Jacobo 2016; Salama 2017). The mixed messages he sent created uncertainty and fear, which were noted in the news stories.

In both the Chaldean and DACA cases, changes in rhetoric and policy during the campaign and after the election of Donald Trump resulted in particular populations being targeted for possible deportation, which understandably created fear in these populations. The relative focus on the issue at the national versus local levels was different for the Chaldeans than for the DACA recipients. Changes in DACA policy affected states such as California, Illinois, and Texas far more than they did Michigan or Detroit. But changes in policy leading to the potential deportation of Chaldeans affected Detroit and Michigan far more than any other state. Of 1,400 Iraqis at risk of deportation nationally, 350 were from Detroit. Of 800,000 DACA recipients at risk of deportation nationally, 6,430 were from Detroit (Maciag 2017; Friess 2017; Hauslohner 2017b).

This data shows the relative importance of the Chaldean issue in the Detroit area.[2] I located forty-one national stories and thirty-two local

---

2. On the national level, the issue of illegal immigration, particularly from Central America, has received much more attention in the news than the issues of Chaldean deportation and refugee relocation, including from the Arab world. However, Chaldean deportation and refugee relocation have reached the national level, albeit in a much more limited way.

stories on the Chaldeans in Detroit, but only seven national stories and twenty-one local stories on DACA in Detroit. Still, there were enough overall parallels in terms of the two issues that I thought a brief comparison would help illuminate the possibilities and limits of the news discourse on the Chaldean deportations.

A few strains of coverage cut across the two issues. First, in both cases, the news coverage emphasized the harm the change in Trump's policies was creating for particular populations. These harms included the possible separation of families, the uncertainty and fear created by being targeted for possible deportation, and the general stress and anxiety the targeted populations were experiencing. I've already discussed these themes in the context of the Chaldean situation. I will now elaborate a bit on how they unfolded in the DACA in Detroit situation.

Early in a Michigan radio story from March 2017, the reporter explained that they interviewed two brothers in the same family. One was a Dreamer and computer science student at the University of Michigan. The other was a US citizen and high school student. Both their parents were undocumented. As a result of Trump's saying at that time that he would end DACA and DAPA, the family, like many others in their situation, was ridden with anxiety. The older brother Javier said about his parents, his brother, and himself,

> They're paranoid. My mom has been very worried. She's just heard about the all the raids in the different workplaces.
>
> We almost feel like they're caging us, our backs against the wall. But so far we haven't encountered anything. We've been—we've been lucky. But yeah, you can definitely feel the tension. You can feel the stress. You can feel the—we're scared. I thankfully have this shield of DACA. But my parents, anything could happen. (Van Buren 2017)

Another Michigan radio story focused on the deportation of the father of an eighteen-year-old DACA recipient, Mia. The story drew a poignant picture of the pain the father's impending deportation was causing. Mia described what she did soon after hearing the news.

I walked through the door and started crying and ran to my dad and started hugging him. I was in his arms, he was just telling me, "It's going to be OK, it's going to be OK." But he has to tell me that, he's my dad. He doesn't want me suffering. But I knew, like, it's not going to be OK, we're going to be separated from my dad. Nothing can be okay from that. (Guerra 2017)

In both cases, the stories conveyed that the deportees and possible deportees were contributing members of society and valued members of their families. However, the exact contours of the worthiness of the people involved and the resulting unfairness of the situation were a bit different.

In the Chaldean case, the fact that they were initially here legally was emphasized, along with the fact that they had lost their immigrant status due to crimes committed a long time ago and that they had subsequently been rehabilitated and become valued members of society, opening businesses and raising families. The case of DACA recipients and their families emphasized that they had done nothing criminal other than having no documentation or being caught in the crosshairs of changing policies. In the Chaldean case, the hypocrisy emphasized was that of Trump promising to protect Christian minorities and then sending them to Muslim nations to face a "death sentence." In the DACA case, the hypocrisy emphasized was that of Trump stating his intention to deport "bad hombres" but instead going after soccer moms and dads (Dwyer 2017). In the case of the DACA recipients themselves, their achievements and potential contributions were further accentuated. Many were students at elite universities, such as the University of Michigan or Wayne State, or were successful young professionals. The "Dreamers" term aptly conveyed the idea that these young people represented the best of the United States (Mejia 2017).

There was a more telling divergence in the news coverage between the two issues. This divergence partly concerned the two communities' different positioning of themselves in relation to the media, but it also had to do with the larger political terrain and the larger terrain of Metropolitan Detroit communities. Overall, the news coverage of the Chaldean issue had a more exclusivist bent than the news coverage of the issue of DACA in Detroit. By *exclusivist*, I mean that the Chaldean community was represented (and represented itself through its spokespeople and their quotes) as belonging to a particular form of Christianity with an ancient lineage. Also, the Chaldeans portrayed themselves as deserving protection from Trump because many of them had voted for him and shared his stance of giving preference to Christians rather than Muslims, and his political stance more generally.

By taking this approach, the news discourse, following from the Chaldean community's self-presentation, remained narrowly circumscribed. Absent in this discourse was a sense of solidarity with other groups targeted by Trump's policies or by anti-immigrant policies and sentiment more generally. Also absent were a sense of protest against these anti-immigrant policies as a whole, and self-consciousness or reflection about the Chaldean community's own positioning or political stance. These absences were particularly apparent when one noticed the presence of these discursive strains in the news coverage about the DACA in Detroit issue.

Michigan United was a prominent source in news coverage on the DACA issue—a broad-based organization fighting for justice for workers and immigrants, among others. But the main spokespeople for the Chaldean issue were representatives of the Chaldean community, and these representatives emphasized the Christian aspect of the issue.

In the news coverage on DACA, the voices of activists from Michigan United and politically conscious Dreamers made it possible to confront the larger anti-immigrant rhetoric and policies of the Trump administration, and also of preceding administrations.[3] The activists could reflect on their own political stance and its ramifications. Beyond this, the news coverage of the DACA in Detroit issue included a few references to the fact that it was not only Dreamers who were being affected by the anti-immigrant policies, but also Mexicans who were not Dreamers as well as people of other ethnic communities. This element of inclusivity was not seen in the coverage of the Chaldean issue. One example of the more inclusive rhetoric surrounding the DACA in

---

3. The ability of the Dreamers to take a more broad-based political stance could also be explained by their long-standing organizing on this issue. This has resulted in a much more thoroughgoing understanding of the interconnections between the experience of different communities and a more sophisticated understanding of the need to build alliances across communities.

Detroit issue was from a Michigan Radio story, in which DACA recipient Maria Ibarra-Frayre critiqued the discourse surrounding the DACA issue. She spoke of

> the narrative we've created around the concept of Dreamers, people who are innocent, people who . . . we defer all the blame to their parents, and who have worked hard, who have assimilated, who in every way fit into the criteria that we impose on immigrants and they represent what we want everyone who comes to the U.S. to do. And that's really problematic because we're throwing our parents under the bus, we're criminalizing people who don't fit into these criteria, simply because they came here when they were at a different age or because they don't speak English. So it really shows the way in which the U.S. wants to create this kind of separation—the deserving immigrant and the non-deserving immigrant.

At a later point in the same story, she said that

> people do not leave their country unless they're being chased out. No one willingly submits themselves to being ridiculed, to being treated as less than a human unless the conditions in their home country are really, really horrible. So allowing ourselves to have a little more sympathy and empathy and welcoming people who are running away from terrible situations that we may never understand but also knowing that no one does this unless they absolutely have to.

Ibarra-Frayre also made the point that "everyone has the notion that Obama gave us DACA but in reality we demanded it." Later in the interview she pointed out that it was Democrats who voted against the Dream Act in 2010 (Mejia 2017).

In allowing Ibarra-Frayre to speak, the coverage went beyond a number of limiting tropes, such as that only Republicans are anti-immigrant, or that only certain kinds of immigrants deserve the support of the general public. Ibarra-Frayre's critique of anti-immigrant discourse and politics could apply just as well to Chaldean or Syrian or Mexican immigrants. There was no corresponding strain in the news discourse on the Chaldean deportations. That discourse was always centered on the particular deservingness of the Chaldean immigrants.

Another instance of this contrast was an extended interview of DACA advocates and activists on radio station WDET. At one point in the story, DACA recipient and University of Michigan student Brenda said,

> I think when it comes to immigration the point is blaming people, blaming my parents or blaming other people's parents, or whoever you want to blame. It's a good game to play. It is. But I think it's more of, as a college student, engaging others with what immigration policy really looks like, how feasible it is for people to actually become legal in the United States and talking the bigger picture and being more logical and think[ing] about it and not blaming people. Because it's easy to blame others but when you engage with immigration policy as a whole there's a lot to be fixed and a lot that has to change. (Henderson 2017)

Once again we witnessed discourse within the DACA in Detroit issue that broadened the scope of the critique and created a basis for solidarity. There were no comparable openings in the discourse on the Chaldean deportations, partly because the representatives of the community made observations and arguments narrowly tailored to the situation, privileges, and challenges of their community. Although ACLU members and the federal judge in Michigan did speak in defense of the Chaldeans being targeted for deportation, they did so as part of their larger agendas related to civil rights and due process. The Chaldean community and its representatives did not articulate a larger agenda, however, to make connections between their own plight and the plight of others.

Perhaps the one exception was a column by Martin Manna, president of the Chaldean Community Foundation and Chaldean American Chamber of Commerce, showing his support for DACA. But even in this column, which showed the economic benefits of immigrants and Dreamers to the Michigan economy, Manna made sure to highlight the economic contribution of Chaldeans. Also, he followed his statement that it is wrong to deport Dreamers with one saying, "In fact, the thought of deporting Chaldeans back to the Middle East where they risk being killed for their religious beliefs is un-American and goes against the principles our country was founded on" (Manna 2017).

The exclusivity of the discourse surrounding the Chaldean deportations becomes even clearer when accounting for the way that right-leaning parts of the Chaldean community as well as the news coverage creates an alterity between the Chaldeans and Muslims. This was broached earlier when discussing the quote from Chaldean Nation positioning the community as being victimized by both a city administration that chose to go ahead with the building of a mosque in Sterling Heights, Michigan, where the Chaldean community is concentrated, and a Trump administration that had promised to protect them and was now willing to deport some of their members. But this alterity was also created by accentuating the persecution the Chaldeans would face at the hands of Muslims if the US government sent them back to Iraq. Even though the argument itself had merit in the context of the deportations, when considered with other instances of seemingly anti-Muslim discourse, it fed into an impression of the community being situated in alterity to Muslims.

Reader Reception of Self-Presentation and Other Representation of Chaldeans

I examined reader comments at the end of a *Slate* article and a *New York Times* article on the Chaldean deportations issue. These comments drove home not only the exclusive positioning of the Chaldean community, but that this positioning has been recognized by non-Chaldeans as being too self-serving and as lacking solidarity with others in similar positions.

Drawing from the *Slate* article first, a comment stated: "First lesson in democracy[:] guard the freedoms of your enemies because the freedoms you protect may be your own." Another reader observed, "So the only difference between the Chaldeans and the Muslims back in Iraq is that the Chaldeans were on the losing side. Cry me a river. There is a reason so many of [*sic*] value tolerance in this country. Attacking that principle can blow back on you personally." In a similar vein, another said,

I live in Detroit and welcome all of our Middle Eastern communities of Chaldeans, Lebanese, Syrians, Yemenis, etc. I'm opposed to these deportations and completely opposed to our sick, self-serving POTUS. That being said I have to ask why these Chaldeans (Catholics) elected to vote for a candidate so utterly bereft of moral and spiritual moorings. What did they really expect? It's not as if this preening narcissist made any secret that he despised anyone not of his class, race, color, and gender. (Gelardi 2017)

Drawing from the *New York Times* article, a reader expressed a similar sentiment:

The scary part is that they felt protected as Christians, they would not be touched by the deportations—and they didn't seem to be concerned about "others." Forget about other groups being deported until it hits home. The primal selfishness of people is really sad to see. (Yee 2017)

Conclusions and Discussion

My analysis centered on the news coverage of the attempted deportation of Chaldeans in June 2017 from the Detroit Metropolitan area. However, a brief comparison with the news coverage of actual or possible deportations of DACA recipients in Detroit and a brief examination of reader comments on the news coverage of the Chaldean deportations allows us to see some of the possibilities and limits of the news discourse. As the news coverage of Syrian refugees to Detroit pointed to the institutional strength of Arab American communities in Detroit, the news coverage of the Chaldean deportations pointed to the institutional strength of the Chaldean community in Detroit, as corroborated by other research (Hanoosh 2011). Leaders from the Chaldean American community were able to speak directly to the issues in the local news media, but they also garnered the support of the ACLU of Michigan. The ACLU filed a class action lawsuit on their behalf, which was in turn taken up by a federal judge in Michigan who was supportive of the lawsuit. Therefore, in the news coverage, the voices of leaders from the community combined with the voices of the

ACLU of Michigan and the federal judge to create a sense of indignation. There was disgust and dismay at the lack of due process; at the potential harm awaiting the Chaldean detainees were they to be deported; and at the unfairness of deporting immigrants who had committed crimes a long time ago, served their sentences, and been rehabilitated.

While all advocates converged regarding these aspects of the situation, the leaders of the Chaldean community greatly heightened the indignation by referring to the "death sentence" the detainees would be subjected to in Muslim-dominated Iraq. There, the Chaldeans had always been a persecuted Christian minority, and conditions for Christian minorities had worsened over time. The Chaldean community leaders also emphasized that they had voted for Trump because he had vowed to protect Christian minorities from Muslim-majority countries and that they felt betrayed by the detainments and attempted deportations.

By accentuating these elements of the situation, the Chaldean community leaders wittingly or unwittingly created an exclusivist discourse. They situated themselves as deserving special protections and consideration, and imputed an alterity with Muslims in Iraq as well as Detroit. This accords with research showing that the Chaldean community in Detroit has become invested in promoting, through the powerful elite institutions it has created, "one *legitimate* Chaldean culture" (Hanoosh 2011, 132). This culture cohered around a few central elements, including an identity as devout Catholics; as hard-working, successful entrepreneurs; and as community- and family-oriented. It was clear in the news coverage that community leaders were using these already existing "uniform identity benchmarks" (127) to advocate on behalf of Chaldeans on the pressing issue of impending deportations.

Hanoosh's research also corroborates that when it came to the sphere of immigration, there was precedent for Chaldeans in the Detroit area representing themselves as the *safe* Iraqi refugees, as not posing a terrorist security threat, in contrast to Muslim refugees from Iraq (2011, 142). Reader comments and a brief comparison to the news discourse on DACA suggested that this aspect of the community's self-presentation through the news discourse might have limited the extent to which momentary sympathy for the issue would be parlayed to longer-term alliances and solidarities. It might also have limited the extent to which activism around the deportations could be joined with the larger struggle of immigrant populations in the United States to critique and effect changes in immigration laws and regimes.[4] DACA recipients and their advocates were able to convey a larger consciousness around immigration issues. This included a recognition that illegality is a legal construction and subject to change as the sociolegal regime on immigration changes (Golash-Boza 2018). In contrast, the news discourse on the Chaldean deportations remained more narrowly circumscribed around the particular community's concerns and political projects. While showing the effectiveness of this discursive approach in the short term, the analysis has raised questions about its implications for the longer term.

---

4. The self-representation of the Chaldean community included positioning the deportations as an exceptional circumstance for this community. On the other hand, the self-representation of DACA activists included a recognition of systemic injustices related to the immigration system, rather than exceptions or one-time aberrations. Although to some extent this could reflect the actual differences between the two situations, what is of greater interest here is the discursive positioning involved, with the exceptional aspect feeding into the self-positioning of the Chaldean community as deserving protection based on its status as a persecuted religious minority in Iraq.

CHAPTER 6

Unsettling Refugee Discourse through Art and Culture

Attempting to Move beyond the Stock Figure of the Refugee

In other chapters we saw how various local and national institutions, such as the media, formal politics, and refugee resettlement agencies, have written their own agendas on the Syrian refugee. To accomplish their goals and missions, they have used the figure of the Syrian refugee to elaborate their own identities and projects and to position themselves at particular junctures in the ongoing history of Michigan and the Detroit Metropolitan area. In this chapter I examine the discursive construction of the figure of the Syrian refugee by cultural and artistic institutions and individuals. Here, too, selection and framing are involved. But in the realm of art and culture, there is some space for consciousness-raising and education of a sort that is distinct from that conveyed by the institutions broached previously; there is often an intent to broaden the consciousness of those who participate.[1]

---

1. The artistic intention of raising consciousness or broadening our horizons is often distorted by the economic contours within which art operates. Frankfurt School theorists put questions of the corruption of culture by culture industries on the table as early as the 1940s, and this continues to be a lively debate in critical media studies

Art and culture sometimes attempt to alter how we see or understand certain phenomena—in this case, not only the situation of Syrian refugees, but the refugees themselves. I will examine a museum exhibit on Iraqi and Syrian refugees, a photo essay by a photographer originally from the Detroit area, and a documentary by students at Ithaca College on Syrian refugees in the Detroit area. My goal is to eke out answers to these questions: How do people and groups "curate" the figure of the refugee and the refugee issue? What frameworks of interpretation of the refugee and the refugee situation do those people or groups create? And to what extent can artists and cultural workers provide ways to see and understand the refugee, including the Syrian refugee, in a way that goes beyond the portrayal by mainstream institutions such as those considered in other chapters?

I found the exhibit *What We Carried* and the photographer Salwan Georges' work through the Arab American National Museum website. I found the documentary *Stateless* by searching on Google Social Searcher using the term "Syrian refugees Detroit." The creations examined here intersect with my main focus, to see how different forms of art broach the question of the Syrian refugee. Also, all the works have some connection to Syrian refugees in the Detroit area or to Iraqi refugees who have come to Detroit via Syria. I then briefly examine a graphic novel created by Leila Abdelrazaq. Although her work is about Palestinian rather than Syrian refugees, I take it up here to show the possibility of retaining a political horizon while creating empathy for refugees through art.[2]

---

and cultural studies (Adorno and Horkheimer 1972). However, compared to other institutions, art still provides some space for ways of seeing and imagining that in some measure go against the grain of the discourses carried by other mainstream institutions. I have approached the artistic creations trying to gauge in what ways and to what extent they open new ways of seeing the refugee.

2. I discovered the *What We Carried* exhibit, Salwan Georges' work, and Abdelrazaq's work through the Arab American National Museum (AANM) website. Lommasson created the exhibit in collaboration with the AANM, and that institution was the first to show it. The AANM also exhibited Salwan Georges' photographs of Iraqi refugees from April 30 to August 21, 2016. In addition, the AANM has exhibited Abdelrazaq's illustrations and murals. Abdelrazaq also conducted a comics and zine workshop at the museum.

Curating the Refugee through a Museum Exhibit

I begin by examining an exhibit partially funded by and premiered at the Arab American National Museum (AANM) in Dearborn from June 4 to October 23, 2016. The full title of the exhibit was *What We Carried: Fragments and Memories from Iraq and Syria.* It was built around personal items the refugees carried with them when they traveled to the United States, with each item inscribed by its owner to provide context for the viewer.[3] Before delving into the actual objects and inscriptions, I examine here the overall framework of the exhibit as conceived by the artist and curators.

As the exhibit curators explain on the AANM website page (www.arab americanmuseum.org/wwc),

> Approximately 140,000 of these refugees have immigrated to the United States, the majority with nothing more than the clothes on their backs and a small memento to remind them of home.
>
> To document their life-changing journey and shed light on the trials and tribulations refugees experience in their search for stability, renowned freelance photographer and author Jim Lommasson has created a project documenting what it means to leave everything behind.

Lommasson is quoted in the description of the exhibit:

> The object photos and stories can help to break down stereotypes and share our common humanity and help to build bridges. Through my project I realized that the objects and stories helped create an intimate empathy for those of us who saw them. The more powerful understanding is the realization of what was left behind. What was left behind was everything else[:] homes, friends, family, school, careers, culture, and history.

---

3. As Lommasson has mentioned in interviews, although he began by interviewing Iraqi refugees, he expanded the focus to include Syrian refugees. Also, as mentioned in the artist's statement on the website of the Japanese American Museum, a venue that carried the exhibit, many of the Syrian refugees are actually Iraqis who found refuge in Syria after the US occupation but were displaced again from Syria after the war began there (http://www.janm.org/exhibits/what-we-carried/artist/).

Here we begin to see some promising departures from the political, administrative, and media discourses examined in other chapters of this book. Lommasson does not speak of the refugee as representing either a threat or an opportunity for the general public, or as a mirror of other people's beneficence. Instead, they are seen as something more, as beings unto themselves with their own life trajectories, their own intense nostalgia, and their own journeys.

Even though refugee agency discourse and the exhibit share certain perspectives, the exhibit attempts to go beyond responding to mainstream discourses or seeing the refugee as merely representing something for the general public. The refugee agency discourse in the "Refugees Welcome" chapter shares with the exhibit the construction of the refugee as a figure of pathos, as having left everything behind, and as someone who resembles most other Americans and shares their humanity.

However, the refugee agency discourse conveyed a more immediate sense of normalizing refugees in response to growing mainstream unease with refugee resettlement, which was especially noticeable after the terrorist attacks in Paris. Lommasson, too, was conscious of the mainstream discourses and to some extent responded to them. For example, in an interview on Michigan Public Radio (Silmi 2019), he referred to the Barbie dolls included in the exhibit. He said that most people expected to see items they associated with an Arab identity, such as teacups with a certain design. "But when we see something like Barbie dolls, we realize, wait a minute, maybe those people that have been othered and demonized and caught up in the travel bans, maybe they're not so different."

Lommasson's bridge-building efforts occurred in a political environment that directly affected Iraqi and Syrian refugees. They were to some extent intended to persuade people to keep their hearts and minds open to the refugee "other." However, in contrast to the refugee agency discourse, he offered an arc for creating empathy as having innate value beyond being an instrument for influencing policy. Lommasson and the curators attempted to frame the exhibit in a way that encouraged people to enter the experience of the refugees, even if momentarily.

An interesting tension developed from the beginning, as the curators introduced the exhibit to viewers. These viewers are meant to develop empathy for individual refugees as they read stories of what refugees carried and what they left behind. At the same time, however, the refugees are a collective, from the beginning. Their individual experiences are part of the 140,000 mentioned in the quote above, and their individual journeys are a key to understanding "the trials and tribulations refugees experience." Jim Lommasson is, by contrast, an individual par excellence: a "renowned freelance photographer and author" giving us a window into the world of the refugees.

At the website Lommasson created for his own showcasing of the exhibit, a viewer could see the incarnation of the exhibit that was shown at the Ellis Island National Immigration Museum in New York from May 25, 2019, to September 2, 2019. The site introduces the viewer to the focus of the exhibit:

> A collaborative photo project by Jim Lommasson with writing by Iraqi and Syrian refugees in America.

Lommasson then shares his artistic vision in the first person.

> I asked each participant to share with me an item they brought with them on their journey to the United States. The objects ranged from family photos to a Qur'an, jewelry to a game of dominoes. I photographed the object and then returned the thirteen-inch by nineteen-inch archival print to its owner to provide personal reflections by writing directly onto the photograph. The participants' additions give voice to the universal plight of refugees throughout time. I hope viewers will imagine themselves making decisions about what they would gather before leaving their homes forever.

Once again, there is a tension between providing a window to refugees' individual experiences and these personal experiences providing a window to a generalized refugee experience. The refugee's volition enters through the choice of an item and through their personal reflection on the item and its significance to them. However, the purpose of the personal inscriptions is to "give voice to the universal plight of refugees." The invocation to viewers to imagine what they would carry with them is indeed an invitation to empathy and to a possible shrinking of the distance between the viewer and refugees. Given the artist's consciousness of the growing suspicion of refugees, particularly those from the Arab world, this gesture is crucial in a world of resurgent nationalisms, with liberal democracies closing their doors.[4]

However, when we are asked to walk in another's shoes, a subtle movement occurs, and the particularities of this historical experience—of Syrian and Iraqi refugees suffused with the geopolitics of receiving countries such as the United States—are partially rubbed out. Lommasson asked viewers to imagine what it would be like to suddenly leave what we call "home" in very difficult circumstances, and what it would be like to reduce a whole world of relationships, connections, and cultural lifeways to a cherished object that can be carried. He asked viewers to think about the intense loss and longing this represents, which in some measure every refugee from anywhere experiences. By foregrounding this shared aspect of the universal refugee, Lommasson seeks viewers' empathy, but not necessarily the viewer's or the refugee's critical political understanding.

A video with Lommasson explaining the exhibit was available on the AANM website page about the exhibit. Interestingly, the video began with a statement that has the potential to be a political interpretation of the Iraq War and ensuing flight of Iraqis, who became refugees. The video opened with Secretary of State Colin Powell warning President Bush "before invading Iraq in 2003" of the potential risk of going to war with Iraq and of the US's responsibility if Iraq were destroyed (Jehl 2004). The quote is inscribed on the screen while an oud[5] plays in the background.

> You are going to be the proud owner of 25 million people. You will own all their hopes, aspirations, and problems. You'll own it all.

The next scene was a still image from CNN with the caption "Pentagon: Beginning of Shock and Awe Campaign." Smoke rose in the still image and a missile exploded in the foreground, while a darabukka played in the back-

---

4. We are able to see that the artist has this consciousness from videos and interviews carried on his website.

5. The oud is a classic instrument akin to a lute or mandolin, played mainly in Arab countries. Its use at this juncture adds poignancy to the events that led millions of Iraqis to have to leave their homes.

ground.[6] It becomes clear that Bush did not heed Powell's advice, starting a train of events leading to the human catastrophe detailed in sparse script on the next screen.

> Over four million Iraqis have fled their homes since 2003.
>
> More than eleven million Syrians have been killed or forced to flee their homes since 2011.

The oud came back in with the darabukka. Then, as the video transitioned to beautiful images of the exhibit itself, starting with the title of the exhibit in Arabic calligraphy superimposed on what looked like a well-worn journal from another world opened to two empty pages, a mellifluous ney began to play in the background.[7] The viewer then saw (in stylized English-language print) one of the titles of the exhibit: "What We Carried: Fragments from the Cradle of Civilization."

World powers waged war in Iraq and Syria, destroying the fabric of an area that gave birth to the first of the world's complex urban centers. What was left to the people who had to flee as a result were fragments of their former lives, epitomized by the objects they chose for display. Rescued from the devastation, the fragments spoke of what was and what could have been.

Lommasson then gave background on the exhibit.

> In the last five years, I've been photographing objects that Iraqi and Syrian refugees have brought with them to America. That sometimes involves many countries and many years. And then I've asked them to write on the photographs why that particular object was so important that they brought it in, above all others. This is a very collaborative project and what the objects speak to is important things, things that mean everything to you. But they also suggest what was left behind, and that's friends, family, school, culture,

---

6. The darabukka is a classic percussion instrument also mainly played in the Arab world. Its use here lends a quickening tone, signaling the warpath President Bush decided to take.

7. The ney is another classic Arabic instrument, in the flute family. Its use here transitions the viewer from a quick recap of the events that led to refugee flight to the beautiful and carefully curated world of the exhibit.

history. I hope one of the takeaways for all of us is if we had to leave our home under cover of darkness, in duress, what would we take with us. I feel that *What We Carried* is a bridge-building project that shares our common humanity and helps break down the sense of us and them.

At this point the political responsibility of the United States that comes from waging war fades into the background. The bridge-building aspect of the exhibit takes the foreground, inviting us to empathize with the refugees, to see our common humanity, and to envision ourselves as possibly being in their shoes.[8]

Taken together, the introductory material of the exhibit provides a framework pointing to the refugee condition as an essentialized human condition, a condition marked by pathos; the political aspect is given only a cursory glance. At several points, the introductory material emphasizes the collaborative aspect of the project. The refugees did in fact choose the objects, and did write on the photographs what the objects meant to them. To that degree their interpretations entered the exhibit. However, they did so within the overall framework and conception of the exhibit as envisioned by the artist in collaboration with the museum curators.

Entering the exhibit itself online at https://whatwecarried.com/, the viewer saw each photograph of an object with the owner's handwritten inscription either in Arabic or in English. Each photograph also had a clear

---

8. In the artist's statement carried on a website page of the Japanese American National Museum (http://www.janm.org/exhibits/what-we-carried/artist/), one of the many venues that carried the exhibit, it again becomes clear that although Lommasson is indeed conscious of US responsibility for the refugees' plight, of the political dimension of the refugee situation, his main mission with the exhibit was to build bridges between people of different backgrounds. In this statement, he mentions that the very inspiration of the exhibit was an Iraqi woman he interviewed early on, who said, "I thank America for removing Saddam Hussein, but did you have to destroy my country?" Toward the end of the artist's statement he does say that "We need to remind ourselves of our good fortune as well as our responsibility for those who have been affected by our reckless interventions in the Middle East." However, collectively, in the artist's statement and the exhibit and the descriptions of it by the artist and others, what takes center stage is feeling "compassion and an intimate empathy," showing us how "similar we all are," helping to "break down xenophobia and share our common humanity and [. . . build] bridges." In a time when many democracies are taking an illiberal turn and there is a call to close doors to refugees and immigrants in a number of locations, this is of course a very important mission. The point is that even though the political aspect was part of the conception of the exhibit, overall it was relegated to the background.

transcription of the inscription, then a hyphen, followed by the inscriber's name, translated into English if the original inscription was in Arabic. The version of the exhibit displayed at the Ellis Island National Immigration Museum included thirty-four photos with inscriptions.

Loss and Nostalgia

The most common theme among the thirty-four entries was the subjects' intense sense of loss and nostalgia for their home, their land, their culture, and their family. Accompanying a photo of a book was a poetic inscription by Haifa Al Habeeb speaking of the pain of sudden separation, but also the pain of loss of a history and the destruction of a civilization: "Alas is today similar to yesterday? Despair, sickness, and foreignness."[9]

Othman Al Ani inscribed on a photo of a domino set: "When I went to see my friends for the last time before leaving my country, they gave this domino set to keep and to remind me of the great times we spent together."[10]

Samir Khurshid, an artist, wrote on a photo of the wedding party of his brother: "I carry this photo wherever I go, I love my family so much and I remember my family and my childhood when I look at the photo, . . . every day . . . every month . . . and every year."

Dhuwiya Al Obaidi carried their mother's glasses, describing their significance in this way: "When I set off from Iraq I [left] many dear things, but I could not leave my mother's glasses."

Iman Shati carried a ceramic decoration piece with Iraqi historic land-

---

9. We learn from a video on Lommasson's website (http://www.lommassonpictures.com/#!/page/478026/video-interviews), one that had accompanied the exhibit at the Arab American National Museum in Dearborn, that the writer of the poem, Haifa Al Habib, was an academic and writer in Iraq, and that she carried with her only books, including the book of archeological artifacts displayed in the exhibit. Many of the artifacts in the book have been destroyed. In her poem, Haifa sheds tears for a history that is being lost. She expresses not only the loss of her connections and her previous life, but the loss of history, and possibly the loss of a civilization.

10. We learn from a video on Lommasson's website that Othman, the owner of the domino set, keeps the set on his bookshelf and looks at it often to remind himself of the good times he used to have with his friends. He also mentions that he doesn't have friends here in the United States who are interested in the game.

marks that Christian neighbors had given as a gift at their departure, and when remembering this moment wrote "They were our neighbors and best friends in our hearts."

Susan Barwary carried her father's coffee cup set, caring for each cup "as if it was a piece of gold" because they "remind me of my father who taught me so much." She couldn't leave the cups despite having left "so many valuable things. . . . I left my friends and those that I have loved, and there were many. . . . I left the job that I loved. . . . I left my home and my memories . . . and my roots." The same person also carried a decorative serving plate to remind her of holidays surrounded by family and the "beautiful, safe days we spent in our home in Iraq."

Nada Al Zebaqr shared a picture of a cell phone that in turn had a picture on the screen of the living room in the home she left behind in Baghdad. She emphasized, "This means home for us."

Diar Hazim Farhan Albozani similarly shared the photo of a cell phone with the picture of a serene-looking place on the screen, writing "This is a memorial photo of my beloved village," knowing that his village would never be the same again after the war.

A woman named Fareda chose to share a photo of her mother and father, saying, "People have one life, and a life without parents means nothing."

Hussein Ali, an artist who fled, wrote, "And when it was impossible for me to carry my mother, my palm tree, and my home, and all those faces that I love, instead I carried only my paints to recreate their faces in a safe land." The photo showed the paints and brushes that helped soothe the pain of separation.

Artist Samir Khurshid also took solace in painting his loved ones, sharing a photo of a painting he was making of his parents. He wrote, "When I became homesick, I started on this painting as a gift of memory for my parents from their son 'Samir' which I will hopefully send to them after the completion." He owned an art gallery in the United States but still carried the painting around and had not finished it yet. As to the reason, he wrote, "I often ask why. . . . I do not know."

Just as Samir carried around the unfinished painting, Kasim carried the two plane ticket stubs on display; they reminded him of when he first left his country.

Mahmoud Khoja carried the keys to the house where he spent his childhood "to remind me of my family, my relatives, and my country."

Dalia Al Tamimi shared a photo of herself as a teenager with two teenage cousins flanking her on either side, leaning in toward her in a gesture of closeness. She wrote, "Whenever I feel the deep missing burning in my heart like fire in chest. I simply hold this picture in my hands and put it as close as possible to my heart to think that they are sitting beside me and calm down the pain that I can't bear of missing all my beloved people."

Endrious Esho expressed poignantly the sense of loss by sharing simply a sheet of paper with an inscription, saying, "I haven't brought anything from my home. . . . We left too many things in our home as well as our childhood and memories of youth. This is a message from an Iraqi refugee to the entire world." Conscious of the public aspect of the enunciation, Esho insisted on the loss of refugees such as himself being registered, being seen and heard.

Interrupted Lives

Another theme that emerged was the fragmenting, breaking, or scattering of things, peoples, and lives, interrupting a wholeness that had existed previously. An inscription accompanying a family photo described the scattering of the family, with the whereabouts of some members not certain. The sister was in Hungary; the brother in "Jordan . . . no maybe Dubai"; another brother in England; the contributor of the object in Portland, Oregon; and the mother "Buried in Dubai or maybe Abu Dhabi."

Schmeiran shared her Kiki and Coco notebooks filled with drawings and entries by her friends. Beside the notebooks was a drawing of a rose shedding two drops of blood and a poetic inscription by Schmeiran. Her poem spoke of the trauma of the sudden departure, the sudden break in the trajectory of one's life in violent circumstances. Schmeiran wrote, "Oh! This is my life that is no longer alive. One night just changed it all." Later in the poem she writes, "That one bomb, it destroyed my land. A mother cries where is my son?" Toward the end of the poem, she says "Past and future will always collide."

In a separate museum entry, Zaid shared a picture of himself with a college classmate. Zaid's inscription on the photo said, "Studying for a future that will never come," speaking of a life trajectory and life plans suddenly interrupted.

Gratitude for Safety

Another recurring theme was gratitude for arriving in the United States, a safe destination. Samir the artist wrote, "I thank the America with all my heart. . . . I thank you UN [United Nations] with all my feelings. . . . I thank you IRCO [Immigrant and Refugee Community Organization in Oregon] with all my passion. . . . Thanks and thanks to my family of Portland, and thanks with all my heart Art Falcon," the art community where he had his gallery. Accompanying the photo of a tea glass and teakettle, the inscription by Ola Hilal included a note of gratitude: "Thank you for the opportunity to meet the people in this beautiful country. I met very nice people with amazing smiles. Thank you for the one who takes photos for these things." Mahmoud, who carried the house keys, wrote, "I thank everyone who helped me." Dr. Baher Butti thanked Jim Lommasson for allowing them to show that there is a whole civilization in Iraq.

Imbued with Meaning

Unlike the discourses taken up in the other chapters, the refugee narratives allow us glimpses of individual refugees capable of interpreting their own experience and imbuing it with meaning. This is true even though the narratives are available only through the frames selected by the exhibition curators and the artist. The framing of the exhibit encouraged viewers to use these particular experiences as a window into the plight of all refugees, but the refugee narratives themselves personalized the experience. The refugees came from particular villages or towns that held great significance for them. They had unique bonds with cousins, mothers, and fathers who had names and faces. Even though the exhibition viewer saw only fragments, the fragments hinted at full lives that had meaning. Life did not begin in the United States; these people were not blank slates to be filled.

Political References

Few narratives interpreted the political aspects or causes of their condition, but when they did, viewers became conscious of the refugees as having political agency. Next to a photo of an Iraqi flag, Ali wrote, "Strangers from around the world occupied our land and they kill our people for a very cheap price. We are tired, we are tired and we want to get some rest."

Dr. Baher Butti wrote below a family photo that he was not sure whether his mother is buried in Dubai or Abu Dhabi. He continued, "I am waiting for my American passport because UAE will not let me visit my mother's grave with my Iraqi passport . . . oh those politicians." Butti specifically addressed the responsibility of the United States for the refugee situation. Accompanying a picture of an annual teachers' party from the 1960s at a school in Baghdad, he wrote,

> In 2003 someone told me that Paul Bremer sent a message to George Bush saying "we are not in the Gulf . . . we are in Mesopotamia." [. . .] It's a pitty [sic] I was not given a chance to show him before going to Baghdad this photo of teachers in school annual party in Baghdad . . . in the 60s . . . I could have told him that Iraqis are modern, and we are civilized enough to build our own democracy . . . Maybe, and just maybe, he could have limited his job to ousting Saddam and not oust the cradle of civilizations itself!

Samir, the artist, showed his inscription emanating like smoke from his drawing of a genie's lamp. The smoke surrounded a dinar (paper currency) with Saddam's image on it. The inscription described his frustration at having to use his artistic talent in service of Saddam's regime. Samir wrote,

> I painted for Saddam 380 portraits. . . . The dictator and his gang managed to put a painting or photo or portrait on all walls, in every book, in the schools, in the government offices, and even in markets and restau-

rants, in every house there was a photo of Saddam, it was more important than the Iraqi flag, even on the Iraqi dinar Saddam is there . . . Saddam . . . Saddam . . . Saddam. . . .

The political narratives in this exhibit were few and far between, however.[11] What came through most forcefully was the sheer weight of it all—the weight of leaving family and friends, of worrying about those left behind, of uncertainty, of long travels—often through transit points, refugee camps, and more. As Ali Ali wrote eloquently, "We have been carrying our miseries for long time on our chests." Or as a poem by contributor Haifa Al Habeeb expressed poignantly: "Alas is today similar to yesterday? Despair, sickness and foreignness. Will my tomorrow be just like my yesterday."[12]

---

11. The paucity of political aspects in the narratives could result in part from the prompt given to the contributors. They were asked to share an object they carried with them, and to reflect on why they chose this object above all others. While this was a very productive prompt in terms of inducing thoughtful reflection and capturing key aspects of the refugee experience, it did open certain doors while closing others. Had the question been about what forces had forced them to leave, the responses would have been different, and possibly far more political. For the purpose of a museum exhibit and as a bridge-building project, however, those prompts might not have worked well. Political narrative can be distancing rather than bridging, and the question "What forces forced you to leave?" might not have yielded compelling stories around which an exhibit could be built. This leads one to ask how the form of an exhibit, and the artist's particular conception for an exhibit, enables certain kinds of narratives while tending to foreclose others. The artist says in some interviews that he originally intended to include photos of the refugees, along with interviews with them, following the pattern of an earlier project he had done with US veterans of the wars in Afghanistan and Iraq. He did not find their narratives compelling enough, however, and switched course, building the exhibit around an object the refugees had carried and their reflections on that object. One can only wonder whether the longer narratives might have carried more political content but have been less compelling aesthetically or from the perspective of connecting with disparate audiences. We know that the exhibit has been presented by venues as diverse as the Arab American National Museum, the Japanese American National Museum, and the Illinois Holocaust Museum, suggesting that the artist's choice generated the potential for bridge-building.

12. The refugee experience is personalized because they are reflecting on their own experience in their own words. Another aspect that helps us see refugees as agential beings is the artistry, the creativity, of the contributors. Included here are poems, drawings, journal entries, paintings, a collage, and more. The refugees are using the fragments at hand to create their unique narratives. Again, these narratives are very much circumscribed within the larger conception of the exhibit, and the contributors were prompted in a specific way to contribute something that fit the artist's and curator's conception. Even then, the narratives themselves have a presence and create their own possibilities to some extent.

Not Solely Refugees

Beyond the themes that emerged in the exhibit, an absence asserts itself, and this absence gains meaning when juxtaposed against the institutional discourses taken up in the rest of the book. Only two of the exhibit contributors referred to themselves as "refugees." Even those two did so self-consciously, knowingly using the "refugee" construct in order to send a particular message.

> My name is Endrious Esho. I am from Nenwah, Iraq. I haven't brought anything from my home. We left home because of ISIS attacks in our areas. We went to Jordan and didn't take anything with us. We left too many things in our home as well as our childhood and memories of our youth. This is a message from an Iraqi refugee to the entire world.

By leading with his name, Endrious was insisting that viewers see him as an individual first—a person with a biography, an identity, from Nenwah [Nineveh], Iraq. Political events forced him to leave behind his memories and childhood. He wanted the world to take responsibility for his condition, for his loss. It was outside forces that made him a refugee; it was not what he was. He conceded this to those who would see him as a refugee, to insist that the world take responsibility for the terrible displacements.

Mahmoud Khoja, the only other person to refer to himself as a "refugee" in the exhibit, still led with "Every man is proud of his country he was born in and spent his childhood. I had to leave my country in the region of Afrin because of the war and lack of security and safety." Only then did he say he immigrated to the United States as a "refugee." He too had a biography, a life history; it was political events that made him a refugee.

The contributors were marked by the experience of sudden departure, loss, difficult journeys, and the interruption of plans and dreams. But they saw themselves as sons, daughters, sisters, cousins, artists or writers, or as people going through difficult circumstances, and not really as "refugees." It was others who saw them as refugees, whether those others were resettlement agencies advocating for them, media players participating in and shaping the discourse about them, or people on the far right creating fear about them.

Oral Histories of Iraqi Refugees

As a partial detour, to understand the degree of identification with the term "refugee" among those displaced from the Arab world who find themselves in the Metro Detroit area, I here examine oral histories of Iraqi refugees. Students in the Center for Arab American Studies (CAAS) program at the University of Michigan-Dearborn, my institutional home, collected, translated, and transcribed these histories. Excerpts from the oral histories were part of an exhibit curated by CAAS faculty and students, *Unsettled Lives: Displaced Iraqis in Metro Detroit*. I mainly examine the oral histories for the degree of identification with the "refugee" label, but I also look at the relationship between the refugee discourse used by the curators and the discourse in the narratives of the refugees themselves. I locate the tensions that arise—tensions that point to how others write *their* stories onto the refugee, even when attempting in good faith to create space for the refugee's own self-representation.

As in the "What We Carried" exhibit, the interviewees spoke of interrupted lives and the difficulty of starting over again in the United States. They spoke of uncertainty, not understanding English, and not having community in places like South Dakota and Florida. They spoke of having to be taken care of like a baby, of neighbors shouting at women because they were unfamiliar with hijab. They spoke of finding relief and comfort in their own cultural and religious community in the Detroit area, while recognizing that living in an Arab community in some ways deters assimilation. And they recognized the hierarchies and tensions between different sections of the Arab community, such as those between the Lebanese, Iraqis, and Yemenis.

While on one or two occasions interviewees used the term "refugee," they used it purely in the past tense. For example, when asked about his journey to the United States, one interviewee said, "I was refugee from Saudi Arabia." As another example, when asked how she ended up in Dearborn after being placed initially in Connecticut, another interviewee explained, "We had come with a group of refugees who were being dropped off in different places. Some of the refugees were heading to Dearborn, Michigan" and that was how they had learned of Dearborn. These were the only two self-references with the term "refugee" from among the seventeen interviews conducted for the project.

The overarching sense that emerges from the interviews was one of *transcending* the refugee condition as they established lives in the Metro Detroit area. While many of the interviewees acknowledged hardships they experienced on arrival, the majority looked back with a sense of accomplishment when considering what they had overcome—a feeling of having made it. The refugee condition was precisely what the interviewees had been working hard to overcome.

Another interviewee expressed this poignantly in an interview. By the time of the interview, he had become a local politician and was also working with the *Washington Post* on a documentary about what it was like to be a refugee in Rafa refugee camp in Saudi Arabia. He described the camp as being in the "middle of nowhere." He bracketed off his time in the camp from his other experiences, and he alluded to its horror only parenthetically. When the interviewer said that they had heard some pretty horrific things about the camp, he responded, "Right! Exactly! You can't imagine!" What this interviewee appreciated about starting again in Dearborn, despite the hardships, was the chance to *move past* the refugee condition, the state of suspension experienced in the refugee camp. He said of the chance to resume a normal trajectory of life, "I'm glad I have the opportunity to be someone. To have a family, to raise kids, you know, to have a future, finish my education, be able to be myself basically."

At other points when Iraqi interviewees referred to the term "refugee" or "refugees," they spoke in the third person or in the past tense. Their personas were those of people who had transcended the refugee condition and could now speak of this condition as an assimilated "other" in relation to the refugee. The interview structure itself encouraged reflection on an earlier state of being a refugee, starting with questions about what it was like when they first arrived in the United States, and then when they arrived in the Metro Detroit area.

Asked about his first impressions of the "community" in Michigan, another refugee interviewed spoke at length about the instability of belonging among the refugees who came from Rafa camp in Saudi Arabia and ultimately resettled in the Metro Detroit area. He described the dilemma he and others experienced:

> Should we staying here or go back? If we go back what is going to happen to our families? If we stay here how are we going to start when—most of us are in thirties and forties and fifties—so it is kind of late to go back to school. Kind of late to start your own business. Most of the community, they failed . . . [goes silent] I mean you can not have a goal and you achieve it. I mean, I am talking about a final goal. Where you want to be? Where you want to stay? What are you going to accomplish in this life? It is hard for everyone. Most people here are always between Iraq and U.S.

At this point the interviewer interjected with "That's the situation with a lot of refugee communities," gesturing toward rendering the participant's description of his own and his friends' experiences as a generalized refugee condition. At several points the interviewees spoke of refugees in the third person.

Toward the end of the interview, the interviewer asked what advice they would give to refugees coming to the country now. The interviewees passed along their insights about getting an education, watching out for deceptive easy credit programs that could land them in trouble, understanding that freedom comes with responsibility, and using the available opportunities to advance in life. Some spoke of wanting to pass on the help they had received. One interviewee said, "I gave my number to the radio station and I told them here's my number if there's any refugees, especially Syrian refugees, I told him here's my number anyone, any family need help give them my number I would like to help because I remember how this guy helped us a lot. I would like to do the same thing for new refugees." Another interviewee addressed the government, speaking of the refugee in the third person: "I know it costs money but when you bring people as refugees, you keep them from suffering in other places and you should help them settle in. You should give them things to help them."

The exhibit itself was pegged as an exhibit on refugees. For example, it emphasized that "Unlike voluntary migrants, refugees are unable to return to their homes. They are often traumatized by experiences of war and have few resources with which to start life in such a different social and economic context." As with the *What We Carried* exhibit, the narratives of the refugees themselves peeked through the overall structure to some extent. They did not speak of themselves as refugees, but as people who had gone through difficult circumstances and had transcended them. There was a recognition that not everyone had "made it," as expressed by an interviewee's silence after he said, "Most of the community, they failed." Yet the overarching story was one of transcendence.

In *What We Carried*, the experience of loss was the major note. In the interviews, transcendence was the major note. In both, the refugees did not primarily see themselves as refugees per se. Rather, the refugee story was written on them as an effort to build bridges with the larger society. Lommasson described the bridge-building aspect of his exhibit in the video on the AANM website, and the curators of "Unsettled Lives" expressed a similar motivation in addressing their prospective audiences. They explained, "We hope this project enables you to see local refugees as neighbors, and not as people to be feared."

Representing the Refugee through a Photo Essay

The bridge-building aspect was also at the forefront of Salwan Georges' photo essay in the *Detroit Free Press* while Georges was a staff photographer there (Georges 2015). In his introduction to the photo essay, Georges worked to normalize the figure of the refugee by saying that he himself was a refugee from Iraq via Jordan and Syria. He wrote, "As I photograph refugees, in every photo, I see myself and my family's story." He implicitly addressed fear and suspicion of the refugee by showing that they had the same aspirations as other people.

> My family's goal in leaving Iraq was like that of many others who come to the U.S. as refugees: They wanted to build a better life for their family and a better future for their kids.

Georges wanted to create a better understanding of the refugee, elicit greater empathy for the refugee, shed light on a struggle that is often "invisible," and attempt to "give a voice to refugees." In fact, the title of the photo essay was *Faces of Refugees Show the Struggle to Resettle in America.* Georges knew he worked in a political environment that created suspicion of the refugee, and that in this environment, bridge-building is important. He wrote in the introduction, "In the U.S., the acceptance of refugees has become controversial as the country tries to understand the complex myriad conflicts in the Middle East."

The essay itself appeared in December 2015. Four of the photos were taken on November 17, 2015, a few days after the Paris attacks. The publication date was probably not coincidental, coming on the heels of the Paris attacks and Governor Snyder's decision to temporarily halt the resettlement of Syrian refugees in Michigan, many of them Iraqi refugees temporarily staying in Syria (Georges 2015). This accords with the observation from the "Destination Detroit" chapter that the local press supported refugee resettlement as a tool for economic revitalization.

The subtitle of the photo essay conveyed authenticity by showcasing Georges' unique vantage point: "Photographer Salwan Georges, who came to the U.S. from Iraq, has made it a mission to document the refugee community."

Georges then also carefully positioned himself as a cultural intermediary. Having been a refugee himself, he understood the experience of his photographic subjects intimately, and he was empowered to tell their stories in a way that mainstream audiences could understand.

> As I photograph refugees, in every photo, I see myself and my family's story. When I was young, experiencing the same things they do, I didn't have the tools to express my voice. But now I hope and wish that, with my photos, I can give a voice to refugees.

The thread of intimate connection between the artist and the subjects runs through the photo essay, as does the normalization of the refugees by placing them in a banal, everyday perspective. In direct contrast to the conservative political rhetoric that vilifies or creates suspicion of refugees, here the refugees are seen as going about their everyday lives, trying to learn the culture, and trying to fit in. The essay's organization mimics the progression of the refugee's arrival and gradual acculturation, from arriving in Metro Detroit to taking English classes, going to places of worship, and working. As with the exhibit *What They Carried*, the artist attempted to create empathy for the refugee struggle.

The first photo was of a family of three arriving in Metro Detroit. Georges commented below the photo, "Seeing their expressions of exhaustion and relief took me back to the moment when I first set foot in the U.S."

The next photo showed a couple practicing their English. Georges conveyed the struggle involved, including the personal observation that it took him five years to become fluent. He also relates that in the meantime people take jobs that don't require English: "When I was in high school I washed dishes and made pizzas. You're in the back room, behind the scenes. That's what a lot of refugees do to survive."

The next photo showed children playing a card game in their bedroom. Below the caption he wrote, "So many young refugees miss out on their education and the experiences of a joyful childhood," adding that he missed six years of school when his family was hiding in Syria.

The next photo showed the Sharaf family, Syrian refugees, shopping at Walmart. In his comments below the photo, Georges commented that child refugees need normalcy. Below another photo Georges wrote,

> What so many refugees have in common is a mission to make a better life for their children. Some refugees can't even speak English, but they've worked to make sure their children have a good education and contribute to the community for generations. That's why they make the long journey.

The impetus for Lommasson's exhibit as well as the photo essay was to elicit people's empathy for refugees and to help people to see our common humanity at a time of growing suspicion toward them. However, whereas Georges' essay was locally rooted and emphasized the struggle of the refugees after arrival, Lommasson's project was designed to be more broadly applicable and emphasized the loss and nostalgia the refugees experienced. Whereas Lommasson relied on the refugees' inscriptions to convey their voices, Georges relied on his intimate connection with the refugees to convey their voices, he having been one of them himself.

Both cases illuminate areas of the everyday lives of the refugees. Georges' approach was akin to the advocacy approach of the refugee agencies seen in the chapter "Refugees Welcome." While Lommasson's exhibit also included an element of advocacy, the design of the exhibit allowed space to inhabit the lifeworld of the refugees in a somewhat deeper way, even if only for a moment.

Defending the Refugee through a Documentary

A short documentary produced by Ithaca College students, titled *Stateless: Syrian Refugees in Detroit*, also intervened in the controversy about resettling refugees from the Arab world and/or Muslim refugees. The film did so by juxtaposing the warnings of anti-Muslim protestors and a local politician in the Metro Detroit area with the words and perspectives of Syrian refugees who had recently resettled in Metro Detroit (McKenzie 2016). The juxtaposition was done in a way that lent credence to the words of the refugees and their advocates and that, by contrast, showed that the fears of the protestors and the politician were unfounded.

The fifteen-minute documentary was shot in the fall of 2015 and released early in 2016 as the presidential campaign was intensifying. Like the museum exhibit and Georges' photo essay, the documentary was created amid the politicization of the refugee issue internationally and in the United States, with immediate implications for key receiving states such as Michigan and key receiving areas such as Metro Detroit. All of these presentations were to some extent artistic creations intending to intervene in the contentious public conversation about the resettlement of refugees, particularly Arab or Muslim refugees.

The documentary opened with clips from CNN segueing into newsclips by the local Detroit NBC and ABC affiliates. After sound bites from President Obama explaining what led to the Syrian refugee crisis, an anchor described the scale of the crisis. Then the presidential candidates Ben Carson and Ted Cruz sounded an alarm about Obama and Clinton's plan to bring more Syrian refugees to the United States. Secretary of State John Kerry explained the plan to bring in more Syrian refugees. Trump said if he were elected, "they're going back." The audience heard a local news anchor from Channel 4 saying, "Caught in the middle are civilians, many of whom are fleeing for their lives, some here to Metro Detroit."

The documentary then zeroed in on an anti-Muslim protest taking place in Dearborn. Local news anchors from Channel 7 introduced the segment by saying, "Back here at home tensions are rising at this hour in Dearborn as an anti-Muslim rally is scheduled for tomorrow," adding that the protest organizers were encouraging demonstrators to carry guns.

The viewer then sees a white woman expressing her concerns.

> I would like to see a moratorium on all immigration. We don't know who is coming into our country. We don't know who's coming over the border. It's dangerous. It could very well be a Trojan horse.

As she said this she carried two signs. One said "Stop Islamicization of America" and the other said "No more refugees." The Trojan horse metaphor was an echo of Trump's rhetoric on the campaign trail. The connection between Islamicization and refugee resettlement was reminiscent of an association repeatedly made on the far-right website Rescue Michigan, which was taken up in an earlier chapter of this book.

Viewers then saw a handful of people gathered on the other side of the protest line. One asked what the gun that one protestor was carrying was for. The white male protester answered, "This is for my protection." The white woman protester then walked closer to the gathered group and asked, "Where are your relatives from?" A woman on the other side answered, "In Syria, in Yarmouk camp, and in Damascus. I have no way of helping them. It's illegal to send them money." The white woman protestor then asked, "Are they Christians?" and the woman on the other side answered, "No." The white woman protestor shrugged her shoulders in response.

The next segment was a talking-head interview with the white woman protestor. The caption revealed her to be "Marsha B., Conservative Activist." She explained

> I only heard about the protests the day before and I said "Bingo! I'm going to that" because I've been very concerned about the Islamicization of Amer-

ica. The protest was held in Dearborn, sometimes affectionately known as Dearbornistan, okay?

The mayor of Dearborn, John O'Reilly, then said about the anti-immigrant protesters:

> They want to denigrate Islam as a faith and as a plot to hurt America. We've had probably Muslims living in Dearborn in good numbers longer than probably any other community which illustrates that there isn't a threat but of course logic doesn't serve sometimes these people.

The next scene was back at the protest, with a protestor saying, "Muslims burn Christians alive." A gun-toting protestor said, "Radical Muslims and moderate Muslims, right? Radicals want to cut your head off. Moderates want 'em to cut your head off."

The white woman protestor then rattled off figures to show the financial burden the refugees represented. The documentary then showed a close-up of her from the interview saying pointedly, "Don't let 'em in."

All this is by way of showing the political environment that constituted the background of the everyday lives of the refugees themselves. The documentary's title appeared next: *Stateless: Syrian Refugees in Detroit*. Viewers found themselves at street level in Hamtramck, a suburb very close to Detroit proper, with two women in hijab going about their business. The documentary then showed a local resident, a refugee himself, helping another refugee who had just arrived with his family from a camp in Jordan and who was temporarily staying in an apartment in Dearborn. The local resident was trying to help the family settle in Hamtramck, close to himself and other refugees. He greeted the refugee warmly and explained the plans to him. He then turned to say to the interviewer, "America is very nice, very nice." The documentary next showed the refugee family being warmly welcomed by a few other refugees who had arrived earlier.

A different refugee, a father, then told his story. He described the conditions that led him to flee Syria with his family, including lack of food, electricity, education, and water, and also the recruitment of youth to fight for the regime.

Next came a blank screen with a caption in large letters: "Paris, France: Friday, November 13, 2015." The documentary showed quick newsclips with national news anchors describing the attack and pointing out the politicization of the issue. Republican presidential candidate Paul Ryan was on the campaign trail saying, "We cannot let terrorists take advantage of our compassion." The film shows a local news anchor at the ABC affiliate announcing Governor Snyder's decision to keep Syrian refugees from entering Michigan.

The documentary cuts to a scene in the office of Tim Kelly, Republican member of the Michigan House of Representatives. He strongly supported Snyder's decision to temporarily halt the resettlement of Syrian refugees in Michigan. He said,

> This is a dangerous movement of people. The head of the FBI has said we don't have the proper vetting service, we don't know if there are some terrorists embedded in these what otherwise would be common refugees. Christians aren't lopping people's heads off. This is, again, scary and it's fearful [*sic*] of a lot of people.

The interview with the representative was then intercut with the interview with the protester Marsha B., with her words echoing the representative's:

> We have a right to be afraid. I mean, what happens when you look at a headline and someone gets blown up. What's the first thing to come to your mind who did it. Don't forget that the Boston bombers came as children refugees. It's not just that they might be terrorists. I don't want their culture here. Their culture, look at the Middle East. All's they do is fight, fight, fight. Look at their cities. They're blown up, they're messes. Do we even want to invite their culture here?

The next scene showed refugees serenely sharing food and tea with each other in an apartment. The culture of hospitality was evident as a family-style meal was set at the table for all to share and as tea was poured for all. As the film showed scenes of hospitality, there was more audio from the Syrian father who fled because of the worsening situation. He spoke of wanting the best education for his children. The resident who was helping them spoke of the refugees' gratitude toward America, saying,

> How could you not be grateful to America? We want to work with America to make this a better environment. This is a new environment for us and we want to help. How would we benefit from harming the community?

In the next scene a child refugee spoke of how Bashar al-Assad was bombing and killing children, and how they were bleeding from here and here and here, pointing to different parts of her body as she said this. She then drew a picture of Bashar bleeding and dying, saying "Since Bashar bombed all the children I drew him being bombed. This is my revenge." The parents then described narrowly escaping when their house was bombed. The father reiterated that he had to escape for his children.

A pediatrician then described what she saw in Al Zataari refugee camp in Jordan, including people who had been tortured and babies who were starving.

The documentary then cut back to Tim Kelly's office. He said,

> They don't want us to be the world's policemen, then why should we be the world's babysitters? Would we be fleeing? I don't think so. Would we be fleeing to Mexico or Canada? I don't think so. No. I think we'd stand and fight. I'm not a xenophobe and I don't think that any of these people asking the president to pause this should be categorized as such. It's just one born out of common sense and concern, that I think we should know full well what we're getting into before we go any further.

From her interview, Marsha B. again chimed in:

> You know, and I always hear this. Oh, it's not American, it's not our values not to accept refugees. They're Muslims! Leave them in the Muslim countries. They don't blend well here. Their culture isn't like American culture, and we'll lose our culture. We'll have no borders, no language, no culture. Do not open our doors to them. I don't care if people think I'm a bigot or not. I think I have good common sense, common sense!

The documentary cut back to the local Hamtramck resident saying the rationale behind the fear was unfounded, that they didn't just come on a boat, that they went through a strict vetting process. He emphasized that the refugees are families who need help, that he himself is a man trying to provide for his family, why would he do anything that would hurt his family? Another refugee vouched for the peaceful nature of the refugees, of the Syrian people, that they are not violent, they are not trouble. As if to demonstrate this, the documentary ended with scenes of refugee children playing in the snow, running through parking lots, and just being kids.

The structure of the documentary, with the constant juxtaposition between a conservative anti-Muslim perspective and the daily lived experience of the refugees, allowed viewers to see for themselves that the fears expressed by a certain section of the local population were unfounded. Every point expressed by the conservative crowd was refuted by the refugees, by their down-to-earth descriptions of why they left, of what they were seeking in their new home, and of why it would be counterproductive for them to cause any harm.

The refugees appeared in family settings, extending a welcome to each other, showing each other gracious hospitality. They spoke of the trauma they experienced in Syria that led them to flee. But they also spoke of their dreams of getting the best education for their children, of escaping violence and living peaceful lives. The figure of threat drawn by the white protesters and Tim Kelly was shown to be a straw figure; actual refugees lived their lives seeking normalcy and adjustment to their new homes. The supposed terrorists turned out to be harmless kids playing in the snow.

Intervening in a Public Conversation

The main purpose of the documentary turned out to be to refute the growing unease about the resettlement of Syrian refugees. Politicians at every level exploited this unease, as is evident from the documentary but also from the "Refugee as Vote Getter" chapter in this book. At some level all three artistic creations taken up here responded to and attempted to intervene in this public conversation. The documentary was almost entirely structured around this mission. Georges' photo essay, while not directly juxtaposing the far-right rhetoric with scenes of refugees in everyday situations, did focus on the banal aspect of refugees' journey of arrival and adjustment to indirectly address growing suspicion. Finally, the museum exhibit also foregrounded the bridge-building aspect. But the choice of objects and the refugees' inscriptions on the photos provided some space for viewers to enter the lifeworlds of the refugees—to experience a bit more deeply and more viscerally their experience of loss, their frustrations, and their pain. For a moment, the label "refugee" disappeared and viewers connected with other humans with names and faces, who were missing a mother, honoring a father, or mourning the loss of a civilization. However, because all three artistic projects had the mission of allaying suspicions of the Arab and/or Muslim refugee other as some part of their horizon, they all helped normalize refugees as benign, as having domestic lives akin to other people's and wanting similar things. These wants include education for their children, the love of friends and family, and the reassurance of familiar practices and objects. As with the other discourses taken up in this book, then, here too the refugee became in some measure a vessel, a floating signifier, to be filled in by others' projects and missions, in this case the mission of improving understanding and acceptance.

Using Art as Activism to Draw the Refugee as a Political Being

In the current environment of growing xenophobia, allaying suspicion of the Muslim other and of Muslim refugees is a political act in itself. But the political per se entered the art discussed thus far only sporadically, and in the background rather than the foreground. The political reasons for the refugees' flight were rarely broached. By contrast, in Leila Abdelrazaq's *Baddawi*, a graphic novel about her father's story as a refugee, the political horizon was in view throughout.[13] The artist's preface set the

13. The kind of political horizon being spoken about here is very different from the "politicization" discussed in the chapter on "Refugee as Vote Getter." The politicians' politicization of the refugee figure was a top-down use of the refugee figure in their effort to succeed as career politicians. Here, the political horizon of Abdelrazaq's novel is much more bottom-up. It is closely related to the activism of a people, the Palestinians, who have been dispossessed of statehood. The hope is to channel the political agency of

tone in this regard. Abdelrazaq began by telling the political story of the Palestinian refugee.

> Today, Palestinians make up the largest refugee population in the world, numbering more than five million. The Palestinian refugee community is made up of survivors of the mass ethnic cleansing, or Nakba, that forced us from our homeland in 1948, and the descendants of those survivors. Some of these five million people don't have citizenship in any country. (11)

She then explained her lineage. She was following in the esteemed footsteps of Palestinian artist and political cartoonist Naji al-Ali, who drew the character Handala, and who in turn became "one of the most prominent symbols of the Palestinian resistance." She informed us that *Baddawi* isn't only about her father; it is about Handala. She further described her book as "a testament to the fact that we have not forgotten," the act of remembering being an utterly political act in this context, "an act of resistance" underpinning the Palestinian struggle for a homeland.

The coming-of-age novel began with scenes of the Nakba or "catastrophe" that took place in 1948. The author clearly laid political responsibility at the feet of the Zionists who conducted "mass ethnic cleansing" in Palestinian villages (11). These were the circumstances in which Abdelrazaq's grandparents fled their village in Palestine and ended up in Baddawi, a refugee camp in northern Lebanon. This was also how Leila's father, Ahmad, came to be born in a refugee camp.

Ahmed's growing-up years were marked by political upheaval. Members of the Lebanese army arrested his friends' fathers and tortured them in the nearby Lebanese army headquarters. When news spread in the camp that Arab armies were preparing to fight the Israelis, the anticipation of a return to Palestine created great excitement, and everyone started to pack up. As she showed him how to make za'atar, Ahmad's mother said, "You know, Ahmad, next time you gather thyme for the za'atar, it will be in Palestine." These hopes were dashed with the defeat of the Arab armies by Israel in 1967 and the beginning of "the longest and most brutal military occupation of modern times in the West Bank and Gaza."

---

a subjugated or subaltern group, not to use the figure of the refugee for careerist political gain.

The 1970s were marked by still more political turmoil. As Ahmed attempted to pursue his studies and discovered his skills in business, chess, mentoring, and academics, major political events shaped his life course at every point. He and his friends witnessed the Israeli and Lebanese army conducting raids and massacres in the camp. When Ahmad's father moved to Beirut, he began school there. However, political events intervened again when Israeli Mossad agents and Phalangists (members of a Christian paramilitary organization in Lebanon) began to target Palestinians in Beirut, and the fifteen-year Lebanese civil war began.[14] Ahmed returned to Baddawi, as the schools in Lebanon were closing due to the war. But there was shelling in Baddawi as well. As Abdelrazaq said, "nowhere was safe for Palestinians." Of Ahmad, her father, she said that he "was always trying to outrun the war," and in doing so, when he finished school he applied to the University of Houston and moved once again.

Using the graphic novel as her medium and keeping her political horizon always in view, Abdelrazaq placed the Palestinian refugee condition on the larger canvas of political history. She assigned clear blame for the displacement of a people while creating empathy for the plight of the refugees through the coming-of-age story of a particular boy, her father. As a result, the refugee here did not become a blank slate on whom to write the story of politics or beneficence and humanity, or to construe as a figure of danger or opportunity. It could be said that in some measure the refugee became a slate on which to write the story of Palestinian resistance. But Abdelrazaq counterbalanced this to some extent by including specific details of Ahmad's life, such as using his skill with marbles to make money off his friends, or his keeping the pellets in his arm after another boy shot at him during a bird-hunting outing. By layering the personal and political aspect throughout, Abdelrazaq was able to create empathy while keeping the political aspect at the center.

---

14. As Abdelrazaq explains in her glossary, Mossad is "The Israeli Institute for Intelligence and Special Operations" (119) and the Phalangists "fought alongside the Lebanese Armed Forces during the Lebanese Civil War in support of the Maronite-dominated Lebanese government" (119).

Conclusion

Art and culture create space to explore refugee lives as worthy in themselves rather than mainly as a threat or opportunity for other people, or a slate on which others can write about their own humanitarianism. Each of the artistic creations opened some doors and not others, but all attempted to connect people with the refugees as human beings who had their own dreams, aspirations, longings, and nostalgia.

Some artists foregrounded the political aspect better than others, such as the graphic novelist Abdelrazaq. Others took audience members more deeply into the emotional lives of the refugees, such as photographer and author Lommasson with his museum exhibit *What We Carried*. All retained some tension between creating understanding of the refugee situation on the one hand and having people see the refugees as something other than emblems on the other hand, as having significance beyond what they represent for the general public.

As with the other institutional discourses, in the voices of the refugees themselves, refugee agency came through in only a limited way. Georges and Abdelrazaq became credible conduits for this agency to some extent, having been refugees or the children of refugees. The students from Ithaca, through the way the documentary is structured, allowed refugees to poke holes in the far-right discourse. Perhaps the most telling glimpse of agency comes from the inscriptions on the photographs in *What We Carried*. On the rare occasion that the general public hears refugee voices, they don't speak of themselves as refugees, revealing the "refugee" to be a construct that serves others' agendas.[15]

---

15. I recognize that there are various subtleties and contradictions in the refusal to see oneself as a refugee, or on the other hand to strategically use the label "refugee" to fit into the agendas of mainstream institutions, including refugee agencies offering assistance during resettlement. Georges himself was a refugee, and he uses this identity to add nuance to his photo essay about Iraqi and Syrian refugees resettling in the Detroit Metropolitan area. Abdelrazaq's father was a refugee, and she uses the political consciousness carved from this experience to show us the refugee experience as infused with political history and the refugee as a political being. Closer to home, when my father spoke of the days of the Partition between India and Pakistan and of how they had to flee without warning to escape interreligious violence, he referred to their refugee condition as a key framing mechanism of their life story. He was marked by the experience; he recalled, for example, his favorite professor being killed in the violence. However, it was a condition he had transcended, and it constituted a very situationally specific part of his identity. One could say that it was not the refugee identity that defined him, but his transcendence of that identity.

Concluding Thoughts

Only from the vantage point of the West is it possible to define the "third world" as underdeveloped and economically dependent. Without the overdetermined discourse that creates the *third* world, there would be no (singular and privileged) first world.

—CHANDRA MOHANTY (1991, 74)

People driven across or being obliged to uproot themselves and go across borders and live in camps, and climb onto the bottom of trains and airplanes . . . enforces a cosmopolitanism of the below because these people *have* to become cosmopolitan, they *have* to learn to live in two cultures, learn another language, make a life in another place. . . . they are living in translation every day of their lives.

—STUART HALL (2017)

What Mohanty says about the definition of the "first world" self as the binary opposite of the "third world" other also applies to the definition of the refugee other from the third world, in contradistinction to the settled self from the first world. In the refugee agency discourse, for example, there were traces of a rescuer-rescued binary, as well as a binary of those with history and agency (those in the place of refuge) and those without (the refugees). In the discourse of the far right, we encountered the binary of the civilized self and the atavistic, uncivilized Muslim refugee other. However, as Hall's words remind us, the "local," in this case Metro Detroit, carries within it the potential to generate cosmopolitanisms (in other words, being used to or welcoming to people and cultures from many parts of the world) from below, or vernacular cosmopolitanisms. These are a kind of non-elite cosmopolitanism forged through having to negotiate with people of different ethnicities and nations just to get on with life, and the processes by which they are achieved can be messy. These everyday cosmopolitanisms in turn have the potential to interrupt or complicate discourses on the refugee.

Following from Dirlik's reflection on the "local" as a "site both of promise and predicament," we could see that Orientalist tropes (ways the West speaks about the Eastern other, as explained in greater detail in the introduction) were not simplistically and unproblematically reproduced at the local level. Rather, the messiness of the local made itself felt. Various local institutions showed traces of Orientalist and even Islamophobic linguistic constructions, but they also talked back to these constructions by making room for a representation of the refugee as ordinary, as human, and as a necessity in turning around America's ailing cities. To show the limits of an Islamophobic discourse put forward by some local politicians about the Muslim refugee, for example, all the documentary *Stateless* had to do was to show the children of actual refugees in Metro Detroit running in the snow. The very banality of the image interrupted the phantasmagoric aspect of the far-right-leaning politicians' rhetoric about the refugee.

The journey of deconstructing the discourses of the refugee in the Metro Detroit area has led us to a central tension. On the one hand, local institutions mimic and reiterate Orientalist tropes of the refugee as an essential other. On the other hand, local pressures and contradictions create openings harkening toward other possible ways to see the refugee. Metro Detroit is a contradictory site at the crossroads of various global, national, and local pressures. These pressures combined to reproduce long-standing and troubling tropes of the refugee, but also to interrupt and complicate these ways of speaking about and seeing the refugee to some extent.

It was at the crossroads of local histories and national and global political currents that the Rescue Michigan website crafted its troubling discourse of the refugee as a civilizational threat. With the Syrian war and subsequent displacement of large numbers of people arose the question of where they would resettle. The long history of Metro Detroit as a hub for refugees and immigrants from the Arab world and from other Muslim-majority countries created the possibility of routing Syrian refugees to the city and its suburbs. It is not just any refugee in the abstract who provoked the discourse of hate and suspicion on the site; it is the specific possibility of routing Muslim refugees to the city that Rescue Michigan responded to.

Layered on top of these considerations was the specific historical moment of the 2016 presidential campaign. Michigan was considered a battleground state. The Rescue Michigan site's creators tried to turn any existing unease about the Muslim refugee other into support for presidential candidate Trump, who used anti-immigrant and anti-refugee rhetoric as a central plank of his campaign. Rescue Michigan therefore wrote its story of suspicion and hate onto the refugee based on its goal of recruiting voters for Trump. The site's creators and contributors did so by populating the site with tropes of the Muslim other already circulating nationally and internationally, and they used these tropes to create fear of the Muslim refugee about to invade Michigan residents' backyards.

The footbath controversy was an important reminder that despite the flames of hate being fanned by the far right, the arena of everyday life can provide buffers and counterpoints against fear and vilification. While far-right bloggers such as Debbie Schlussel attempted to rouse resistance against the footbaths, at the campus level her rhetoric simply washed away in the ordinariness of the situation. It was rendered a nonissue partly because other accommodations, such as a reflection room or serving halal chicken in the salad bar at the cafeteria, had created no harm. While controversies do arise around accommodations in the Metro Detroit area, such as a controversy surrounding the call to prayer in Hamtramck, these are generally resolved through deliberation and do not rise to the level of acrimony characteristic of the far right (Leland 2004). Processes of everyday, messy cosmopolitanism (Georgiou 2013) at the ground level help to provide an important counterpoint to Islamophobic discourses being circulated at the local, national, and international levels (Lean 2017; Esposito and Kalin 2011).

The refugee agency discourse pushed in the opposite direction than the far-right discourse, working assiduously to normalize the refugee and dilute any sense of threat in the eyes of the general population. However, refugee agencies still participated in Orientalist discourse, albeit of a different shade than that of the far right. In attempting to dilute any threat associated with refugees, the agencies depoliticized and dehistoricized them. They were painted as generally apolitical beings shorn of history, ready for members of the general public to write their beneficence on them. The security, stability, and orderliness of the host society was contrasted with the instability, violence, and disorderliness of the places the refugees fled. Also, these agencies accentuated the gratitude of the refugees. In both the far-right and the refugee agency discourse, therefore, the refugee was painted as a figure with little or no agency, including interpretational agency.

Whether on refugee websites or through advocacy in the local press, refugee agencies worked hard to dilute any perception of threat that the refugee represented. While some problematic aspects of this attempt at normalization have been discussed, other facets of the normalization process worked against painting the refugee as a distant other or as a foil to a US subject who has agency. For example, the testimonials on the websites and in local news stories showed in a matter-of-fact manner the preparations being made for specific refugee families, the adjustments the families made in trying to settle in the city, the businesses they established, and the hopes they had for their children. On the "USCRI in Detroit" part of the US Committee for Refugees and Immigrants website, for example, the story of Detroit interlaces with the story of the refugee, with each trying to find their footing again after devastating losses and disruption, both "seeking a new horizon." In contrast to the verbiage on the same websites showing the refugee as someone to be rescued, there is a glimpse of the intertwined fates of a city in decline and a people forced to flee political violence. As with the *Stateless* documentary, the very banality of the everyday lives of the refugees interrupts any larger narratives about the refugee as an empty slate on whom to write the story of our largesse. We see the nitty-gritty of the process of resettlement. This includes putting the electrical bill in the landlord's name for the first month of the refugee family's stay in their new apartment, taking the refugee family to their first appointments, and placing toys on the children's beds to welcome them. The concreteness and ordinariness in the video works against a sense of an America of mythic proportions. While there is still a sense of an upward trajectory for the refugee families on arrival in the United States, it is depicted as a gradual climb with twists and turns.

The larger horizon within which the refugee agencies advocated for the refugees had to do with their own raison d'être as the conduits for refugee resettlement, on which their own economic survival depended. Nonetheless, they were effective advocates for the refugees, both through their websites and in their advocacy efforts in the local press. The discourse they created in defense of the refugees was multidimensional, in some ways reproducing Orientalist tropes but in other ways interrupting them.

Like refugee agency discourse, formal political discourse harbored internal contradictions. Politicians leaning to the far right used much softer yet still recognizable elements of the discourse seen on the Rescue Michigan website. But many other politicians at various levels came to the defense of refugees and their resettlement in Metro Detroit and the state of Michigan. For example, in January 2016, state Senator Patrick Colbeck attempted to pass a state Senate resolution urging Governor Snyder to continue his position of pausing the resettlement of Syrian refugees into Michigan (Gray 2016). He defended his position by saying that "America will always be a nation of immigrants" but in the past these immigrants "have loved America and were not seeking to fundamentally transform America." Gary Kubiak, then president of the Southeast Michigan 912 Tea Party, backed Colbeck's resolution and underlined the distinction between past immigrants and the Syrian refugees, saying that they are not only "unvettable" but that "they're changing Michigan dramatically." The resolution was easily tabled, pointing to the marginality of this discourse in the state legislature, and harkening to the strength of the Arab community as a significant political constituency. The institution building that the Arab community has done for over a century acts as an important counterweight to political discourses of suspicion.

These pushes and pulls were also evident in Governor Snyder's rhetorical balancing act during the 2016 presidential election. The issue of Syrian refugees was politicized on the heels of the terrorist attacks in Paris in 2015, and was further politicized by Trump's rhetoric on the campaign trail in 2016. Once that happened, Snyder was caught among the various political currents. He had to balance long-standing support for refugee relocation from the Arab world, including from the already-settled Arab American population in the state, against the security concerns being expressed by sections of the local population and by fellow Republicans. He had to balance important economic considerations against the suspicion of Syrian refugees from right-leaning sections of the population and from the Republican Party. Thus, we could see the various pressures at play in the rhetoric of even a single politician.

By contrast, national news outlets such as Breitbart and Fox News exploited the issue of Syrian refugees being routed to Detroit to pander to their audiences on the far right. They amplified suspicion of Syrian refugees and pitted economically marginalized local communities against Syrian refugees. Here we did not see the messiness of the local applying discursive brakes on far-right discourse.

The clearest instance of the counterweight exerted by the local, or even the hyperlocal, against discourses of suspicion came from Hamtramck. Saad Almasmari, a Yemeni American immigrant, was elected to the City Council. National outlets emphasized the peculiarity of a city council with a Muslim majority and accentuated nervousness about the city's changing demographics. The far right also latched onto the event, birthing the moniker "Shariaville, USA" for Hamtramck. However, the local mayor, most residents, and Almasmari himself refused to politicize the Muslim aspect in relation to the election. As he said when speaking to the *Guardian*, "It was a regular election, just like any other election. . . . People choose whomever they want." The refusal to politicize the Muslim aspect provided an important counterpoint to discourses of suspicion and unease.

In Hamtramck the disassociation of the Muslim aspect from the election provided an important counterweight to local but especially national discourses of suspicion. However, in news discourse about Chaldeans in Metro Detroit threatened with deportation, disassociation from Islam served a very different rhetorical purpose. The Christian aspect of the community was foregrounded to convey a general sense that the community deserved protection from deportation. While the disassociation from the Muslim aspect was not overt, it was imputed by the refrain that the Chaldeans were a community of ancient Christian lineage and were promised protection by President Trump on that basis. The community was painted as deserving protection *because* of their religion, not despite it. This contrasted with refugee advocate discourse working hard to paint the Syrian refugee as deserving rescue and protection *despite* their religion. In both cases, the work done to elaborate the discursive construction of the refugee became visible. Religious affiliation was deployed differently in the discourse, depending on the interests and projects at hand.

One of the most important local aspects serving to interrupt Orientalist discourses of the refugee was the economic aspect. As the "Destination Detroit" chapter made evident, economic necessity created a strong countercurrent to discourses of suspicion, hate, and even rescue. When it came to Syrian refugee relocation in Detroit and the specific instance of building a housing complex to welcome Syrian refugees, it was clear from the stories that economic considerations were at the forefront, and these considerations created a favorable frame of interpretation. The current status of Detroit as a city experiencing population loss and in need of revitalization created the larger context from which the local news frames emanated. This created a strong tendency for the news to play a developmental role, championing and supporting immigration as an instrument of economic revitalization. In addition, it became clear that Detroit's long-standing strength as a hub for Arab immigration (Rignall 2000; Schopmeyer 2000, 2011) contributed to the favorable frame of interpretation.

One element allowing for this favorable framing was the eloquent advocacy for refugee relocation by a range of advocates. Refugee advocates were able to make a case for refugee relocation, and in economic terms many people saw the fate of Michigan as tied to the prospect of revitalization by immigrant communities, including Syrian refugees. Some local politicians, such as Governor Snyder and L. Brooks Patterson, got caught up in the national pushback against Syrian refugees after the Paris attacks. These politicians participated in this pushback based on their own political calculations. In contrast, at the local level refugee advocates, Syrian American advocates, and Arab American advocates effectively reframed their arguments to make a strong case for the uninterrupted relocation of Syrian refugees to the Detroit area.

While the economic aspect in the news stories was the most important countercurrent to Orientalist discourses, these discourses were still present. As in the refugee agency discourse, but to varying degrees in all the discourses studied here, the refugee was rarely if ever represented as a subject capable of agency, including interpretational agency. Almasmari was perhaps an exception, but he was not represented as a refugee but rather as a former immigrant and now a Yemeni American citizen.

In the arena of public culture, not surprisingly, we see the most conscious attempt to provide alternative ways of seeing and understanding the refugee, going beyond already existing Orientalist tropes. Public culture created a necessary and important space for attempts to go beyond the administrative discourses on the refugee and to provide an important counterpoint to discourses of suspicion and hate being circulated at various levels. Whether through a documentary, photo essay, graphic novel, or museum exhibit, this discourse attempted to break through the discursive construct of the refugee as an entity to be administered or as primarily a threat or opportunity for Americans. There was an attempt to see refugees as entities unto themselves, as having history, as having experienced deep loss but also as harboring dreams and hopes, and as essentially human. These were all bridge-building projects working strenuously to create empathy for the refugees. Museumgoers, audience members, and readers were asked to try to walk in refugees' shoes, if only for a moment—to ask, for example, what they would choose to carry if they had to suddenly leave.

Here, too, however, contradictions arose. The refugee was still curated in these creations, and as a curated figure entered the discourse in very particular ways. While these works opened a window to the refugee experience as an essentially human experience, as in the other institutional discourses examined here, there was only a limited sense of the refugee as having interpretational agency, and an even more limited sense of the refugee as having political agency. As in the other discourses, acknowledgment of the political conditions that turned the humans into refugees was also very limited—with the notable exception of Abdelrazaq's graphic novel about the displacement of the Palestinian refugee.

When the different discourses are considered together or in juxtaposition with each other, the fact that the refugee is a discursive construct becomes evident. At the end of the day, as Malkki shows in her work, the term "refugee" started as an administrative construct created in the aftermath of World War II, and it continues to be largely an administrative construct (1995). It is the vulnerability of this figure of loss, the figure to be managed, that makes the refugee eminently available as a floating signifier on which various institutions can inscribe their own projects, and on which the post-industrial region of Metro Detroit can inscribe its fears and hopes. At the end of the day there is no essential refugee, but rather there are actual people in various stages of transition and settlement, loss and gain, unbecoming and becoming.

Perhaps the most important counterpoint to Orientalist tropes of the refugee is the refusal of the term "refugee" itself. More than anywhere else, in the artistic creations we glimpse self-definition in the negation, self-definition through the prism of transcendence.[1] On the rare occasions when someone referred to themselves as a refugee in the created works, it was in the sense of looking back at a transcended former self, or with a self-consciousness of having been rendered a refugee by larger forces. Or it was a conscious political act, taking a name created by others and using it to turn a critical eye on dominant institutions and processes. Making visible the constructedness of the term "refugee," and refusing the term itself, might yet be the most powerful first step in returning the Orientalist and neocolonial gaze directed at the refugee.

---

1. Arendt begins her famous essay "We Refugees" with "In the first place we don't like to be called 'refugees.'" She points to the layers of complexity contained in the label "refugee" by leading with a self-consciousness about the label. Gatrell (2013) points to the varied ways in which refugees understand, position themselves in relation to, and sometimes strategically use the "refugee" label, depending on their particular circumstances of displacement and aspects of their overall situation once they are resettled.

References

Introduction

Agamben, G. (1998). *Homo sacer: Sovereign power and bare life*, trans. Daniel Heller-Roazen. Stanford: Stanford University Press.

Ali, W., & Duss, M. (2011, March). Understanding sharia law: Conservatives' skewed interpretation needs debunking. Center for American Progress. https://cdn.ame ricanprogress.org/wp-content/uploads/issues/2011/03/pdf/sharia_law.pdf

Arab America. (2022). Michigan. https://www.arabamerica.com/michigan/

Arendt, H. (2007a). Guests from no-man's land. In J. Kohn & R. H. Feldman (eds.), *The Jewish writings*, 211-13. New York: Schocken Books.

Arendt, H. (2007b). We refugees. In J. Kohn & R. H. Feldman (eds.), *The Jewish writings*, 264-74. New York: Schocken Books.

Azam, J. (2018). Last, first, middle. In V. T. Nguyen (ed.), *The displaced: Refugee writers on refugee lives*, 23-34. New York: Abrams Press.

Bailey, S. P. (2015, November 21). In the first majority-Muslim U.S. city, residents tense about its future. *Washington Post*. https://www.washingtonpost.com/nat ional

BBC News. (2016, March 11). Syria: The story of the conflict. *BBC News*. https://www.bbc.com/news/world-middle-east-26116868#:~:text=%20Syria:%20T he%20story%20of%20the%20conflict

Bomey, N., & Gallagher, J. (2013, September 15). How Detroit went broke: The answers may surprise you—and don't blame Coleman Young. *Detroit Free Press*. https://www.freep.com/story/news/local/michigan/detroit/2013/09/15/how -detroit-went-broke-the-answers-may-surprise-you-and/77152028/

Bradley, B. (2015, November 9). The blight-fighting solution for saving 40,000 Detroiters from eviction. *Next City*. https://nextcity.org/features/view/detroit-for eclosures-tax-auction-loveland-technologies-jerry-paffendorf

Carlisle, J. (2015, August 2). The last days of Detroit's Chaldean Town. *Detroit Free Press*. https://www.freep.com/story/news/columnists/john-carlisle/2015/08 /01/

Center for Arab American Studies, University of Michigan-Dearborn. (2019). *Unsettled Lives: Displaced Iraqis in Metro Detroit*. https://www.arcgis.com/apps/Ca scade/index.html?appid=7561c077f0dc41dbb0dec27153d3d9cd

Dalby, B. (2017, June 9). Anti-sharia rallies met by counter-protesters across US. *Patch.* https://patch.com/michigan/detroit/anti-sharia-rallies-muslim-leaders -across-u-s-brace-conflict

Denvir, D. (2012, September 25). Dearborn: Where Americans come to hate Muslims. *Bloomberg City Lab.* https://www.bloomberg.com/news/articles/2012-09 -25/dearborn-where-americans-come-to-hate-muslims

Doucet, B. (2017a). Introduction: Why Detroit matters. In B. Doucet (ed.), *Why Detroit matters: Decline, renewal, and hope in a divided city,* 1-29. Bristol, UK: Policy Press.

Doucet, B. (2017b). *Why Detroit matters: Decline, renewal and hope in a divided city.* Bristol, UK: Policy Press.

Enns, D. (2004). Bare life and the occupied body. *Theory & Event* 7 (3). https://doi .org/10.1353/tae.2004.0019

Esposito, J. L., & Kalin, I. (2011). *Islamophobia: The challenge of pluralism in the twenty-first century.* Oxford: Oxford University Press.

Fair, J. E. (1996). The body politic, the bodies of women, and the politics of famine in U.S. television coverage of famine in the Horn of Africa. *Journalism and Mass Communication Monographs* 158: 1-45.

Felton, R. (2015, November 15). Michigan town said to have first majority Muslim city council in U.S. *Guardian.* https://www.theguardian.com/us-news/2015 /nov/15/michigan-muslim-majority-city-council-hamtramck-detroit

Fiddiyan-Qasmiyeh, E., Loescher, G., Long, K., & Sigona, N. (2014). Introduction: Refugee and forced migration studies in transition. In E. Fiddiyan-Qasmiyeh, G. Loescher, K. Long, & N. Sigona (eds.), *The Oxford handbook of refugee and forced migration studies,* 1-18. Oxford: Oxford University Press.

Gatrell, P. (2013). *The making of the modern refugee.* Oxford: Oxford University Press.

Grossberg, L. (1996). History, politics, and postmodernism: Stuart Hall and cultural studies. In D. Morley & K. H. Chen (eds.), *Stuart Hall: Critical dialogues in cultural studies,* 151-73. London: Routledge.

Guyton, T. (2017). My Detroit. In B. Doucet (ed.), *Why Detroit matters: Decline, renewal, and hope in a divided city,* 271-74. Bristol, UK: Policy Press.

Haddad, K. (2017, October 19). Study: Economic impact of refugees in Southeast Michigan nearly $300M in 2016. *Click on Detroit.* https://www.clickondetroit .com/news/2017/10/19/study-economic-impact-of-refugees-in-southeast-mi chigan-nearly-300m-in-2016/

Hall, S. (1980). Cultural studies: Two paradigms. *Media, Culture, and Society* 2: 57-72.

Hall, S. (1984a). The culture gap. *Marxism Today* 28 (January): 18-23.

Hall, S. (1984b). Reconstruction work. *Ten-8* 16, 2-9.

Hall, S. (1985). Signification, representation, ideology: Althusser and the post-structuralist debates. *Critical Studies in Mass Communication* 2 (2): 91-114.

Hall, S. (1988). *The hard road to renewal: Thatcherism and the crisis of the left.* London: Verso Books.

Hamdi, T. K. (2013). Edward Said and recent Orientalist critiques. *Arab Studies Quarterly* 35 (2): 130-48.

Hartzell, S. L. (2018). Alt-White: Conceptualizing the "Alt-Right" as a rhetorical bridge between white nationalism and mainstream public discourse. *Journal of Contemporary Rhetoric* 8 (1/2): 6-25.

House, G. (2019, July). Freedom of expression: The power of owning our voices. Talk presented at Concert of Colors Forum on Community, Culture, and Race, Dearborn, MI.

Howell, S., & Feldman, R. (2017). Visions in conflict: A city of possibilities. In B. Doucet (ed.), *Why Detroit matters: Decline, renewal, and hope in a divided city*, 209-20. Bristol, UK: Policy Press.

Howell, S., & Jamal, A. (2009). The aftermath of the 9/11 attacks. In Detroit Arab American Study Team (eds.), *Citizenship and Crisis: Arab Detroit after 9/11*, 69-100. New York: Russell Sage Foundation.

Howell, S., & Jamal, A. (2011). Backlash, part 2: The federal law enforcement agenda. In N. Abraham, S. Howell, & A. Shyrock (eds.), *Arab Detroit 9/11: Life in the terror decade*, 87-104. Detroit: Wayne State University Press.

Howell, S., & Shryock, A. (2011). Cracking down on diaspora: Arab Detroit and America's war on terror. In N. Abraham, S. Howell, & A. Shryock (eds.), *Arab Detroit 9/11: Life in the terror decade*, 67-86. Detroit: Wayne State University Press.

International Rescue Committee. (2018, December 11). Migrants, asylum seekers, refugees and immigrants: What's the difference? https://www.rescue.org/artic le/migrants-asylum-seekers-refugees-and-immigrants-whats-difference

Jackson, C. (2017, June 9). Critics blast anti-sharia law march to be held in Southfield on Saturday. *WXYZ Detroit*. https://www.wxyz.com/news/region/oakland -county/critics-blast-anti-sharia-law-march-to-be-held-in-southfield-on-sa turday

Jones, R. (2017). *Violent borders: Refugees and the right to move*. London: Verso.

Jouppi, S. (2017, August 8). CuriosiD: How did Detroit become a center for Arabs in the United States? WDET. https://wdet.org/posts/2017/08/08/85592-curiosid -how-did-detroit-become-a-center-for-arabs-in-the-united-states/

Kinney, R. J. (2016). *The beautiful wasteland: The rise of Detroit as America's postindustrial frontier*. Minneapolis: University of Minnesota Press.

Lung-Amam, W. S. (2017). *Trespassers? Asian Americans and the battle for suburbia*. Oakland: University of California Press.

Luthra, R. (1995). The "abortion clause" in U.S. foreign population policy: The debate viewed through a postcolonial feminist lens. In A. Valdivia (ed.), *Feminism, multiculturalism, and the media*, 197-216. Thousand Oaks, CA: Sage.

Malkki, L. H. (1995). Refugees and exile: From "Refugee Studies" to the national order of things [PDF file]. *Annual Review of Anthropology* 24: 495-523.

Mani, L. (1998). *Contentious traditions: The debate on sati in colonial India*. Berkeley: University of California Press.

McKirdy, E. (2016, June 20). UNHCR: More displaced now than after WWII. *CNN*. https://www.cnn.com/2016/06/20/world/unhcr-displaced-peoples-report/ind ex.html

Mohanty, C. T. (1991a). Introduction. In C. T. Mohanty, A. Russo, & L. Torres (eds.), *Third World women and the politics of feminism*, 1-47. Bloomington: Indiana University Press.

Mohanty, C. T. (1991b). Under Western eyes: Feminist scholarship and colonial discourses. In C. T. Mohanty, A. Russo, & L. Torres (eds.). *Third World women and the politics of feminism*, 51-80. Bloomington: Indiana University Press.

moore, j. C. (2017). You may not know my Detroit. In B. Doucet (ed.), *Why Detroit matters: Decline, renewal, and hope in a divided city*, 177-82. Bristol, UK: Policy Press.

Morton, S. (2003). *Gayatri Chakravorty Spivak*. New York: Routledge.

Nayeri, D. (2018). The ungrateful refugee. In V. T. Nguyen (ed.). *The Displaced: Refugee writers on refugee lives*, 137-50. New York: Abrams Press.

Nguyen, V. T. (2018). Introduction. In V. T. Nguyen (ed.), *The Displaced: Refugee writers on refugee lives*, 11-22. New York: Abrams Press.

Quraishi-Landes, A. (2016, June 24). Five myths about sharia. *Washington Post*. https://www.washingtonpost.com/opinions/five-myths-about-sharia/2016/06/24/7e3efb7a-31ef-11e6-8758-d58e76e11b12_story.html

Rubin, N. (2017, June 10). Protestors in Southfield rally against Islamic law. *Detroit News*. https://www.detroitnews.com/story/news/local/oakland-county/2017/06/10/protesters-southfield-rally-islamic-law/102707996/

Said, E. (1978). *Orientalism*. New York: Pantheon Books.

Said, E. (1981). *Covering Islam: How the media and the experts determine how we see the rest of the world*. New York: Pantheon Books.

Schopmeyer, K. (2000). A demographic portrait of Arab Detroit. In N. Abraham & A. Shyrock (eds.), *Arab Detroit: From margin to mainstream*, 61-94. Detroit: Wayne State University Press.

Schopmeyer, K. (2011). Arab Detroit after 9/11: A changing demographic portrait. In N. Abraham, S. Howell, & A. Shryock (eds.), *Arab Detroit 9/11: Life in the terror decade*, 29-66. Detroit: Wayne State University Press.

Shryock, A., & Abraham, N. (2000). On margins and mainstreams. In N. Abraham & A. Shryock (eds.), *Arab Detroit: From margin to mainstream*, 15-38. Detroit: Wayne State University Press.

Shryock, A., Abraham, N., & Howell, S. (2011). The terror decade in Arab Detroit: An introduction. In N. Abraham, S. Howell, & A. Shryock (eds.), *Arab Detroit 9/11: Life in the terror decade*, 1-28. Detroit: Wayne State University Press.

Spivak, G. C. (1988). Can the subaltern speak? In C. Nelson and L. Grossberg (eds.), *Marxism and the interpretation of culture*, 271-316. Champaign: University of Illinois Press.

Spivak, G. C. (1990). *The postcolonial critic: Interviews, strategies, dialogues*. Sarah Harasym (ed.). New York: Routledge.

Stanovsky, D. (2017). Remix racism: The visual politics of the "alt-right." *Journal of Contemporary Rhetoric* 7 (2/3): 130-38.

Stonebridge, L. (2018). *Placeless people: Writing, rights, and refugees*. Oxford: Oxford University Press.

Sugrue, T. (2014). *The origins of the urban crisis: Race and inequality in postwar Detroit* (rev. ed.). Princeton: Princeton University Press.

University of Michigan. (2004, July 29). U-M Detroit Arab American study portrays a complex population. *Michigan News*. https://news.umich.edu/u-m-detroit-arab-american-study-portrays-a-complex-population/

Walsh, D. (2017, June 6). Report highlights immigrants' economic contribution to Detroit. *Crain's Detroit Business.* https://www.crainsdetroit.com/article/20170 606/news/630741/report-highlights-immigrants-economic-contribution-det roit

Wright, T. (2014). The media and representations of refugees and other forced migrants. In In E. Fiddiyan-Qasmiyeh, G. Loescher, K. Long, & N. Sigona (eds.), *The Oxford handbook of refugee and forced migration studies,* 460-72. Oxford: Oxford University Press.

Zwiek, S. (2014, July 9). What explains Michigan's large Arab American community? Michigan Radio. https://www.michiganradio.org/arts-culture/2014-07-09 /what-explains-michigans-large-arab-american-community

Chapter 1

Airgood, B. (2017, November 26). Congo refugee leads French worship service in Grand Rapids church. *MLive Michigan.* https://www.mlive.com/news/grand-ra pids/2017/11/from_the_congo_to_grand_rapids.html

Asher, T. (2015, November 19). Patterson: Syrian refugees in Pontiac would present "imminent" danger. *Fox 2 Detroit.* http://www.fox2detroit.com/news/local-ne ws/patterson-syrian-refugees-in-pontiac-would-present-imminent-danger

Bauer, W., & Thawnghmung, E. (2017). The Burmese immigration to Michigan: American Baptists are part of the story! https://www.abc-mi.org/the-burme se-immigration-to-michigan-american-baptists-are-part-of-the-story!.html

Berman, L. (2015, November 16). Snyder takes a too-hasty retreat from Syrian refugees. *Detroit News.* https://www.detroitnews.com/story/opinion/columnists/la ura-berman/2015/11/16/berman-opinion-hasty-retreat-refugees/75908552/

Burke, M. N. (2015, November 16). Snyder among governors not taking Syrian refugees. *Detroit News.* https://www.detroitnews.com/story/news/nation/2015/11 /16/syrian-refugees-governors-glance/75868806/

Cassidy, J. (2015, August 28). Isis and the curse of the Iraq war. *The New Yorker.* https://www.newyorker.com/news/john-cassidy/isis-and-the-curse-of-the-ir aq-war

Christian Reformed Church. (2018, April 11). Refugee resettlement a beautiful, "God-sized" challenge. https://www.crcna.org/news-and-views/refugee-reset tlement-beautiful-god-sized-challenge

Cohen, P. (2017, May 29). Immigrants keep an Iowa meatpacking town alive and growing. *New York Times.* https://www.nytimes.com/2017/05/29/business/eco nomy/storm-lake-iowa-immigrant-workers.html

Congolese refugee high schoolers get training at U-M (2019, April 25). *Michigan News.* https://news.umich.edu/congolese-refugee-high-schoolers-get-traini ng-at-u-m/

de Four, S. (2015, November 23). We must keep our border, our hearts open to refugees. *Detroit Free Press.* https://www.freep.com/story/opinion/readers/2015/11 /23/must-keep-border-hearts-open-refugees/76277904/

Detroit has space, need for Syrians (2015, November 8). *Wisconsin State Journal.* Retrieved September 26, 2017, from LexisNexis Academic Database.

Dickerson, B. (2015, November 17). Detroit talks tough on refugees, flunks social studies. *Detroit Free Press.* https://www.freep.com/story/opinion/columnists/brian-dickerson/2015/11/17/snyder-refugees/75936716/

Dickson, J. D. (2015, November 29). Rev. Jackson: Welcome Syrian refugees to Mich. *Detroit News.* https://www.detroitnews.com/story/news/local/wayne-county/2015/11/29/panel-urges-michigan-welcome-syrian-refugees/76547502/

Eagan, P. (2015, September 29). Snyder: Michigan exploring steps to take in Syria refugees. *Detroit Free Press.* https://www.freep.com/story/news/politics/2015/09/29/snyder-michigan-exploring-steps-take-syria-refugees/73030078/

Eagan, P., & Warikoo, N. (2015, November 15). Snyder suspends Syrian refugee effort in Michigan. *Detroit Free Press.* https://www.freep.com/story/news/local/michigan/2015/11/15/snyder-suspends-efforts-settle-syrian-refugees/75825736/

Erb, R. (2015, November 29). Jackson: U.S., Michigan must welcome Syrian refugees. *Detroit Free Press.* https://www.freep.com/story/news/local/michigan/2015/11/29/jackson-us-michigan-must-welcome-syrian-refugees/76540306/

Fitzgerald, T., & Hannah, M. (2015, November 29). In presidential race, all eyes are now on security. *Philadelphia Inquirer.* https://www.inquirer.com/philly/news/politics/20151129_All_EYES_ON_SECURITY.html

Free Press readers (2015, October 13). We shouldn't be afraid of Syrian refugees. *Detroit Free Press.* https://www.freep.com/story/opinion/readers/2015/10/13/afraid-syrian-refugees/73890832/

Gillespie, P. (2017, July 27). The opioid crisis is draining America of workers. *CNN Business.* https://money.cnn.com/2017/07/07/news/economy/opioid-epidemic-job-market/index.html

Heinlein, G. (2015, November 19). Activists demand Snyder accept Syrian refugees. *Detroit News.* https://www.detroitnews.com/story/news/politics/2015/11/19/activists-demand-snyder-accept-syrian-refugees/76052606/

Hinds, J. (2015, November 20). Michael Moore: I'll house Syrian refugees in Traverse City. *Detroit Free Press.* https://www.freep.com/story/entertainment/movies/2015/11/20/michael-moore-filmmaker-syrian-refugees-governor-rick-snyder/76132262/

Holmes, S. M., & Castañeda, H. (2016). Representing the European refugee crisis in Germany and beyond: Deservingness and difference, life and death. *American Ethnologist, 43*(1): 12-24. https://doi.org/10.1111/amet.12259

House, G. (2019, July). Freedom of expression: The power of owning our voices. Talk presented at Concert of Colors Forum on Community, Culture, and Race, Dearborn, Michigan.

Howell, S., & Jamal, A. (2011). Backlash, Part 2: The federal law enforcement agenda. In N. Abraham, S. Howell, & A. Shyrock (eds.), *Arab Detroit 9/11: Life in the terror decade,* 87-104. Detroit: Wayne State University Press.

Hughbanks, V. (2016, June 8). Syrian refugees flock to Michigan. *Detroit News.* https://www.detroitnews.com/story/opinion/2016/06/08/syrian-refugees-flock-michigan/85630462/

Karoub, J. (2015, October 18). As some Syrian refugees arrive, state makes case for more. *Detroit Free Press*. https://www.freep.com/story/news/local/michigan/wa yne/2015/10/18/syrian-refugees-michigan/74181518/

Kelley, I. (2015, December 4). Patterson fumes as Syrian refugee plan in Pontiac proceeds. *Fox 2 Detroit*. http://www.fox2detroit.com/news/local-news/patters on-fumes-as-syrian-refugee-plan-in-pontiac-proceeds

la Corte, M. (2015, November 30). Syrian refugees an asset to U.S. *Detroit News*. https://www.detroitnews.com/story/opinion/2015/11/30/la-corte-syrian-refu gees-immigration-michigan/76541356/

LaFranchi, H. (2015, November 17). Can White House stop refugee program from becoming a political football? *Christian Science Monitor*. Retrieved September 26, 2017, from LexisNexis Academic Database.

Laitin, D. D., & Jahr, M. (2015, May 14). Let Syrians settle Detroit. *New York Times*. https://www.nytimes.com/2015/05/15/opinion/let-syrians-settle-detroit .html

LIRS (Lutheran Immigration and Refugee Service) (2013, November 1). Resettling Congolese refugees—Lutheran Social Services of Michigan offers insights. https://www.lirs.org/resettling-congolese-refugees-lssm/

Malkki, L. H. (1992). National Geographic: The rooting of peoples and the territori-alization of national identity among scholars and refugees [PDF file]. *Cultural Anthropology* 7 (1): 24-44.

Malkki, L. H. (1995). Refugees and exile: From "Refugee Studies" to the national order of things [PDF file]. *Annual Review of Anthropology* 24: 495-523.

Opinion. (2015, September 21). *Crain's Detroit Business*. Retrieved September 26, 2017, from LexisNexis Academic Database.

Packer, G. (2015, November 9). America's apathy about the Syrian refugees. *New Yorker*. https://www.newyorker.com/magazine/2015/11/09/powerful-gestures

Parikh, J. C. (2012, May 24). Burmese Americans find a home in Battle Creek. *Second Wave*. https://www.secondwavemedia.com/southwest-michigan/features /burmese0524.aspx

Philo, G., Briant, E., & Donald, P. (2013). *Bad news for refugees*. London: Pluto Press.

Pickering, S. (2001). Common sense and original deviancy: News discourses and asylum seekers in Australia [PDF file]. *Journal of Refugee Studies* 14 (2): 169-86.

Rahal, S. (2019, April 12). Michigan becomes haven for Congo refugees. *Detroit News*. https://www.detroitnews.com/story/news/local/michigan/2019/04/12 /michigan-becomes-haven-congo-refugees/3287895002/

Ramirez, C. E. (2016, June 9). Michigan tops other states in number of Syrian refugees. *Detroit News*. https://www.detroitnews.com/story/news/local/michigan /2016/06/09/michigan-tops-states-number-syrian-refugees/85629610/

Rignall, K. (2000). Building the infrastructure of Arab American identity in Detroit: A short history of ACCESS and the community it serves. In N. Abraham & A. Shyrock (eds.), *Arab Detroit: From margin to mainstream*, 49-60. Detroit: Wayne State University Press.

Riley, J. (2009, December 11). Christian couple adopts eight Burmese refugee children. *Christian Post*. https://www.christianpost.com/news/christian-couple-ad opts-8-burmese-refugee-children.html

Rubin, N. (2016, November 28). Rubin: Syrian refugees find a new home—and Batman. *Detroit News*. https://www.detroitnews.com/story/opinion/columnists/neal-rubin/2016/11/21/syrian-refugees-dearborn-samaritas-batman/94445532/

Runyon, C. (2018, May 22). Jenison sponsors welcome arrival of Burmese refugee family. *MLive Michigan*. https://www.mlive.com/jenison/2018/05/sponsors_welcome_arrival_of_bu.html

Shopmeyer, K. (2000). A demographic portrait of Arab Detroit. In N. Abraham & A. Shyrock (eds.), *Arab Detroit: From margin to mainstream*, 61-94. Detroit: Wayne State University Press.

Shopmeyer, K. (2011). Arab Detroit after 9/11: A changing demographic portrait. In N. Abraham, S. Howell, & A. Shyrock (eds.), *Arab Detroit 9/11: Life in the terror decade*, 29-66. Detroit: Wayne State University Press.

Stafford, K. (2015, December 18). Scientist who fled Syria arrives "home" in Michigan. *Detroit Free Press*. https://www.freep.com/story/news/local/michigan/2015/12/18/scientist-syria-refaai-hamo-michigan/77483350/

Thawnghmung, M. (2017, March 22). Martha Thawnghmung: Why we matter. *Battle Creek Enquirer*. https://www.battlecreekenquirer.com/story/opinion/columnists/2017/03/22/martha-thawnghmung-why-we-matter/98292530/

Thiele, R. (2018, April 23). Burmese refugees find mental health challenges in Michigan. WKAR. https://www.wkar.org/post/burmese-refugees-find-mental-health-challenges-michigan#stream/0

Walsh, D. (2015, September 21). One square mile, thousands of lives: Local activists want to rebuild North Town with help of Syrian refugees. *Crain's Detroit Business*. Retrieved September 26, 2017, from LexisNexis Academic Database.

Warikoo, N. (2015, November 18). Oakland County to Pontiac: Stop Syrian refugee housing. *Detroit Free Press*. https://www.freep.com/story/news/local/michigan/oakland/2015/11/18/oakland-county-pontiac-stop-syrian-refugee-housing/76008598/

Warikoo, N. (2015, November 20). Syrian refugee family arrives in Metro Detroit. *Detroit Free Press*. https://www.freep.com/story/news/local/michigan/2015/11/20/syrian-refugee-family-arrives-metro-detroit/76122550/

Warikoo, N. (2015, November 23). Detroit mayor: Our city welcomes refugees. *Detroit Free Press*. https://www.freep.com/story/news/local/michigan/detroit/2015/11/23/detroit-mayor-our-city-welcomes-refugees/76275426/

Williams, C., & Hicks, M. (2015, November 18). Patterson to Pontiac: Don't take Syrian refugees. *Detroit News*. https://www.detroitnews.com/story/news/local/oakland-county/2015/11/18/brooks-patterson-pontiac-syrian-refugees/76017962/

Zong, J., & Batalova, J. (2017, January 12). Syrian refugees in the United States. *Migration Information Source*. https://www.migrationpolicy.org/article/syrian-refugees-united-states

Chapter 2

Abbas, T. (2017). Ethnicity and politics in contextualizing far right and Islamist extremism. *Perspectives on Terrorism* 11 (3): 54-60.

Abu-Lughod, L. (2013). *Do Muslim women need saving?* Cambridge, MA: Harvard University Press.

Barrett, J. (2016, June 30). Video: The greatest threat to America: "Civilization Jihad." *Daily Wire.* https://www.dailywire.com/news/video-greatest-threat-america-civilization-jihad-james-barrett

Beauchamp, Z. (2017, February 2). A video claiming refugees are a Muslim plot to colonize America has nearly three million views. *Vox.* https://www.vox.com/world/2017/2/2/14475264/refugees-syrian-muslim-video-sharia

Bhabha, H. (1994). *The location of culture.* New York: Routledge.

Bradley, S. (2017, May 10). Questioner told to "shut up" by presenter at Secure Michigan presentation in Alma. *Morning Sun.* https://www.themorningsun.com/news/nation-world-news/questioner-told-to-shut-up-by-presenter-at-secure-michigan/article_76db734c-5261-563b-a74a-38869c3eff33.html

Clarion Project. (2015, December 10). By the numbers: The untold story of Muslim opinions and demographics [video file]. https://www.youtube.com/watch?v=pSPvnFDDQHk

Corcoran, A. (2015). *Refugee resettlement and the Hijra to America.* Washington, DC: Center for Security Policy Press.

Counter Jihad (2016, June 29). Killing for a cause: Sharia law and civilization jihad [video file]. https://www.youtube.com/watch?v=7zd2yLNpv_A&t=26s

Ellis, E. G. (2018, August 10). How big is the alt right? Inside my futile quest to count. *Wired.* https://www.wired.com/story/unite-the-right-charlottesville-alt-right-inside-my-futile-quest-to-count/

Elsheikh, E., Sisemore, B., & Lee, N. R. (2017). Legalizing othering: The United States of Islamophobia. Berkeley, CA: Haas Institute. file:///C:/Users/rashm/Documents/Book%20in%20progress/haas_institute_legalizing_othering_the_united_states_of_islamophobia.pdf

Goyette, J. (2016, April 1). How an environmental lobbyist became an influential anti-refugee blogger. *PRI's The World.* https://www.pri.org/stories/2016-04-01/she-was-once-environmental-lobbyist-now-she-blogs-against-refugees

Gramsci, Antonio. 1971. *Selections from the prison notebooks.* New York: International Publishers.

Hall, S. (1988). *The hard road to renewal: Thatcherism and the crisis of the left.* London: Verso Books.

Harris, S. (2015). *Waking up: A guide to spirituality without religion.* New York: Simon and Schuster.

Hartzell, S.L. (2018). Alt-white: Conceptualizing the "Alt-Right" as a rhetorical bridge between white nationalism and mainstream public discourse. *Journal of Contemporary Rhetoric* 8 (1/2): 6-25.

Hohmann, L. (2016). *Stealth invasion: Muslim conquest through immigration and the resettlement jihad.* Washington, DC: WND Books.

Hohmann, L. (2017, April 2). Meet "next Obama" groomed to make political history. *WND.* https://www.wnd.com/2017/04/meet-the-next-obama-groomed-to-make-political-history/

Laitner, B. (2016, November 17). L. Brooks Patterson draws fire for speaker's anti-refugee views. *Detroit Free Press.* https://www.freep.com/story/news/local/michigan/oakland/2016/11/17/l-brooks-patterson-refugees/94047262/

Lean, N. (2017). *The Islamophobia industry: How the right manufactures hatred of Muslims*. London: Pluto Press.

Lewin, T. (2007, August 7). Universities install footbaths to benefit Muslims, and not everyone is pleased. *New York Times*. https://www.nytimes.com/2007/08/07/education/07muslim.html

Mani, L. (1998). *Contentious traditions: The debate on sati in colonial India*. Berkeley: University of California Press.

Narayan, U. (1997). *Dislocating cultures: Identities, traditions, and Third World feminism*. New York: Routledge.

Neiwert, D. (2018, April 3). The alt-right media bubble is in trouble. *Vice*. https://www.vice.com/en_us/article/j5axa7/the-alt-right-media-bubble-is-in-trouble

Refugee Resettlement Watch (2017, May 19). Ann Corcoran: Michigan on the brink [video file]. https://www.youtube.com/watch?v=PuDsRxaTPSo

Schlussel, D. (2007, May 30). Exclusive: So long church/state separation: University of Michigan to fund Muslim footbaths. http://www.debbieschlussel.com/1347/exclusive-so-long-churchstate-separation-university-of-michigan-to-fund-muslim-footbaths/

Simpson, J. (2015). *The red-green axis: Refugees, immigration, and the agenda to erase America*. Washington, DC: Center for Security Policy Press.

Spivak, G. C. (1988). Can the subaltern speak? In C. Nelson and L. Grossberg (eds.), *Marxism and the interpretation of culture*, 271-316. Champaign: University of Illinois Press.

Stanovsky, D. (2017). Remix racism: The visual politics of the "alt-right." *Journal of Contemporary Rhetoric* 7 (2/3): 130-38.

Warikoo, N. (2018, October 15). Number of refugees in Michigan plunges as Trump restricts immigration. *Detroit Free Press*. https://www.freep.com/story/news/local/michigan/2018/10/15/refugee-admissions-drops/1607544002/

Youmans, W. (2011). Domestic foreign policy: Arab Detroit as a special place in the war on terror. In N. Abraham, S. Howell, and A. Shyrock (eds.), *Arab Detroit 9/11: Life in the terror decade*, 269-86. Detroit: Wayne State University Press.

Chapter 3

ABC (2015, November 17). Barbara Walters asks Donald Trump about banning Syrian refugees. [Video] Available at YouTube, https://youtu.be/fa7XKKr61Ng

Aghajanian, L. (2017, February 9). What it's like to live in Hamtramck, a majority-Muslim city in Michigan, right now. *Teen Vogue*. https://www.teenvogue.com/story/hamtramck-michigan-majority-muslim-city

Ansari, T. (2018, April 24). A Republican running for governor in Michigan is using unfounded conspiracy theories against a Muslim American rival. *BuzzFeed News*. https://www.BuzzFeednews.com/article/talalansari/reublican-muslim-conspiracy-theories-democrat-michigan-gover

Benkler, Y., Faris, R., Roberts, H., & Zuckerman, E. (2017, March 3). Study: Breitbart-led right-wing media ecosystem altered broader media agenda. *Columbia Journalism Review*. http://www.pressandguide.com/news/hammoud-calls-on-sen

-patrick-colbeck-to-resign-after-controversial/article_f22fd846-b02f-5d38
-a577-306ce57d276a.html

Boyle, M., & Hahn, J. (2016, September 3). Exclusive: Trump slams "crazy" Bill Clinton plan to give Detroit jobs to Syrian refugees. Breitbart. https://www.brei tbart.com/politics/2016/09/03/exclusive-donald-trump-slams-bill-clinton-pl an-to-give-detroit-jobs-to-syrian-refugees/

Clement, S. (2016, June 11). How black voters could determine the 2016 election. *Washington Post*. https://www.washingtonpost.com/news/the-fix/wp/2015/06 /11/how-black-voters-could-determine-the-2016-election

Egan, P. (2018, May 11). He's Michigan's most conservative Republican candidate for governor. *Detroit Free Press*. https://www.freep.com/story/news/local/mich igan/2018/05/11/patrick-colbeck-michigan-governor-candidate/480985002/

Felton, R. (2015, November 15). Michigan town said to have first majority Muslim city council in U.S. *Guardian*. https://www.theguardian.com/us-news/2015 /nov/15/michigan-muslim-majority-city-council-hamtramck-detroit

For Abdul El-Sayed "the path hasn't changed" despite primary loss. (2018, August 13). *Stateside*, Michigan Radio. https://www.michiganradio.org/post/abdul-el -sayed-path-hasnt-changed-despite-primary-loss

Gamboa, S. (2015, June 16). Donald Trump announces presidential bid by trashing Mexico, Mexicans. NBC News. https://www.nbcnews.com/news/latino/donald -trump-announces-presidential-bid-trashing-mexico-mexicans-n376521

Georgiou, M. (2013). *Media and the city: Cosmopolitanism and difference*. Cambridge, UK: Polity Press.

Gov. Snyder wants more Syrian refugees, "would love to see" Michigan's Middle Eastern population grow (2015, September 29). CBS Detroit. https://detroit.cb slocal.com/2015/09/29/gov-snyder-wants-more-syrian-refugees-would-love -to-see-michigans-middle-eastern-population-grow/

Gray, K. (2016, January 26). Syrian refugee resolution tabled after intense debate. *Detroit Free Press*. https://www.freep.com/story/news/politics/2016/01/26/syri an-refugee-resolution-tabled-after-intense-debate/79366104/

Hahn, J. (2016, August 29). Video—Bill Clinton: Rebuild Detroit with Syrian refu gees. Breitbart. https://www.breitbart.com/politics/2016/08/29/bill-clinton-ca lls-for-rebuilding-detroit-with-syrian-refugees/

Harris, G., Sanger, D. E., & Herszenhorn, D. M. (2015, September 10). Obama in creases number of Syrian refugees for U.S. resettlement to 10,000. https:// www.nytimes.com/2015/09/11/world/middleeast/obama-directs-administrati on-to-accept-10000-syrian-refugees.html

Hayward, J. (2016, September 2). Ben Carson slams Clinton plan to move Syrian refugees to Detroit: "We need to take care of our own people" first. Breitbart. https://www.breitbart.com/radio/2016/09/02/ben-carson-slams-clinton-plan -move-syrian-refugees-detroit-need-take-care-people-first/

Hicks, M. (2015, November 6). Hamtramck elects first majority-Muslim city coun cil. *Detroit News*. https://www.detroitnews.com/story/news/local/wayne-coun ty/2015/11/06/hamtramck-elects-first-majority-muslim-city-council/75272 654/

Illing, S. (2019, March 22). How Fox news evolved into a propaganda operation. *Vox.* https://www.vox.com/2019/3/22/18275835/fox-news-trump-propaganda-tom-rosenstiel

Inskeep, S., & Taylor, J. (2015, November 20). Governor who started stampede against refugees says he only wants answers. NPR. https://www.npr.org/2015/11/20/456713306/governor-who-started-stampede-on-refugees-says-he-only-wants-answers

Kingsley, P. (2015, November 15). Why Syrian refugee passport found at Paris attack scene must be treated with caution. *The Guardian.* https://www.theguardian.com/world/2015/nov/15/why-syrian-refugee-passport-found-at-paris-attack-scene-must-be-treated-with-caution

Klein, A. (2017, November 9). Trump nominee for career tech position being pulled due to offensive blog posts. *Education Week.* https://www.edweek.org/ew/articles/2017/11/09/trump-nominee-for-careertech-position-being-pulled.html

Laitin, D. D., & Jahr, M. (2015, May 14). Let Syrians settle Detroit. *New York Times.* https://www.nytimes.com/2015/05/15/opinion/let-syrians-settle-detroit.html

Lawler, E. (2015, November 17). After Syrian refugee stance, is Michigan's Rick Snyder still the most pro-immigration governor? *MLive Michigan.* https://www.mlive.com/lansing-news/2015/11/after_syrian_refugee_stance_is.html

Mahtesian, C. (2016, June 15). What are the swing states in 2016? *Politico.* https://www.politico.com/blogs/swing-states-2016-election/2016/06/what-are-the-swing-states-in-2016-list-224327

McCarthy, T. (2015, September 10). Obama calls on U.S. to resettle "at least 10,000" Syrian refugees in 2016 fiscal year. *Guardian.* https://www.theguardian.com/world/2015/sep/10/syrian-refugees-obama-us-admit-more-fiscal-2016

McGraw, D. J. (2015, September 29). The GOP immigration plan to save Detroit—and Syria. *Politico.* https://www.politico.com/magazine/story/2015/09/detroit-saved-by-syrian-immigrants-rick-snyder-immigration-gop-213206

Monkovic, T. (2016, February 17). Clinton, Sanders, and the underrated power of the black voter. *New York Times.* https://www.nytimes.com/2016/02/18/upshot/clinton-sanders-and-the-underrated-power-of-the-black-voter.html

Nashrulla, T. (2018, April 27). A Republican peddling anti-Muslim conspiracy theories in Michigan was called a "coward" on the Senate floor. *BuzzFeed News.* https://www.buzzfeednews.com/article/tasneemnashrulla/republican-muslim-conspiracy-theories-colbeck-coward

Novak, M. (2017, May 10). Fox News got Trump elected and Fox News is the reason he'll stay in power. *Gizmodo.* https://gizmodo.com/fox-news-got-trump-elected-and-fox-news-is-the-reason-h-1795080589

Omi, M., & Winant, H. (1994). *Racial formation in the United States: From the 1960s to the 1990s.* New York: Routledge.

Oosting, J. (2018a, April 25). Colbeck under fire for Muslim conspiracy claims. *Detroit News.* https://www.detroitnews.com/story/news/politics/2018/04/25/colbeck-el-sayed-muslim-conspiracy/34235679/

Oosting, J. (2018b, May 10). "Islamophobia" charge rocks Michigan governor debate. *Detroit News.* https://www.detroitnews.com/story/news/politics/2018/05/10/islamophobia-charge-rocks-michigan-governor-debate/34765749/

Pluta, R. (2016, November 3). Michigan community clashes over embrace of immigrants. NPR. https://www.npr.org/2016/11/03/500506308/michigan-community-clashes-over-embrace-of-immigrants

Rahal, S. (2018a, March 26). Michigan sees sharp drop in refugees. *Detroit News*. https://www.detroitnews.com/story/news/politics/2018/03/26/refugees-michigan-decline/33284833/

Rahal, S. (2018b, June 26). Protesters rally against Trump travel ban in Detroit. *Detroit News*. https://www.detroitnews.com/story/news/local/detroit-city/2018/06/26/protesters-rally-against-trump-travel-ban-detroit/735334002/

Ramirez, C. E. (2016, June 9). Michigan tops other states in number of Syrian refugees. *Detroit News*. https://www.detroitnews.com/story/news/local/michigan/2016/06/09/michigan-topsstates-number-syrian-refugees/85629610/

Stranahan, L. (2016a, August 10). Twin Falls refugee rape special report: Why are the refugees moving in? Breitbart. https://www.breitbart.com/politics/2016/08/10/twin-falls-refugee-rape-special-report-refugees/

Stranahan, L. (2016b, August 25). Turkish Chobani owner has deep ties to Clinton Global Initiative and Clinton campaign. Breitbart. https://www.breitbart.com/politics/2016/08/25/turkish-chobani-owner-has-deep-ties-to-clinton-global-initiative-and-campaign/

Vitali, A. (2015, October 1). Donald Trump in New Hampshire: Syrian refugees are "going back." NBC News. https://www.nbcnews.com/politics/2016-election/donald-trump-new-hampshire-syrian-refugees-are-going-back-n436616

Warikoo, N. (2015a, November 6). Hamtramck elects Muslim-majority city council. *Detroit Free Press*. https://www.freep.com/story/news/local/michigan/wayne/2015/11/05/hamtramck-elects-muslim-majority-city-council/75237920/

Warikoo, N. (2015b, November 23). Detroit mayor: Our city welcomes refugees. *Detroit Free Press*. https://www.freep.com/story/news/local/michigan/detroit/2015/11/23/detroit-mayor-our-city-welcomes-refugees/76275426/

Chapter 4

Castles, S. (2003). Towards a sociology of forced migration and social transformation. *Sociology* 77 (1): 13-34.

Gilmore, L. (2005). Autobiography's wounds. In W. S. Hesford & W. Kozol (eds.), *Just advocacy: Women's human rights, transnational feminisms, and the politics of representation*, 99-119. New Brunswick, NJ: Rutgers University Press.

Hesford, W. S. (2005). *Kairos* and the geopolitical rhetorics of global sex work and video advocacy. In W. S. Hesford & W. Kozol (eds.), *Just advocacy: Women's human rights, transnational feminisms, and the politics of representation*, 146-72. New Brunswick, NJ: Rutgers University Press.

Hesford, W. S., & Kozol, W. (2005). Introduction. In W. S. Hesford & W. Kozol (eds.), *Just advocacy: Women's human rights, transnational feminisms, and the politics of representation*, 1-32. New Brunswick, NJ: Rutgers University Press.

Malkki, L. H. (1995). Refugees and exile: From "Refugee Studies" to the national order of things [PDF file]. *Annual Review of Anthropology* 24: 495-523.

Malkki, L. H. (1996). Speechless emissaries: Refugees, humanitarianism, and de-historicization. *Cultural Anthropology* 11 (3): 377-404.

Smith, S. (2005). Belated narrating: Grandmothers telling stories of forced sexual servitude during World War II. In W. S. Hesford & W. Kozol (eds.), *Just advocacy: Women's human rights, transnational feminisms, and the politics of representation*, 120-45. New Brunswick, NJ: Rutgers University Press.

Chapter 5

Albom, M. (2017, July 2). Why deport this Iraqi refugee? *Detroit Free Press*. https://www.northjersey.com/story/opinion/contributors/2017/07/02/why-deport-iraqi-refugee/441729001/

Allen, R. (2017, June 12). Iraqi Christians fear Metro Detroit ICE raids, deportations a "death sentence." *Detroit Free Press*. https://www.freep.com/story/news/local/michigan/2017/06/12/iraqi-christians-ice-raids-deportations/388743001/

Bach, T. (2017, June 21). Why Michigan's Iraqi Christians thought Trump would spare their loved ones. *Christian Science Monitor*. https://www.csmonitor.com/USA/Society/2017/0621/Why-Michigan-s-Iraqi-Christians-thought-Trump-would-spare-their-loved-ones

Barros, A. (2017, August 11). Detroit Iraqi Christians fearful after deportation raids. *Voice of America*. https://www.voanews.com/a/detroit-iraqi-christians-fearful-deportation-raids/3981466.html

Brayman, L. (2017, July 5). Is it still a Muslim ban if Christian refugees are punished? *Foreign Policy*. https://foreignpolicy.com/2017/07/05/is-it-still-a-muslim-ban-if-christian-refugees-are-punished-iraqi-chaldean-christians-trump/

Dwyer, D. (2017, February 1). He said he would go after "bad hombres": This order allows him to go after soccer moms. *State of Opportunity*, Michigan Radio. https://stateofopportunity.michiganradio.org/post/he-said-he-would-go-after-bad-hombres-order-allows-him-go-after-soccer-moms-0

Editorial Board (2017, June 21). Putting Iraqis in harm's way. *Washington Post*. Retrieved September 20, 2017, from LexisNexis Academic Database.

Ferretti, C. (2017, June 15). ACLU sues feds to stop Chaldean deportations. *Detroit News*. https://www.detroitnews.com/story/news/local/detroit-city/2017/06/15/aclu-lawsuit-chaldeans/102895284/

Friess, S. (2017, July 24). U.S. judge halts deportation of more than 1,400 Iraqi nationals. Reuters. https://www.reuters.com/article/us-usa-immigration-iraqis/u-s-judge-halts-deportation-of-more-than-1400-iraqi-nationals-idUSKBN1AA04Z

Gelardi, C. (2017, September 4). When ICE came for the Chaldeans. *Slate*. https://slate.com/news-and-politics/2017/09/michigans-iraqi-chaldean-community-is-fighting-to-protect-dozens-of-people-from-deportation.html

Golash-Boza, T. M. (2018). *Forced out and fenced in: Immigration tales from the field*. New York: Oxford University Press.

Guerra, J. (2017, April 12). "We're going to be separated from my dad": A family's final days together before deportation. *State of Opportunity*, Michigan Radio. https://stateofopportunity.michiganradio.org/post/were-going-be-separated-my-dad-familys-final-days-together-deportation

Hanoosh, Y. (2011). Fighting our own battles: Iraqi Chaldeans and the war on terror. In N. Abraham, S. Howell, & A. Shyrock (eds.), *Arab Detroit 9/11: Life in the terror decade*, 126–50. Detroit: Wayne State University Press.

Hauslohner, A. (2017a, April 28). A charter flight left the U.S. carrying eight Iraqis. A community wonders who will be next. *Washington Post*. https://www.washingtonpost.com/national/a-charter-flight-left-the-us-carrying-8-iraqis-a-community-wonders-who-will-be-next/2017/04/28/a4ce9418-293c-11e7-b605-33413c691853_story.html?utm_term=.3dd7e232f210

Hauslohner, A. (2017b, June 12). Dozens of Iraqi nationals swept up in immigration raids in Michigan, Tennessee: ICE officials made large numbers of arrests as it works to process "backlog" of 1,400 Iraqis the U.S. government wants to deport. *Washington Post*. Retrieved June 5, 2019, from ProQuest Database.

Henderson, S. (2017, September 6). Detroit DACA recipients vow to "continue the fight." *Detroit Today*, WDET. https://wdet.org/posts/2017/09/06/85713-detroit-daca-recipients-vow-to-continue-to-fight/

Hijazi, S. (2015, September 4). Sterling Heights mosque controversy spills across Chaldean and Muslim communities. *Arab American News*. https://arabamericannews.com/2015/09/04/sterling-heights-mosque-controversy-spills-across-chaldean-and-muslim-communities/

Hohmann, L. (2017, June 13). U.S. sending Christians back to Iraq to face "slaughter." *WND*. https://www.wnd.com/2017/06/trump-sending-christians-back-to-iraq-to-face-slaughter/

Jacobo, J. (2016, October 19). Donald Trump says he will get "bad hombres" out of U.S. ABC News. https://abcnews.go.com/Politics/donald-trump-bad-hombres-us/story?id=42926041

Karoub, J., & Caldwell, A. (2017, June 12). Immigration arrests of dozens of Chaldeans prompt protest. AP News. https://www.apnews.com/348f11271b704d5291d4652d0091edb1

Lah, K., Sutton, J., Hassan, C., & Sterling, J. (2017, June 12). ICE arrests in Metro Detroit terrify Iraqi Christians. CNN. https://www.cnn.com/2017/06/12/politics/detroit-ice-iraqi-christians/index.html

Maciag, M. (2017, September 5). DACA recipients by state: Federal statistics on numbers of Deferred Action for Childhood Arrivals (DACA) participants for each state. *Governing: The Future of States and Localities*. https://www.governing.com/archive/daca-approved-participants-by-state.html

Manna, M. (2017, October 10). Column: Protect immigrants, DACA. *Detroit News*. https://www.detroitnews.com/story/opinion/2017/10/10/immigrants-daca/106476988/

Mejia, M. (2017, September 27). Dreamer weighs in on the stress of being in the political crosshairs; Detroit DACA recipients vow to "continue to fight." *Stateside*, Michigan Radio. https://www.michiganradio.org/post/dreamer-weighs-stress-being-political-crosshairs

Salama, V. (2017, February 2). Trump to Mexico: Take care of "bad hombres" or U.S. might. AP News. https://www.apnews.com/0b3f5db59b2e4aa78cdbbf008 f27fb49

Savage, D. G. (2019, November 12). DACA Timeline: The rise and resilience of the "Dreamers" Program. Los Angeles Times. https://www.latimes.com/politics/sto ry/2019-11-12/timeline-on-daca

Smith, P. J. (2017, July 27). Federal judge blocks Catholic Chaldeans' deportation to Iraq—for now. National Catholic Register. http://www.ncregister.com/daily-ne ws/federal-judge-blocks-catholic-chaldeans-deportation-to-iraq-for-now

Valverde, M. (2018, January 22). Timeline: DACA, the Trump administration, and a government shutdown. Politifact. https://www.politifact.com/truth-o-meter /article/2018/jan/22/timeline-daca-trump-administration-and-government-/

Van Buren, A. (2017, March 16). We're scared: Two brothers, one a citizen, one not, endure uncertainty under Trump. State of Opportunity, Michigan Radio. https://stateofopportunity.michiganradio.org/post/were-scared-two-brothers -one-citizen-and-one-not-endure-uncertainty-under-trump

Yee, V. (2017, July 4). After backing Trump, Christians who fled Iraq fall into his dragnet. New York Times. https://www.nytimes.com/2017/07/04/us/iraqi-chri stians-deport.html

Chapter 6

Abdelrazaq, L. (2015). Baddawi. Washington, DC: Just World Books.

Adorno, T. W., & Horkheimer, M. (1972). The culture industry: Enlightenment as mass deception. In J. Cumming (trans.), Dialectic of Enlightenment, 94-137. New York: Herder & Herder.

Center for Arab American Studies, University of Michigan-Dearborn. (2019). Un-settled lives: Displaced Iraqis in Metro Detroit. https://www.arcgis.com/apps/Cas cade/index.html?appid=7561c077f0dc41dbb0dec27153d3d9cd

Georges, S. (2015, December 19). Faces of refugees show the struggle to resettle in America. Detroit Free Press. https://www.freep.com/story/opinion/contributors /2015/12/19/photographer-syrian-refugees-detroit/77489858/

Jehl, D. (2004, April 17). The struggle for Iraq: Policy; wary Powell said to have warned Bush on war. New York Times. https://www.nytimes.com/2004/04/17 /world/the-struggle-for-iraq-policy-wary-powell-said-to-have-warned-bush -on-war.html

Lommasson, J. (2016, June 4-October 23). What we carried: Fragments and memories from Iraq and Syria. Dearborn, MI: Arab American National Museum. http://ara bamericanmuseum.org/wwc

Lommasson, J. (2018, May 19-August 5). What we carried: Fragments and memories from Iraq and Syria. Los Angeles: Japanese American National Museum. http:// www.janm.org/exhibits/what-we-carried/

Lommasson, J. (2019, May 25-September 2). What we carried: Fragments and memo-ries from Iraq and Syria. New York: Ellis Island National Immigration Museum. https://whatwecarried.com/

McKenzie, C. (2016, March 1). IC students document struggles of Syrian refugees in Detroit. *IC News.* https://www.ithaca.edu/ic-news/releases/ic-student-doc umentary-contrasts-syrian-refugee-life-with-anti-muslim-protests-41079/

Moriarty, E., Basciano, H., Holland, M., Dellert, S., & Margolis, J. (2016). *Stateless: Syrian refugees in Detroit.* Ithaca, NY. Vimeo. vimeo.com/150790193

Silmi, M. (2019, June 18). Dearborn exhibit on refugees and immigration is on display at Ellis Island. Michigan Radio. https://www.michiganradio.org/post/dear born-exhibit-refugees-and-immigration-display-ellis-island

Concluding Thoughts

Arendt, H. (2007b). We refugees. In J. Kohn & R. H. Feldman (eds.), *The Jewish writings*, 264-74. New York: Schocken Books.

Dirlik, A. (1996). The global in the local. In R. Wilson & W. Dissanayake (eds.), *Global/local: Cultural production and the transnational imaginary*, 21-45. Durham: Duke University Press.

Esposito, J. L., & Kalin, I. (2011). *Islamophobia: The challenge of pluralism in the twenty-first century.* Oxford: Oxford University Press.

Gatrell, P. (2013). *The making of the modern refugee.* Oxford: Oxford University Press.

Georgiou, M. (2013). *Media and the city: Cosmopolitanism and difference.* Cambridge: Polity Press.

Gray, K. (2016, January 26). Syrian refugee resolution tabled after intense debate. *Detroit Free Press.* https://www.freep.com/story/news/politics/2016/01/26/syri an-refugee-resolution-tabled-after-intense-debate/79366104/

Lean, N. (2017). *The Islamophobia industry: How the right manufactures hatred of Muslims.* London: Pluto Press.

Leland, J. (2004, May 5). Tension in Michigan city over Muslims' call to prayer. *New York Times.* https://www.nytimes.com/2004/05/05/us/tension-in-a-michigan -city-over-muslims-call-to-prayer.html

Malkki, L. H. (1995). Refugees and exile: From "Refugee Studies" to the national order of things [PDF file]. *Annual Review of Anthropology* 24:495-523.

Mohanty, C. T. (1991b). Under Western eyes: Feminist scholarship and colonial discourses. In C. T. Mohanty, A. Russo, & L. Torres (eds.). *Third World women and the politics of feminism*, 51-80. Bloomington: Indiana University Press.

Rignall, K. (2000). Building the infrastructure of Arab American identity in Detroit: A short history of ACCESS and the community it serves. In N. Abraham & A. Shyrock (eds.), *Arab Detroit: From margin to mainstream*, 49-60. Detroit: Wayne State University Press.

Shopmeyer, K. (2000). A demographic portrait of Arab Detroit. In N. Abraham & A. Shyrock (eds.), *Arab Detroit: From margin to mainstream*, 61-94. Detroit: Wayne State University Press.

Shopmeyer, K. (2011). Arab Detroit after 9/11: A changing demographic portrait. In N. Abraham, S. Howell, & A. Shyrock (eds.), *Arab Detroit 9/11: Life in the terror decade*, 29-66. Detroit: Wayne State University Press.

Today's Remedy. (2017, March 8). *Stuart Hall on cosmopolitanism* [Video]. YouTube. https://www.youtube.com/watch?v=zcaGhyYvMlo

Index